THE GETTY HEXAMETERS

The Getty Hexameters

Poetry, Magic, and Mystery in Ancient Selinous

Edited by

CHRISTOPHER A. FARAONE
AND DIRK OBBINK

OXFORD
UNIVERSITY PRESS

OXFORD
UNIVERSITY PRESS

Great Clarendon Street, Oxford, OX2 6DP,
United Kingdom

Oxford University Press is a department of the University of Oxford.
It furthers the University's objective of excellence in research, scholarship,
and education by publishing worldwide. Oxford is a registered trade mark of
Oxford University press in the UK and in certain other countries

© Oxford University Press 2013

The moral rights of the authors have been asserted

First Edition published in 2013

Impression: 1

All rights reserved. No part of this publication may be reproduced, stored in
a retrieval system, or transmitted, in any form or by any means, without the
prior permission in writing of Oxford University Press, or as expressly permitted
by law, by licence, or under terms agreed with the appropriate reprographics
rights organization. Enquiries concerning reproduction outside the scope of the
above should be sent to the Rights Department, Oxford University Press, at the
address above

You must not circulate this work in any other form
and you must impose this same condition on any acquirer

British Library Cataloguing in Publication Data
Data available

Library of Congress Control Number: 2013947223

ISBN 978-0-19-966410-8

As printed and bound by
CPI Group (UK) Ltd, Croydon CR0 4YY

Links to third party websites are provided by Oxford in good faith and
for information only. Oxford disclaims any responsibility for the materials
contained in any third party website referenced in this work.

Preface

Kenneth Lapatin

In 1981 the J. Paul Getty Museum acquired six fragments of an inscribed lead tablet as gifts from Dr. Max Gerchik (JPGM 81. AI.140.2.1-6). Soon after they arrived at the Museum, publication of the tablet was entrusted to Dr. Roy Kotansky, who then worked as an assistant to Getty antiquities curator Jiri Frel, and toIzed Dr. David Jordan. This proved more complex than anticipated, although a preliminary edition of the text has recently appeared.[1] These two scholars are also preparing fuller treatments of the Hexameters individually.

In the meantime, at the initiative of Christopher A. Faraone, Professor of Classics at the University of Chicago and a former Getty Villa Scholar-in-Residence, a workshop focusing on the Hexameters was hosted at the Getty Villa on 5 November 2010. Scholars from the United States and Europe gathered in Malibu for this one-day event, which centred on a close reading of the text utilizing photographs, drawings, and, most importantly, the lead fragments themselves, which were made available to the participants for close examination and analysis. Invited speakers, most of whose revised papers appear in the following pages, then addressed various aspects of the Getty Hexameters, and vigorous discussion ensued. The J. Paul Getty Museum and the Getty Villa Programming Committee are grateful to Professor Faraone, to the Center for the Study of Ancient Religions at the University of Chicago, and to all who participated in the Getty Hexameters Workshop for their contributions to the success of that event, to this publication, and to the diffusion of knowledge, which was the principal mandate of the museum's founder.

---

[1] Kotansky and Jordan (2011).

Contents

Figures, Plates, and Tables — ix
Abbreviations — xi
List of Contributors — xiii

Introduction — 1
Christopher A. Faraone and Dirk Obbink

Greek Text and Translation of the Getty Hexameters — 10

1. The Getty Hexameters: Date, Author, and Place of Composition — 21
   Jan N. Bremmer

2. The Hexametric Incantations against Witchcraft in the Getty Museum: From Archetype to Exemplar — 31
   Richard Janko

3. Spoken and Written Boasts in the Getty Hexameters: From Oral Composition to Inscribed Amulet — 57
   Christopher A. Faraone

4. The *Ephesia Grammata*: Genesis of a Magical Formula — 71
   Alberto Bernabé

5. The *Ephesia Grammata*: *Logos Orphaïkos* or Apolline *Alexima Pharmaka*? — 97
   Radcliffe G. Edmonds III

6. Magical Verses on a Lead Tablet: Composite Amulet or Anthology? — 107
   Christopher A. Faraone

7. Myth and the Getty Hexameters — 121
   Sarah Iles Johnston

8. The Immortal Words of Paean — 157
   Ian Rutherford

9. Poetry and the Mysteries — 171
   Dirk Obbink

Appendix: The Inscribed Lead Tablet from Phalasarna, Crete	185
Bibliography	189
Subject Index	201
Index of Ancient Works and Texts	210
Index of Foreign Words	216

Figures, Plates, and Tables

FIGURES

Figure 1 Line-drawing of the Getty Hexameters Tablet (front, tracings by Kassandra Jackson) — 16

Figure 2 Line-drawing of the Getty Hexameters Tablet (back, tracings by Kassandra Jackson) — 19

PLATES

Plate 1 Photo of the Getty Hexameter Fragments (The J. Paul Getty Museum, Villa Collection, Malibu, California. Unknown artist, Lamella Fragment (comprised of 6 unjoined fragments), 4th century BC, Lead) — 15

Plate 2 Lead Tablet with the Getty Hexameters (The J. Paul Getty Museum, Villa Collection, Malibu, California. Unknown artist, Lamella Fragment (comprised of 6 unjoined fragments), 4th century BC, Lead) — 17

Plate 3 Lead Tablet with the Getty Hexameters (The J. Paul Getty Museum, Villa Collection, Malibu, California. Unknown artist, Lamella Fragment (comprised of 6 unjoined fragments), 4th century BC, Lead, Gift of Dr. Max Gerchik.) — 18

Plate 4 Orpheus, seated with lyre (now missing) and plectrum, life-size, in terracotta. Sicily, early 5th century BC. (The J. Paul Getty Museum, Villa Collection, Malibu, California Unknown, Detail of Sculptural Group of a Seated Poet and Sirens (2) with unjoined fragmentary curls (304), 350–300 BC., Terracotta with Polychromy) — 175

Plate 5 Orpheus, seated with lyre (now missing) and plectrum, and singing Sirens group, life-size, in terracotta. Sicily, early 5th century BC. (The J. Paul Getty Museum, Villa Collection, Malibu, California Unknown, Sculptural Group of a Seated Poet and Sirens (2) with unjoined fragmentary curls (304), 350–300 BC., Terracotta with Polychromy) — 176

TABLES

Table 2.1	A reconstruction of the archetype of the Getty tablet, with facing translation	40
Table 6.1	Phalasarna and Getty compared	114
Table 6.2	Refrains and rubrics summary	117

Abbreviations

A note on abbreviations and transliteration
Wherever possible, the abbreviations used within this volume for ancient authors, scholarly journals, collections of texts, and the like are those found in the second edition of the *Oxford Classical Dictionary*. In transliterating ancient Greek names it has seemed reasonable, if not entirely consistent, to use the familiar Latinized spelling for those names for which this has become normal English usage (for example, 'Socrates' or 'Heracles'), and in other cases to use a direct transliteration of the Greek to avoid confusion (for example, 'Dike' rather than 'Dice'). The divine name or title Paean presents special problems, because it is represented in this volume in several dialectical variations. We have therefore used 'Paean' wherever a general reference is made to the god or the epithet or 'paean' to refer generally to the song.

AMC	M. Meyer, and R. Smith (eds), *Ancient Christian Magic: Coptic Texts of Ritual Power* (San Francisco, 1994)
Borghouts	J. F. Borghouts, *Ancient Egyptian Magical Texts*. Nisiba 9 (Leiden, 1978)
CEG	P. A. Hansen, *Carmina Epigraphica Graeca saeculorum VIII–V a. Chr. n.* (Berlin and New York, 1983)
G&J	F. Graf, and S. I. Johnston, *Ritual Texts for the Afterlife. Orpheus and the Bacchic Gold Tablets* (London, 2007)
GMA	R. Kotansky, *Greek Magical Amulets*, Vol. 1, Papyrologica Coloniensia 22.1 (Opladen, 1994)
Heim	R. Heim, *Incantamenta Magica Graeca–Latina, Jahrbücher für classische Philologie* Suppl. 10 (Leipzig, 1892)
PGM	K. Preisendanz *et al.* (eds), *Papyri Graecae Magicae. Die griechischen Zauberpapyri*. 2nd ed. 2 vols. (Stuttgart, 1973–74)
PMG	D. L. Page, *Poetae Melici Graeci* (Oxford, 1962)
SEG	*Supplementum Epigraphicum Graecum* (Leiden)
SGD	D. Jordan, 'A Survey of Greek *Defixiones* Not Included in the Special Corpora', *GRBS* 26 (1985) 151–97.
SM	R. Daniel and F. Maltomini, *Supplementum Magicum*, 2 vols., Papyrologica Coloniensia 16.1 and 2 (Opladen, 1990–91)

SMA	C. Bonner, *Studies in Magical Amulets Chiefly Graeco-Egyptian,* University of Michigan Studies, Humanistic Series 4 (Ann Arbor, 1950)
TrGF	B. Snell, S. Radt, and R. Kannicht, *Tragicorum Graecorum Fragmenta.* 2nd ed. 5 vols. (Göttingen, 1968–2004)
VS	H. Diels and W. Kranz, *Die Fragmente der Vorsokratiker.* 6th ed. 3 vols. (Zurich, 1951)

List of Contributors

Alberto Bernabé is Professor of Greek Philology at the University Complutense (Madrid). His main research interests are Greek literature, religion, and philosophy. He is editor of *Poetae Epici Graeci* (2nd ed. 1996) and *Orphicorum fragmenta* (2004–7), and coeditor (with Francesc Casadesús) of *Orfeo y la tradición órfica: un reencuentro* (2008).

Jan N. Bremmer was Chair of Religious Studies at the Faculty of Theology and Religious Studies at the University of Groningen, where he was dean of the faculty for nearly ten years (1996–2005), before his retirement in 2006. He has been a member of the Institute of Advanced Study in Princeton (2000), Inaugural Getty Villa Professor at the Getty Research Institute (Los Angeles: 2006–7), and Visiting Leventis Professor at Edinburgh (2007). He specializes in Greek, Roman, early Christian, and contemporary religion, and the historiography of ancient religion. Among his many publications are the books *Greek Religion and Culture, the Bible, and the Ancient Near East* (2008), *The Rise and Fall of the Afterlife* (2002), and *Greek Religion* (Greece and Rome: New Surveys in the Classics no. 24, second edition 1999). He has edited *The Strange World of Human Sacrifice* (2007), and (with Andrew Erskine) *The Gods of Ancient Greece* (2010).

Radcliffe G. Edmonds III is Associate Professor and Chair of the Department of Greek, Latin, and Classical Studies at Bryn Mawr College. In addition to a number of articles on ancient magic, the Orphica, and Platonic philosophy and myth, he has published the books *Myths of the Underworld Journey: Plato, Aristophanes, and the 'Orphic' Gold Tablets* (2004) and *Redefining Ancient Orphism: A Study in Greek Religion* (forthcoming). He has edited *The 'Orphic' Gold Tablets and Greek Religion: Further Along the Path* (2011), a collection of essays with texts and translations of the tablets.

Christopher A. Faraone is the Frank C. and Gertrude M. Springer Professor of the College and the Humanities at the University of Chicago. His work is primarily concerned with ancient Greek religion and poetry. He is co-editor (with D. Dodd) of *Initiation in Ancient*

Greek Rituals and Narratives: New Critical Perspectives (2003), (with L. McClure) of *Prostitutes and Courtesans in the Ancient World* (2005), and (with F. Naiden) of *Ancient Victims, Modern Observers: Reflections on Greek and Roman Sacrifice* (2011). He is the author of *Talismans and Trojan Horses: Guardian Statues in Ancient Greek Myth and Ritual* (1992), *Ancient Greek Love Magic* (1999), and *The Stanzaic Architecture of Ancient Greek Elegiac Poetry* (2008).

Richard Janko is the Gerald F. Else Distinguished University Professor of Classical Studies at the University of Michigan. He has published extensively on a wide range of topics, which include Homeric poetry and diction, the Greek language and its dialects, and the weirder aspects of Greek religion such as Empedocles, Orphism, and the Derveni papyrus. His most recent book is *Philodemus On Poems Books 3-4, with the Fragments of Aristotle's On Poets* (Oxford University Press, 2011). He is a Fellow of the American Academy of Arts and Sciences, and of the American Philosophical Society.

Sarah Iles Johnston is Arts and Humanities Distinguished Professor of Religion and Professor of Classics at Ohio State University in Columbus, Ohio. She is the general editor for the volumes *Religions of the Ancient World: A Guide* (2004) and *Ancient Religions* (2007), and the author of numerous articles and books on Greek religion, including *Ancient Greek Divination* (2008), *Restless Dead: Encounters Between the Living and the Dead in Ancient Greece* (1999), *Hekate Soteira* (Amer. Class. Studies no. 21, 1990), and (with Fritz Graf) *Ritual Texts for the Afterlife: Orpheus and the Bacchic Gold Tablets* (2007).

Kenneth Lapatin is Associate Curator of Antiquities with the J. Paul Getty Museum. His areas of specialization are ancient Mediterranean art and archaeology (particularly the Aegean Bronze Age, Greek, and Roman), historiography, forgery, reception, and luxury arts. He has conducted fieldwork in Caesaria Martima (Israel), Rome, and Corinth. His main publications include *Chryselephantine Statuary in the Ancient Mediterranean World* (2002), and *Mysteries of the Snake Goddess: Art, Desire, and the Forging of History* (2001).

Dirk Obbink is the University Lecturer in Papyrology and Greek Literature and Tutor and Fellow in Classics at Christ Church College, University of Oxford. The recipient of a MacArthur fellowship, he has published widely on Greek religion, philosophy, and poetry, and is a career papyrologist and text editor, including editions of *Philodemus On Piety* I (1996), Anubion, *Carmen astrologicum elegiacum* (2006), and (with Roger Bagnall) *Columbia Papyri* X (1996), as well as numerous volumes of *The Oxyrhynchus Papyri*, of which series he serves as a General Editor.

Ian Rutherford is Professor of Greek at the University of Reading. He studied at Oxford, has taught at Harvard, and has been a visiting fellow at the Center for Hellenic Studies in Washington DC. He has published widely on Greek and Near Eastern religion, wandering poets, and intercultural aspects of myth and religion, especially Anatolia and Hittite. His many publications include the books *Pindar's Paeans. A Reading of the Fragments with a Survey of the Genre* (2001) and *Greek Religion and Hittite Religion* (forthcoming OUP). He has edited a volume of the *Journal of Ancient Near Eastern Religions* (vol. 6, 2006) on connections between Greek religion and the Orient, and (with Jas Elsner) *Pilgrimage in Greco-Roman and Christian Antiquity. Seeing the Gods* (2005).

Introduction

Christopher A. Faraone and Dirk Obbink

The nine chapters collected in this volume address one enigmatic but important text, written on a large lead tablet of uncertain provenance and date. Dialect and alphabet point to a Doric city in Sicily. Selinus has a good claim and this is, in fact, the on-going assumption in all the chapters. A date in the latter part of the fifth century BC seems likely. Its purpose is not entirely clear, but there is agreement that this is a ritual and presumably magical text, composed almost entirely in dactylic hexameters and designed to protect a house or a city from some unspecified danger. The Getty tablet is—as the subtitle of this volume suggests—of enormous interest to scholars and students of early Greek poetry, magic, and mystery religions, and as such we have invited scholars from various backgrounds and interests to give us their thoughts and insights. We do not aim, however, at any comprehensive or fully integrated study nor do we claim any authoritative text or interpretation. The intention of the present volume is—as was the goal of the conference that lies behind it—to expose this text (and the myriad questions it prompts) to wider scrutiny by offering a number of different and not entirely converging studies. Our goal in this introduction, then, is to present some general questions and problems surrounding the Getty Hexameters in order to give some context to the contributions that follow.

As a prelude, it is important to stress that our Getty text is part of a small but growing corpus of similarly inscribed and dated lead tablets from Crete and West Greece. The sizeable and nearly intact example from Phalasarna, Crete has been known for quite some time, although it seems to be of somewhat later date, perhaps as late as the third century BC.[1] But more recently fragments of earlier texts in the same series have turned up in Himera and Selinus in Sicily and in western Locri on the Italian mainland.[2] Variations within the text of the Getty Hexameters themselves and among the parallel texts from West Greece and Crete offer our contributors fodder for assessing the origin and transmission of these texts, which seem to have been orally composed and reperformed a number of times before they were eventually inscribed in lead during the Classical and early Hellenistic periods. Their transformation from oral song to inscribed text is documented by a number of our contributors, more than one of whom observe the similarity, in this respect, of these lead amulets to the longest of the Orphic–Dionysiac gold tablets, which also preserve sequences of hexameter verses and have also turned up in West Greece and Crete. As poetry, then, these lead tablets and the Getty text in particular (because of its much greater length and better state of preservation) offer us an exciting opportunity to study how hexametrical poetry was orally composed, transmitted, and eventually preserved on lead tablets in the Classical period.

Another important issue is the extent to which the Getty Hexameters, together with the parallel texts from West Greece and Crete, provide us with evidence for the early practice of magic in ancient Selinus and elsewhere. Such practices would hardly be surprising, of course, in Sicily, the home of the poet Empedocles, who declared in a hexameter poem his ability to control the weather, plague, and floods, and even to bring back a man from the dead; or in Crete where the poet Epimenides likewise composed curative and oracular hexameters. The Getty Hexameters also raise the question of private versus public magic, for they begin by boasting of their protective power when hidden in a 'house of stone', suggesting a private function. But elsewhere in the text we find references to incantations designed to protect armies, ships, flocks, and handicrafts, all of which point to an entity larger than a single house. Does this text, then, prescribe the use of magic for the wider purposes of community welfare? Even more intriguing are the nature and date of the incantations. The Getty tablet preserves two of the earliest versions of what would eventually

---

[1] For text and annotated translation see the Appendix to this volume. Jordan (1992) and Brixhe and Panayotou (1995) are the most recent studies and supply earlier bibliography.

[2] Jordan (2000a and b) and Rocca (2009).

become the most famous of ancient Greek incantations, the so-called *Ephesia Grammata*, which in Roman times are described and transmitted as a series of nonsense words or sounds recited as a kind of mumbo-jumbo or abracadabra to protect people and places.

But the Getty Hexameters reveal for the first time that these *Ephesia Grammata* were originally composed as comprehensible dactylic hexameters, which seem to have devolved over time into the nonsense of the later Roman versions. This process of devolution, surprisingly enough, is documented by the two versions in the Getty Hexameters themselves: the first in full-blown dactylic hexameters, and the second in faltering verse, fragmentary phrases, and incomprehensible strings of letters. Several of our contributors, then, explore the ways in which the nonsense version developed from the poetic one through both textual confusion and creative phonetic play, while at the same time eventually becoming frozen in their nonsense form and then transmitted well into the late antique period. The Getty Hexameters, in short, provide us with crucial evidence for the transformation of oral songs to text, as well as the transformation of verse incantations into prose formulae.

This gives rise to what is perhaps the most important aspect of the Getty tablet as evidence for the history of ancient Greek myth and religion: the original poetic version of the *Ephesia Grammata* seems to offer a kind of *hieros logos* or sacred discourse, naming in different ways the three goddesses most closely connected with both the Eleusinian mysteries and with the underworld: Demeter, Persephone, and Hecate. Two of these deities, however, are referred to rather obliquely in the narrative that mysteriously describes the descent at milking time from the 'garden of Persephone' of a she-goat bursting with milk and described as 'the four-footed attendant of holy Demeter'. Then Hecate appears holding torches and screaming in a barbaric voice as she leads into the deepening night a male god whose identity is either suppressed or lost in a nearby lacuna. This is a truly enigmatic narrative that raises two obvious questions: was the text originally composed and used as a kind of ritual hymn or liturgy in a mystery cult, or connected in some other way to Eleusis, where Demeter, Persephone, and Hecate appear, the last with torches? And if these hexameters do originate in such a cultic context, why were they placed here in a magical text apparently used for protection? A number of our contributors take up the challenge, some suggesting, for example, that the general theme of salvation in mystery cults is appropriate to wider concerns for protection and safety, both in this world and the next, while others assert that the association with the mysteries is a much later development or that the Getty narrative operates on a more sophisticated level as a *historiola* ('little tale'), a narrative form known from later magical texts, whose recitation and resolution offers a pattern of cure intended by the Getty text.

There is one final mystery in our Getty text: the prominence of the healing god Paean as the sender and even the composer of healing incantations collected on the tablet. As a god closely connected with and eventually assimilated to Apollo and Asclepius as healers, his appearance amidst hexameters aimed at the protection of a house or city needs no special pleading, of course, but it is the reiteration of his name and expertise that raises eyebrows. He appears no less than four times in similar verses that punctuate the Getty Hexameters at odd intervals and that seem to serve as refrains to a continuous paeanic song or incantation. The text closes with a brief reference to Heracles and his destruction of the many-headed Hydra by means of Apollo's arrows—yet another nod to an Apolline world that seems at odds with the earlier narrative concerned with the three goddesses of Eleusis.

No one approach is likely to solve all the many intriguing questions and problems posed by this text. The fact that scholars of considerable erudition have pondered this text for nearly three decades from all three angles—as poem, as incantation, and as evidence for cult—without reaching anything like consensus testifies to its complexity and challenges. But since the editing and constitution of the text has now reached a point of relative fixity, we felt it was time to take stock and record a number of divergent positions and conclusions, fully welcoming areas of contention and disagreement, and in full expectation that the debate will continue.

We begin our volume, then, by offering an excellent set of photographs (courtesy of the Getty Villa), new drawings traced from these photographs, and a simple, unadorned, and rather conservative Greek text (with annotated translation) to serve as a neutral reference point, both for the chapters that follow and for future discussion. For completeness's sake, we also include in the Appendix a similarly conservative text and translation of the lead tablet from Phalasarna, Crete. Our contributors were asked to use these texts as a starting point for their inquiries, but not to be bound by them in any way, and

Introduction

indeed, a number of variations and emendations to the text and translation appear in the pages that follow.

In the first chapter, 'The Getty Hexameters: Date, Author, and Place of Composition', Jan Bremmer attempts, on the basis of an inventory of lexical parallels, to contextualize our tablet in time and place, without necessarily presupposing any understanding of the form of the text or the function of its narrative. As a result he suggests a surprisingly early date, given the magical nature of the text and especially the nonsense version of the *Ephesia Grammata*: as early as 409 BC, but perhaps unsurprisingly before the cut-off date of the destruction of Selinus by the Carthaginians in that same year. Central to his dating are the use of the *digamma* in one place in the text (together with its absence elsewhere), and telling parallels with similar expressions in Euripides, which put the text in a fifth-century BC milieu. Bremmer also draws attention to the fact that there may have been a theatre in the sanctuary of Demeter in Selinus (many major mystery sites had prominent performance spaces), which reminds us that Aeschylus and Euripides had their works performed as far afield as Sicily and Macedonia. The series of parallel texts for both the Getty Hexameters and the Orphic–Dionysiac gold tablets betray a similar geographical reach and suggest a further connection to mystery texts in general, as shown, for example, by Pindar's second *Olympian Ode*, composed for a Sicilian tyrant, or the Derveni papyrus, a late fifth-century BC papyrus found in Macedonia that offers a running commentary on an Orphic theogonic poem that was apparently used for ritual purposes.

In the second chapter, 'Hexametric Incantations Against Witchcraft in the Getty Museum: from Archetype to Exemplar', Richard Janko also dates the Getty Hexameters to the fifth century BC and offers a detailed description of the lead tablet itself. More importantly, Janko reconstructs the archetype or original form of the text, which began life as an orally composed song, either an incantation or paean in hexameters, designed to overcome witchcraft, poison, and disease. The archetype he posits reveals the sometimes composite nature of the hexameters, as well as their modes of transmission, both oral and written. Janko's reconstruction thus gives a fascinating glimpse of what the text might have looked like in a more consciously composed poetic version, perhaps one intended more for public, rhapsodic recitation than magical incantation. It is also suggestive of how much it may have been transformed in even the earliest stages of written transmission, i.e. how labile the text could be and how susceptible to the sorts of errors and corruption we expect from manuscript transmission in a much later period. To what extent we can see in the Getty Hexameters copyists working creatively on this tradition in transmission is an issue discussed in several other chapters in the volume (Edmonds and Bernabé).

In Chapter 3, 'Spoken and Written Boasts in the Getty Hexameters', Christopher Faraone sets out to isolate the ritual efficacy of the Getty Hexameters, by drawing parallels with boasts in early Greek literary texts, such as that of Demeter in her *Homeric Hymn*, or that of the satyr chorus in Euripides' *Cyclops*, who claim to know an Orphic charm to protect themselves against the ogre. Faraone argues that like these literary texts, the Getty Hexameters repeatedly make boasts about the efficacy of orally performed speech, which insist on the expertise and authority of the oral performer and invoke Paean as the divine source for the incantations they preserve. But elsewhere on the same tablet we also find a boast about the power of these verses simply as inscribed text, without any reference to human expertise or divine composition. Faraone attributes this difference to the fact that the Getty Hexameters still have one foot in the oral world of performance, in which the performer/composer would have had a more visible role and greater stake in the success of the rite, again as in the case of Empedocles. In the later tradition, more importance would be accorded to the object upon which the poetic verses were inscribed.

In the fourth chapter, 'The *Ephesia Grammata*: Genesis of a Magical Formula', Alberto Bernabé traces the complete history of the *Ephesia Grammata*, both their early evolution from hexameter verse to prose formula and their later transmission in fixed form from Late Antiquity to the medieval period, providing full texts and translations at every stop. In addition to treating the lexical components of the formulae in the Getty Hexameters, he concentrates on their transmission in fixed formulae unconnected to the original words. Most puzzling is the fact that the Getty tablet, one of our earliest testimonies, contains both a poetic and a prose version, and Bernabé, after entertaining the possibility of development in either direction, ends up supporting the idea that the prose version represents some kind of devolution of the hexameterical verses. He also finds important links between these formulae and the Orphic tradition, which he suggests may go back to a mystery tradition surrounding the use of these texts in the Sanctuary of Demeter Malophorus at Selinus.

Radcliffe Edmonds takes a different approach in the fifth chapter, 'The *Ephesia Grammata*: *Logos Orphaïkos* or Apolline *Alexima Pharmaka*?', in which he questions the idea that the *Ephesia Grammata* originated in some kind of mystery cult or liturgy. He points out that—aside from a very late magical recipe from Egypt that labels the *Grammata* as an 'Orphic *Logos*'—none of the numerous quotations and allusions to them suggest any connection with the mysteries. Stressing the repeated invocations of Paean and his *alexima pharmaka*, he argues that the formulae of the Getty and Phalasarna tablets deploy this formula against harmful creatures and magical attacks, and that in the later testimonia the *Grammata* become a kind of general protective spell, especially useful against demonic attack. He stresses the fact that on the early lead tablets, healing and protective gods such as Paean, Zeus Alexikakos, and Iatros are invoked, rather than the gods typically associated with the mysteries, and that it is only quite late in the history of the *Grammata* that the original connection with Paean and healing is lost, and the tradition is connected with other prestigious figures in magic, such as Orpheus or the Idaean Dactyls, all of whom have deep associations with mystery cults.

In Chapter 6, 'Magical Verses on a Lead Tablet: Composite Amulet or Anthology?', Christopher Faraone addresses the problem of the repeated verses in the Getty Hexameters. He explores two possibilities: first, that these repetitions operate as single verse refrains in a long hexametrical incantation, much like the refrain in Theocritus' second *Idyll*; and second, that they serve as rubrics to divide and introduce a number of different incantations within the Getty Hexameters. In the first case, this suggests that Theocritus, a native of Syracuse, may recall a Sicilian form of incantatory refrain in his poem composed in the Hellenistic period, and in the second that both the Getty and Phalasarna tablets may have originally been designed as handbooks or anthologies of protective incantations to be consulted and used as needed. If he is correct in his second suggestion, the Getty text would have anticipated by many centuries the later handbooks of magical spells, such as that of the great magical papyrus in Paris (*PGM* IV), although there are partial parallels in the magical prescriptions in Hesiod's *Works and Days*.

Sarah I. Johnston's 'Myth and the Getty Hexameters', the seventh chapter, focuses on the narrative aspects of the Getty Hexameters, insofar as they can be seen to offer a series of what historians of religion have called *historiolae*, i.e. truncated or under-nourished narratives that suggest a story pattern akin to myth (and the way myth works in ritual), but without telling a particular version so explicitly. Rather, they suggest by means of allusion, invocation, and naming of divinities, places, and events: i.e. what one might consider to be the material of myth. She reviews the nature and function of *historiolae* as mythic narrations embedded in performative texts and compares them suggestively to the narrative verses in the Getty Hexameters, where the action of leading the goat down from the mountains takes on a whole new significance—in the context of the fundamental action of 'milking'—that symbolically is thought to benefit the whole community, not just individuals within it. Johnson, moreover, sees the Getty *historiola* not so much as a fixed performative strategy, but rather as an experiment in the evolution of ritual techniques that developed under the influence of Egypt and the Near East. If so, the Getty text is probably unique, rather than part of a definitive tradition or genre.

In Chapter 8, 'The Immortal Words of Paean', Ian Rutherford's paper focuses closely on the form of the text and the central role in it of *Paean* (or should we call him Apollo?). He alone among the contributors notes that *Paean*'s personal role in the Getty Hexameters is quite unusual for the god and for the paeanic genre as it came to be established in and known from the literary tradition, where the word Paean/paean can serve as the name of an independent god, the epithet of saviour gods, such as Apollo or Asclepius, and as a shout used, like a refrain, to punctuate paeanic songs that plead for safety and healing. Rutherford comes close to positing, in fact, that paeans had originally been composed as purificatory songs such as the Getty Hexameters, i.e. consisting mainly of ritual incantations with less or no emphasis on myth or even localized cult per se. As such, the Getty Hexameters could be seen as a kind of proto-paean, i.e. without the baroque embellishment of choral metre and myth we find in Pindar and Bacchylides, but with greater emphasis on the desired effect. If he is correct, this would have far-reaching implications for the notion of the origin and development of lyric genre in early Greek poetry, and would show the explicit effects of change on a genre in a living cultic context.

In the ninth and final chapter, 'Poetry and the Mysteries', Dirk Obbink presents a general survey of the association between poetry and the mysteries, mystery rites, and mystery religions of the Graeco–Roman worlds. He suggests that the Getty Hexameters provide, for the first time, concrete evidence that the mysteries provided a definitive context for the composition and performance of poetry, an idea (he points out) that was more or less recognized in antiquity and one that sheds new light on our understanding of texts as early as the *Homeric Hymn to Demeter* and Aristophanes' *Frogs* and beyond. Indeed, some scholars, such as Richard Seaford and Walter Burkert, have gone so far as to suggest that the entire corpus of Greek tragedy may have originally been devoted to the performance of poetry and stories that had significance mainly in the mysteries of Dionysus with which the aristocratic elite of late fifth-century BC Athens was obsessed. Since these stories and dramatic performances travelled well in the ancient Greek world, he suggests that some of the itinerant oracle composers, who populate Aristophanes' *Birds* and *Knights*, may have carried the poetic texts of the mysteries back and forth between West Greece and Athens like an electrical conduit, following routes of trade, diplomacy, colonization, and the proliferation of oracle shrines and mystery cults.

In conclusion, the Getty Hexameters mark what must be the tip of the iceberg for lost genres of poetic, magical, and religious texts in the ancient world, whose scant survival is perhaps explained by the contradictory instructions at the start of the Getty Hexameters to both inscribe these verses and conceal them. This collection of papers, then, attempts to go underground with the verses to ferret out what originally inspired and motivated them, who used and adapted them, and how they can give us new insights into better-known texts such as Aristophanes' *Frogs* or Theocritus' second *Idyll*. In many ways these conclusions point surprisingly to the late fifth century BC as a period of transformation, not only from verbal song to written verse, and from simple healing paeans in hexameters to more complex lyric songs, but also from verse to abracadabra, from narrative to *historiolae*, and which saw, perhaps, the invention of the first handbook of magical spells. While in the end, many aspects of the Getty Hexameters remain enigmatic, with important details to be worked out in generations and discoveries to come, the body of evidence for poetry, magic, and mystery is so much the richer for their seeing the light.

GREEK TEXT AND TRANSLATION OF THE GETTY HEXAMETERS[1]

Side A, column i

----

traces?

1 [c.3]ΤΑΙΣ[c.2]...καὶ οὐκ ἀτέλεστ᾿ ἐπ[α]ε̣ίδῳ.
   ὅστις τῶνδ᾿ ἱερῶν ἐπέων ἀρίσημα καλ⟨ύ⟩ψ⟨ει⟩
   γράμματα κασσιτέρωι κεκολαμμένα λᾶος ἐν οἴκωι,
   οὔ νιν πημανέουσιν ὅσα τρέφει εὐρεία χθών
5 οὐδ᾿ ὅσα πόντωι βόσκει ἀγάστονος Ἀμφιτρίτη.
   Παιήων, σὺ δὲ πάντοσ᾿ ἀλέξιμα φάρμακα πέμπεις
   καὶ τάδ᾿ ἐφώνησας ἔπε᾿ ἀθάνατα θνητοῖσιν·
   ὅσσα κατὰ σκιαρῶν ὀρέων μελαναυγεῖ χώρωι
   Φερσεφόνης ἐκ κήπου ἄγει πρὸς ἀμολγὸν ἀνάγκη[ι]
10 τὴν τετραβήμονα παῖς ἁγίην Δήμητρος ὀπηδόν,
   αἶγ᾿ ἀκαμαντορόα νασμοῦ θαλεροῖο γάλακτος
   βριθομένην· ἕπεται ⟨δὲ⟩ θεαῖς π̣ε̣πιθοῦσα φαειναῖς
   [λ]αμπά⟨σιν⟩· [Ε]ἰνοδίαι δ᾿ Ἑκάτ⟨η⟩ι φρικώδει φωνῆι
   [βα]ρ̣βάρ⟨ω⟩ι ἐκκλάζουσα θεὰ θεῶι ἡγεμονεύ[ει]·
15 [c.5].[c.2]ι· αὐτοκέλευστος ἐγὼ διὰ νύκτα { . }
   [c.8–9].ι προμολοῦσα λέγω [θ]εοφρασ[c.4]
   [c.8–9] θνητοῖσι δὲ̣ δαίμο[ν]ος ἀγλα[αδώρου]
   [c.9–10]ΟΣΤΕΛΕΣ̱[1–2]ΝΧΑ[3–4]ΩΙΚΕΘ[c.6]
   [c.11–12]Ι̣ΚΑΙ[..].[c.10–12]Σ[c.6]
20 [c.12–13]ΤΑΔΩ[c.20]

Side A, column ii

----

21 [c.10–11]ΝΤΑ[c.3]...ΔΕ[c.24–26]
   [c.6–7]ωντ᾿ ἀνόμων ο̣[ἴκ]ων ἀπο χε[c.10–11]
   [Παιήων,] σὺ γὰρ αὐτὸς ἀλέξιμα φάρμα[κα πέμπεις]
   [c.6–7]γου κατάκουε φ[ρ]ασὶν γλυκὺν ὕ[μνον]
25 [c.6 ἀ]ν̣θρώποισιν ἐπιφθέγγεσσθαι ἄν[ωγα]
   [c.5–6]ωι κἂν εὐπολέμωι καὶ ναυσίν, ὅτα[ν κήρ]
   [c.7 ἀ]νθρώποις θανατηφόρος ἐγγύ[θεν ἔλθηι]
   [c.6–7]ι̣ προβάτοις καὶ ἐπὶ τέχναισι βροτ[c.4–5]
   [c.6 φ]θέγγεσσθαι ἐν εὐφρόνηι ἠδὲ κατ᾿ [ἦμαρ]

---

[1] Letters marked in ⟨ ⟩ indicate editorial additions to restore original orthography or expected reading.

Greek Text and Translation 11

30 [c.6–7]ν ἔχων ὅσιον {σιον} στόματος θυ[c.4–5]
    [c.6 ἔ]σστι πόλει· τὰ γὰρ ἀρχῆς ἐστιν ἀρίστ[α·]
    [Παιήων, σὺ δ]ὲ πάντοσ' ἀκεσσφόρος ἐσσι καὶ ἐσθ[λός]
    [c.8–9]κι κατασκια αασια ασια ἐνδασι[c.5–6]
    [c.8–9]δε· ἀμολγὸν ⟨δ'⟩ αἴξ· αἶγα βίαι ἐκ κ[ήπου
35 τῶι δ' ὄνομα Τέτραγος ηηδ[
    ΤΕΤΡΟΑΝ ἄρ' ἄγε Τέτραγ[c. 5? ἀνε-]
    μώλιος ἀ[κ]τὲ ὑδάτων ιο[
    ὄλβ[ι]ος ὦι [κα]τὰ δὲ σκεδαθ[ῆι κατ' ἀμα-]
    ξιτὸν 'ἰὼ' [καὶ] φρασὶν αὐ[τὸς ἔχηι]
40 [μακάρων κατ'] ἀμαξιτὸ[ν αὐδάν]
    [c.10 Τ]ετραγ[ος
    [c. 16]ε[.

Side B, column i
- -
43 [c.9–10]κηι θν[- - -]
    [c.8–9]ο κέλεσ[θ]ε [- - -]
    [c.8]ΩΣΕΙΣ [. .] κ[c.6] .. [- - -]
    [c.6] Διὸς υἱός [.]ιστε[π]άγκακ[ον - - -]
47 υἱω]νός τε Διός· μνῆσαι δ' Ἑκάτοιο Φ[οίβου
    [c.7–8]ε[ι]ς τόξξων, καὶ Ὕδρης πολυ[- - -]
    [Πα]ι[ή]ων, ὁ γὰρ αὐτὸς ἀλέξιμα φάρμακα πέ[μπει,]
    [οὐ]κ ἂν δ⟨η⟩λήσαιτ' οὐδεὶς {ουδαι} πολυφαρ[μακ - - -]

TRANSLATION[2]

Side A, column i
(traces of letters?)
1 .... and I sing incantations that are not ineffective.
2 Whoever hides in a house of stone the notable letters
3 of these sacred verses[3] inscribed on tin,
4 as many things as broad Earth nourishes shall not harm him
5 nor as many things as much-groaning Amphitrite rears in the sea.
6 Paean, for in every direction you send averting charms[4],

---

[2] Letters marked in [ ] indicate corresponding elements editorially supplied in the Greek text according to expected orthography or expression.
[3] Or: 'words'.
[4] Or: 'charms that are averting of everything'.

7   and you spoke these immortal verses[5] to mortal men:
8   "As down the shady mountains in a dark-and-glittering land
9   a child leads out of Persephone's garden by necessity for milking
10 that four-footed holy attendant of Demeter,
11 a she-goat with an untiring stream of rich milk
12 laden; and she follows, trusting in the bright goddesses
13 with their lamps. And she[6] leads Hecate of the Roadside,[7]
14 the foreign divinity, as she cries out in a frightening voice:
15 'I by my own command through the night . . .
16 . . . having sallied forth, I recount divinely [uttered?] . . .
17 . . . to mortals and of the goddess[8] of the splendid [gifts]'"
18–20 (individual letters and traces of letters)

Side A, column ii
21 [traces of letters]
22 . . . of/from lawless h[ou]ses . . .
23 [Paean,] for you yourself [send] averting charms,
24 give ear in your mind to sweet h[ymnic song]!
25 I command you to utter for mortals . . .
26 whenever [doom] among the . . . good-at-war, and the ships
27 [comes] near bringing death to mortals.
28 . . . [and]near the flocks-and-herds and the handiworks of mo[rtals]
29 . . . uttering night and by [day]
30 . . . keeping pure of mouth
31 . . . is for/to the city, for best are the things from the beginning(?).
32 [Paean, for you] in every direction are cure-bringing[9] and exce[llent].
33 ". . . kataskia assia asia endasia
34 a she-goat for milking . . . the she-goat from the g[arden by] force!
35 and for the one who has the name of sw[eet] Tetragos,
36 TETROAN lead, then, Tetrag[
37 . . . windy headland of the waters . . . .
38 Blessed is the one for whomever from overhead "Iô" is scattered
39 on the carriage-way [and] whoever him[self] [down along] the
40 carriage-way [holds] in his heart the speech [of the blessed]:
41 . . . T]etrag[os . . .
42 [a single letter]

[5] Or: 'words'   [6] The 'child'? (see, however, next note).
[7] Perhaps the text should be emended to make Hecate the subject, who leads a 'divinity' (Paean?).
[8] Persephone?
[9] Or: 'you are bringing a cure to everything'.

Greek Text and Translation 13

      Side B, column i
43 [letters and traces of letters]
44 ...command...!
45 [letters and traces of letters]
46 ...son of Zeus,...completely evil...
47 ...with your bow...and of the Hydra, many-....
47 of the [so]n of Zeus. And be mindful of the Far-Shooting A[pollo...
48 ...with your bow...and of the Hydra, many-....
49 [Pa]e[a]n, for he himself [sends] averting charms,
50 Nor would anyone harm [us?][10] armed with powerful dr[ugs]...

---

[10] The parallel texts have a direct object: 'me' (Phalasarna) and 'him' (*Hymn to Dem.* 227); see Ch. 3 in this volume.

Greek Text and Translation 15

Plate 1. Photo of the Getty Hexameter Fragments (The J. Paul Getty Museum, Villa Collection, Malibu, California).

Fig. 1. Line-drawing of the Getty Hexameters Tablet (front, tracings by Kassandra Jackson).

Plate 2. Lead Tablet with the Getty Hexameters (The J. Paul Getty Museum, Villa Collection, Malibu, California).

Plate 3. Lead Tablet with the Getty Hexameters (The J. Paul Getty Museum, Villa Collection, Malibu, California. Gift of Dr. Max Gerchik).

Fig. 2. Line-drawing of the Getty Hexameters Tablet (back, tracings by Kassandra Jackson).

1

The Getty Hexameters: Date, Author, and Place of Composition

Jan N. Bremmer

After his initial foray into elucidating several lead tablets with lines from our text,[1] David Jordan and his colleague Roy Kotansky have recently published a preliminary edition of the opisthographic lead tablet from the Getty Villa. This is the fullest text thus far of a series of hexameters, some of which may date back to the early fifth century BC.[2] The authors tentatively assign the tablet under consideration to the late fifth or the early fourth century BC and 'are inclined to take seriously the possibility that *Mal* (our text) is from Selinus'. They also interpret some passages from the text as 'the traditional *legomena* of a rite of initiation into the worship of Demeter and Kore',[3] but that interpretation is not immediately obvious, and the meaning of the text as a whole still remains enigmatic and problematic. In the following I will try to narrow down the date of the text of the tablet, to adduce additional arguments that the tablet derives from Selinus, and to say something about the literary culture of the author of these fascinating Getty Hexameters. I will do this via a running commentary on Column i. Although the other Columns provide evidence as well and are interesting in their own right, Column i with lines 1–20 will be sufficient to prove my argument.

---

[1] Jordan (1988), (2000a and b), (2001).
[2] Jordan (2000b) 106 notes that the tablet from Himera with a version of lines 33–38 of the Getty tablet 'could no doubt as easily belong to the second as to Prof. Manni Piraino's proposed first half of the (fifth) century'.
[3] Jordan and Kotansky (2011) 54 (initiation), 55 (date, Selinus).

So let us start with line 1. The combination οὐκ ἀτέλεστα, 'not ineffective', is Homeric and occurs both in the *Iliad* (IV.167-8) and *Odyssey* (XVIII.345). On the other hand, the verb ἐπαείδω does not occur before Aeschylus (*Ag.* 1021) and Herodotus (I.132.3), where it is used of the Magi's singing of a theogony and fits the frequent allusions to the latter's singing.[4] Chris Faraone has noted that a form of τελεῖν ἐπαοιδήν often occurs in the final lines of many late erotic charms,[5] which he rightly calls a popular coda and which, as he observes, was already parodied by Aristophanes.[6] We note the same position of ἐπαοιδή here, and although it does not occur very often in early Greek literature, ἐπαείδων also occurs at line end in Aeschylus' *Agamemnon* (1021). Last but not least, we also note that the combination of οὐκ ἀτέλεστα and ἐπαείδω is a variant of τελεῖν ἐπαοιδήν, but strikingly occurs at the beginning of our poem, as opposed to its expected position at the end. It is clear from these observations on οὐκ ἀτέλεστα ἐπαείδω that Jordan's translation 'I do not utter the profane' is completely off the mark. The expression has nothing to do with initiation. In fact, the idea of an initiation into the worship of Demeter and Kore is rather odd. We know, of course, of initiations into mysteries, but no Greek was ever officially initiated into the worship of the major gods.

In line 2, I note the striking combination of 'holy words (verses?)', which does not occur in Greek literature before the turn of the era. It is clearly not a variant of *hieroi logoi*, which at the time of the tablet always refers to some kind of Pythagorean or Orphic work or practice. The expression *hieros logos* occurs first in the Egyptian part of Herodotus, which brings us to the period around the 430s BC.[7] For Herodotus, however, a *hieros logos* was a secret tale, which was especially and perhaps exclusively connected with rites that reminded him of mysteries Samothracian, Orphic, and/or Bacchic.[8] In short, it seems to me that 'holy words' is quite a remarkable expression.

---

[4] Hdt. VII.191; Xen. *Cyr.* VIII.1.23; Catullus 90.5; Strabo XV.3.14; Curt. Ruf. III.3.9, V.1.22; Dio Chrys. XXXVI.39, 42; Paus. V.27.5, cf. De Jong (1997) 362-4; Bremmer (2008) 246.

[5] For the noun, see Lanata (1967) 46-51; Boyancé (1972²) 33-59; Furley (1993); West (2007) 327.

[6] Faraone (1992), (2010) 147-8, and this volume, Ch. 3.

[7] Hdt. II.51.4, II.48.3, II.62.2, II.81.2 = *OF* 43, 45, 650 Bernabé,

[8] For the expression *hieros logos*, see most recently Bremmer (2010b) 331-33; Parker (2011) 22.

The same is true for the idea of words carved on tin and hidden in the house of stone. Carving on tin was not wholly unknown in magical circles and is mentioned in several late antique spells and medical prescriptions.[9] The contrast with stone, on the other hand, seems to be meant for literary effect, but might also suggest a place of preservation that will last a very long time. In lines 2 and 3 we have the repetition of forms of κολάπτω with κολάψας and κεκολαμμένα, although it is not clear to me why the author thought this repetition necessary, and a scribal mistake does not seem impossible (cf. the text above, p. 1). The verb κολάπτω occurs with γράμμα in an epigram of the *Greek Anthology* (IX.341) where it means 'engraving', which is its normal meaning (see also *AP* App. 678; *IG* XIV.256; Schol. Oppian I.559). One reason for its use might be that magical texts by and large seem to avoid the verb γράφω,[10] although precisely γράφω and its *composita* are well attested in Selinuntine *defixiones*.[11]

In line 4 εὐρεῖα χθών is already Homeric (*Il.* XI.741), just as in line 5 βόσκει ἀγάστονος Ἀμφιτρίτη (*Od.* XII.97). The same is true for *Paiêôn*, who, although still independent in Mycenaean times and in the *Iliad* (V.401, 900), soon ended up as an epithet of Apollo and Asklepios.[12] It is interesting to note that in the few passages in Homer (*Il.* V.401 and 900), Hesiod (F 307 M/W), and Solon (fr. 11 West²) in which his name occurs, *Paiêôn* is nearly always connected with φάρμακα. Although it is true that ἀλέξιμα is a new word, the expression ἀλεξιφάρμακα already occurs in the Syracusan Sophron (F 3 K/A) and is well attested for Plato (*Pol.* 279–80, *Alc.* 132b, *Leg.* XII.957d). It seems reasonable to suspect that our author adapted existing vocabulary here, the more so as the line seems to have been inspired by Hesiod's αὐτὸς Παιήων, ὅς ἁπάντων φάρμακα οἶδεν (F 307 M/W). Again, the combination of ἔπεα ἀθάνατα in line 7 is unparalleled, and one wonders about the connection with the already-quoted 'holy words'. Is this an attempt to raise the status of the incantation? Is there perhaps influence from Empedocles? I also note the juxtaposition of 'immortal' with 'mortals' in ἀθάνατα θνητοῖσιν, which may have been inspired by *Od.* XIX.593, ἀθάνατοι

---

[9] Daniel and Maltomini (1992) no. 74.9, 94.37, 96 A 23.
[10] Avram (2007) 394–5, but see Graf (1997) 125.
[11] Willi (2008) 318 n. 42; add Dubois (2008) no. 26 (Selinus, c.500 BC), 77 (Agrigentum, c.500 BC).
[12] Rutherford (2001) 13–17; Graf (2009) 81–4.

θνητοῖσιν or [ἀ]θάναται θνηταῖσιν in the Dorian *Meropis* (F 4.3), even though the combination of 'mortal' and 'immortal' is rather normal in Homer. In any case, we seem to have here a speech of *Paieôn* in which he has not wholly lost his independent role: Apollo Iatros is especially prevalent in Ionia and its colonies, and not attested in fifth-century Sicily.[13]

Let us now turn to the intriguing *historiola*, which Sarah Johnston elucidates in an inventive and stimulating manner in Chapter 6 of this volume. Her proposal presupposes a religious transfer from Egypt, to Phoenicia, and to Sicily. This is certainly not impossible, as Chris Faraone has shown,[14] and indeed, as I have argued elsewhere, there are a number of indications that the Greeks derived the ancestor of their curse tablets from the Carthaginians.[15] Yet even if this transfer took place, one must observe that no specific Egyptian detail has survived the journey in this very literary text. Moreover, although milk together with honey and/or wine signifies a '*seelige Gegenwart*', as Fritz Graf has expressed it, it is extremely rare that milk is mentioned on its own as a paradisiacal signifier, perhaps only in Euphorio (*Suppl. Hell.* 430 ii 24 Lloyd-Jones/Parsons) in connection with the maenads.[16] Johnston also notes that, unlike in the Egyptian *historiolae*, the goddesses do not act in our text. Finally, the healing power of milk was noted by Greek medicinal authors as well,[17] as Johnston observes, which means that Greek ritual specialists did not need Egyptian examples to think of milk in connection with *Paieôn*.

However this may be, after this 'historiolic' interlude let us continue with our commentary. Confirmation that our hexameters derive from Selinus also comes from the following lines, of which the ultimate significance still remains rather obscure. Yet at first sight the meaning is clear. In lines 8–12 we hear of a youth who brings a goat for milking from Persephone's garden in the mountains. It is, of course, not surprising that the goat comes from the mountains, as goats are typically herded in marginal areas of land. In line 8 the 'shaded mountains' are already Homeric (*Il.* I.157; *Od.* VII.268), but

---

[13] Graf (1985) 250; Ustinova (2009).
[14] Faraone (1995).
[15] Bremmer (2010a) 18–19.
[16] See the collected evidence in Bremmer (2002) 121–2, Graf (1980) 214–15.
[17] Herzog-Hauser (1932) 1573–6; Richter (1972) 419–20.

Date, Author, and Place of Composition

the adjective σκιαρός instead of σκιερός is not attested before Pindar (O. 3.14, 18, F 129 Maehler), and has a Doric flavour.[18] Yet the most intriguing and revealing word in this line is undoubtedly the oxymoronic μελαναυγής, which is an invention of Euripides in his *Hecuba* (152) and extremely rare in Greek literature: it occurs otherwise only in the Chaldean Oracles (fr. 163 des Places: with thanks to Radcliffe Edmonds) and the Orphic *Argonautica* (513).[19] Moreover, it cannot be chance that the original noun it belonged to in Euripides, ναsμός, occurs only three lines later (line 11). Although it has now also turned up in Aeschylus' *Psychagôgoi* (F 273a.13 Radt), ναsμός is relatively popular in Euripides.[20] As the *Hecuba* dates from the middle or late 420s BC,[21] we have here a clear *terminus post quem* for our Getty Hexameters. And when we take into account that Selinus was destroyed by the Carthaginians in 409, we may assign our composition to the in-between period.

Unfortunately, we cannot identify the κῆπος of Persephone (line 9), the spelling of whose name follows the tradition of Hesiod (*Th.* 914) and the Homeric *Hymn to Demeter* (56, 360, etc.) rather than the Homeric 'Persephoneia'. Was this a particular garden?[22] Or was it an old name that survived locally? As it is somewhat surprising to find a garden located in the mountains, it might be an expression for a sanctuary, as seems to be the case in Pindar, who speaks of Gardens of the Charites (O. 9.27), Aphrodite (P. 5.24), and Zeus (P. 9.53). It is also Pindar who calls Agrigentum Φερσεφόνας ἕδος, (P. 12.2), whereas he elsewhere, like Bacchylides (3.1–2), just calls the goddess 'the daughter' (O. 6.96), perhaps in accordance with the 'soft' taboo on the name of this ἄρρητος κόρη and other underworld powers.[23] In any case, the archaeological remains do not seem to point to a particular garden in Demeter's temple at Selinus.

---

[18] See also Gow on Theocr. 18.44; Janko, this volume, Ch. 2. Could the later texts with σκιερός not be adaptations of the Homeric example?

[19] Herrmann, *ad loc.*, also compares Orph. H. 23.1: κυαναυγέτιν.

[20] Eur. *Hipp.* 225, 653; *Hec.* 152; F 223.143 Kannicht.

[21] Collard (1991) 34–5.

[22] For Greek gardens, see Carroll-Spillecke (1989) and (1992); Osborne (1992).

[23] For the expression see Eur. *Hel.* 1306–7 with Kannicht *ad loc.* and F 63 Kannicht; Carcinus *TrGF* 70 F 5.1; Henrichs (1991) 178–81. For other underworld powers note *Il.* XIV.274; Hes. *Th.* 767; Soph. *Ajax* 571, *El.* 110 with Finglass *ad loc.*, 292, *OC* 1548; Eur. *Or.* 37, probably parodied by Euboulos F 64 K/A; [Eur.] *Rh.* 963.

When does the milking (line 9) take place? Jordan and Kotansky think that it happened at dusk because the goat is brought down from the mountains.[24] However, in a learned study, Calvert Watkins has shown that there is a connotation of darkness to ἀμολγός.[25] We should therefore probably conclude that the scene takes place in the early morning when it is still dark, given that the text also mentions λαμπάδας in line 13.

In line 10 the goat is called the 'four-footed holy attendant' of Demeter. Although *composita* with -βάμων (-βή-) occur in Aeschylus, Sophocles, and Empedocles,[26] the 'four-footed' goat probably derives again from Euripides, who was the only author to use the word τετραβάμων in archaic and classical Greek. He uses it at least five times, although for a bear, horses, the Trojan horse, and the Sphinx, but not for goats.[27] As regards the goat being an attendant, we must first note that whereas Homer and Hesiod use the verb ὀπηδεῖν, the noun ὀπηδός first appears in the Homeric *Hymn to Hermes* (450), Aeschylus (*Supp.* 985, 1022, *Ag.* 426), and Pindar (*N.* 3.8, F 95.3 Maehler). Yet the noun occurs here at line end, as the verb also always does in Homer and Hesiod. Now the striking fact in the description of the goat is the close connection that is proclaimed between it and Demeter, and, presumably, by implication also with Persephone. As is well known, in the Greek world it was normally pigs, especially pregnant ones,[28] which were sacred to Demeter, whereas Persephone particularly enjoyed sacrifices of rams.[29] Of all the Sicilian sanctuaries, only Selinus contains the bones of sheep and goats near the altars of Demeter.[30]

The goat is said to be 'weighed down with an unceasing stream of rich milk' (lines 11–12). This is probably a poetic exaggeration, but goats do produce more milk than sheep.[31] Rather striking is the word ἀκαμαντορόας, as this is a *hapax*, found only in Bacchylides' *Fifth Ode* (180), an ode that was written to celebrate the victory of Hiero of Syracuse and his stallion Pherenicus in the Olympic horse race of 476 BC, even though applied to the Alpheios.[32] Milk of goats could

---

[24] Jordan and Kotansky (2011) 58.   [25] Watkins (2009).
[26] Willi (2008) 217.
[27] Eur. *El.* 477, *Tr.* 516, *Hel.* 376, *Phoen.* 792, 808; see also the discussion by Janko, this volume, Ch. 2.
[28] Bremmer (2005); Clinton (2005).   [29] Graf (1985) 282.
[30] Hinz (1998) 146f.   [31] Degen (2007).
[32] Cairns (2010) 75; see also the discussion by Janko, this volume, Ch. 2.

not be kept long and was usually drunk where it was produced. Martin West (on *Works and Days* 590) comments that the kids of goats were born in the spring and that milk could be obtained for several months from them. The Greeks did not like the cows' milk, and the mention of the goat's milk should therefore not surprise us, even though the combination θαλερὸν γάλα (11) seems to be unique and another innovation of our author.

Who brought the goat down from the mountains? Our text is not very informative and just says παῖς. It seems typical of the marginal position of the goat that we have very little information about who actually tended goats in antiquity, although it is clear that in the pecking order of tending animals, goatherds occupied the bottom of the herding ladder.[33] Anyone who searches via Google for 'girls/boys tending goats' will find examples from many parts of the world, showing that both boys and girls are charged with looking after goats. In Greece we have the examples of Branchus and Daphnis tending a flock of goats; Callimachus (*Ep.* 22 Pf.) describes a Cretan goatherd who has been abducted by a nymph from the mountains and thus, surely, was a youngish lad; and Ovid tells of a small girl tending two goats on a mountain.[34] Given the female company of Persephone, Demeter, and Hecate we should probably think of a young girl as the goatherd in our text.

Our author is similarly innovative with his expression of θεαῖς... φαειναῖς, 'bright goddesses', in line 12, as normally φαεινός never seems to be applied to living persons, only to things. The torches of line 13 fit the darkness in which the scene unfolds, but we should also not forget that torches were typical of the goddesses Demeter and Persephone and often mentioned in Sicily, sometimes in the shape of cross-torches;[35] Timoleon was even shown the way to Sicily by a torch and used the torch on his coins.[36]

---

[33] Berman (2005). Stephanie West (per email 28 November 2011) notes this interesting parallel: 'Eleanor Latimore, *Turkestan Reunion* (New York, 1934) Ch.3 (1994 ed. p. 83) (from a letter home, nomads migrating through the snow): "The men drove pony herds ahead to trample a path, then came the women with the household goods roped onto camels, and last of all the larger children driving the flocks of sheep and goats".'

[34] Branchus: Varro F 252 Cardauns; Conon *FGrH* 26 F 33. Daphnis: Longus I.7, 8, 10, etc. Ovid: *Fasti* IV.511.

[35] For this type, see Klöckner (2010).

[36] Diod. Sic. XVI.66.3–5; Plut. *Tim.* 8.1.3–4; Hinz (1998) 24 and *passim*.

In line 13 we also find the combination Εἰνοδία Ἑκάτη. This combination occurs in literature first in Sophocles' *Rhizotomoi* (F 353.2),[37] but once again Euripides proves to be more interesting. Twice he calls Hecate the daughter of Demeter, once in the *Ion* (1048) and once in the *Phaethon* (F 781.268 Kannicht).[38] This close connection between the goddesses was also reflected on the cultic level, as Hecate occupied a small *temenos* in the southeastern corner of the temple of Demeter in Selinus next to the Propylaea,[39] which has been identified by an inscription (*SEG* 34.971): once again a unique indication of a local characteristic, as we do not find other sanctuaries of Hecate in connection with Demeter and Persephone in Sicily.[40]

The verb ἐκκλάζω in line 14 is very rare in older Greek literature, but occurs once in Euripides' *Ion* (1204) as the shrieking of a bird, just as the simplex occurs twice in Sophocles as the shrieking of birds: κακῷ / κλάζοντας οἴστρῳ καὶ βεβαρβαρωμένῳ (*Ant.* 1001–2) and ἢ τοὺς ἄνω κλάζοντας ὄρνεις (*OT* 965). The juxtaposition θεὰ θεῷ derives from Hesiod (*Th.* 381). Finally, αὐτοκέλευστος in line 15 is the earliest occurrence of this word: the next time we find it is in Xenophon's *Anabasis* (IV.5.4), while θεόφραστος in line 16 is also very rare in older Greek literature, and occurs first in Pindar (F 165 Maehler).

It is time to come to a close, as lines 17–20 of Column i are too fragmented to analyse fully. Looking back at what we have found, we can conclude the following. As the quotation from Euripides' *Hecuba* shows, our text was composed in the last decade(s) before the destruction of Selinus in 409 BC.[41] Given that Jordan and Kotansky also arrive at the same approximate date on the basis of the letter-forms, it seems probable that the text of our tablet, even if it incorporated earlier verses, was actually composed at that time, not just copied; in other words, we may well have here the actual archetype of our text.[42] It also seems clear that Selinus was the place of composition, not only because it was probably found there,[43] but also because our text

---

[37] Radt and Lloyd-Jones (Loeb), probably wrongly, do not capitalize εἰνοδία.

[38] Her name is rejected by Kannicht in Euripides F 308.4, probably rightly. For the older Hecate, see Johnston (1990) 21–28; Sarian (1992).

[39] Sarian (1992) notes the importance of the localization.

[40] Hinz (1998) 148 with plate 35 on 146.

[41] Similarly, Richard Janko, this volume, Ch. 2, with additional linguistic and historical arguments.

[42] For the author, see also Faraone, this volume, Ch. 6.

[43] See also Janko, this volume, Ch. 2.

displays knowledge of characteristics of Demeter's cult that must have been familiar only to locals.

Finally, our author clearly was an erudite and sophisticated man, who knew his literature very well. In addition to being original enough to coin new combinations of words, he obviously knew Homer and Hesiod, but also, in varying degrees of probability, Bacchylides, Pindar,[44] Aeschylus, Sophocles, and Euripides.[45] Considering his scope of knowledge, we may even wonder if there was not a theatre close to the temple of Demeter, as 'many theatrical structures in Sicily are found in close proximity to sanctuaries associated with chthonic cults'.[46] There is the famous story of Plutarch that Euripides' songs saved many Athenian prisoners in Syracuse's stone quarries.[47] Our text is one more eloquent testimonial to this popularity of Euripides in Sicily.[48]

---

[44] See also Janko, this volume, Ch. 2, on Col. ii.4.
[45] See also the Conclusion (§6) of Janko, this volume.
[46] Wilson (2007) 354, referring to Todisco (2002) 29.
[47] Satyr. *Vit. Eur.* = F 6 Fr. 39 XIX Schorn; Plut. *Nic.* 29; Hornblower (2008) 18.
[48] I am most grateful to Martin Hose for his comments and to Suzanne Lye for her editing of my English.

2

The Hexametric Incantations against Witchcraft in the Getty Museum: From Archetype to Exemplar

Richard Janko

2.1. INTRODUCTION

The two lead sheets in the John Paul Getty Museum containing magical hexameters almost certainly come from Selinus, since they were obtained from the same person as the Selinuntine *lex sacra* and *defixiones* from the same city.[1] They form a document that is extraordinary not only in itself, but also because it belongs with two groups of spells written on lead that clearly had an existence almost as widespread and long-lasting as the B series of the Orphic gold leaves, which circulated from the late fifth century BC down to the first century BC, from Sicily and Magna Graecia through Crete to Thessaly.[2] The authors of the *editio princeps* have identified cognate early texts from Himera and Selinus[3] itself in Sicily, Locri Epizephyrii in Magna Graecia, and Phalasarna in Crete, and later tablets from Rome and Egypt that are now in Duke and Cologne respectively, as well as in a Michigan papyrus that includes one verse from this text. These

---

[1] Jordan and Kotansky (2011) 54. For the *lex sacra* see Jameson, Jordan, and Kotansky (1993), and for the other items from the same lot Kotansky and Curbera (2004).

[2] See now Bernabé and Jiménez San Cristóbal (2001); Pugliese Caratelli (2003); Tortorelli Ghidini (2006); Graf and Johnston (2007); Tzifopoulos (2010).

[3] Rocca (2009) nos. 6–7. The fact that the versos of both inscriptions are essentially identical to the rectos except that the script runs in the opposite direction is surely a magical practice: one must be sure that the deity hears the text, whichever way he or she prefers to read it.

parallels show that the spells were diffused as far as Egypt and survived until late in the Roman Empire, even if the Duke tablet exhibits them in a profoundly garbled state and largely transliterated into Roman script. The geographical distribution of these texts is more explicable than it might seem, since the major trade route of the Mediterranean ran from Syria via Cyprus to western Crete, and then along the coast as far as western Sicily.[4] They would first have been diffused by wandering seers and oracle-mongers such as we see most vividly in Aristophanes' *Knights* and *Birds*,[5] disreputable people who peddled hexametric spells and oracles of various kinds, which were perhaps most in demand in times of crisis such as the desperate last decades of the fifth century BC.

2.2. THE ORIGINS AND PHYSICAL RECONSTRUCTION OF THE TEXT

As the editors have suggested, the Getty Hexameters were copied from a version in the Selinuntine alphabet, without eta and omega and with the down-turned epsilon that has resulted in the corruption $αγαι$ for $ἄγει$ (line 9). Given this fact and their magical contents, this material seems likely to have come from Selinus, and indeed specifically from the adjacent chthonic sanctuaries of Demeter Malophorus and Hecate there;[6] one may compare the celebrated *lex sacra*, which is also written on lead and deals with chthonic cult, but is in the Selinuntine alphabet rather than the Ionic one. There are also signs that our text underwent metagrammatism from a copy that lacked a sign for the aspirate *h*; and, like the tablets from Heraclea and many vases from Magna Graecia, it uses for the aspirate the sign ⊢, which seems first to have appeared in Sicily, and more precisely at the nearby town of Himera in 410 BC.[7] The sheets on which the

---

[4] This sea route is as old as the Minoans: see Janko (2008) 584–6 with fig. 14.6 on p. 579.
[5] *Eq.* 1000–97, *Av.* 959–91.
[6] Demeter and Persephone (or Hecate?) are called Malophorus and Pasikrateia respectively in ll. 5–6 of the inscription from Temple G at Selinus: see Calder (1963) = Meiggs and Lewis (1969) no. 38 and Dubois (1989) no. 78. However, there is no sign of these epithets in this tablet.
[7] This symbol seems first to be found on Himeraean tetradrachms of 410 BC, e.g. Kraay and Hirmer (1966) no. 71, as is noted by Jordan and Kotansky (2011) 55 n. 8. Of course it is possible that the die-cutter brought this innovation from elsewhere.

hexameters are written surely date from the last quarter of the fifth century BC or shortly thereafter.[8] In the latter half of the fifth century the East Ionic alphabet was being introduced throughout the Greek world;[9] this alphabet arrived at Selinus around the middle of the fifth century, when it also reached nearby Himera, together with Gela, Rhegium, Tarentum, and Thurii.[10] However, the texts themselves may be earlier, and may, of course, have heterogeneous origins. Before we can proceed to approach these texts, we need to review how they can be reconstructed. To this end, we must briefly consider the physical form of the leaden sheets on which they are incised. Are we dealing with a single text or several? If so, in what order do the present two sheets go?

The sheets are similar to each other, since the tapering shapes and relative widths of the four segments of *ensemble* 1 (the editors' frr. 1–4) resemble those of the two surviving segments of *ensemble* 2 (their frr. 5–6). The two sheets formerly constituted one single folded sheet, with one or more segments lost in between.[11] When this sheet was folded, *ensemble* 2 lay outside *ensemble* 1, since its segments are wider than are those of *ensemble* 1: the approximate ratios between the segments, moving from the left of *ensemble* 1 to the right of *ensemble* 2, are 4.2 : 4.9 : 3.8 : 2.7 : lost : 5.1 : 4.8. *Ensemble* 2 was folded with its blank side outermost; however, this side was originally the verso, since the other side is the only one that has writing and was therefore used first. *Ensemble* 1, when folded, contained the interior layers, as its middle segments are narrower than are the two segments of *ensemble* 2; once again the side with less writing on it, in this case only eight lines, which again must be called the verso, was folded so that it faced the exterior of the packet. Whoever folded these two sheets intended to protect the writing to the maximum extent possible.

---

[8] Jordan and Kotansky (2011) 54–5. The D-shaped form of rho, Jeffery's ρ2 in Jeffery (1961) 34, 325, is frequent in Samian and Milesian inscriptions of the sixth century and the first half of the fifth (e.g. Jeffery, 1961, pl. 63 nos. 16, 19, pl. 64 nos. 34, 39); hence the script is unlikely to date from the fourth century.

[9] Threatte concludes that at Athens the period of transition in private documents is 480–430, and that 'Ionic script was employed by most persons for private purposes by the last quarter of the century' (1980, 33). But he also notes the paucity of evidence for Ionic script in book-rolls shown on fifth-century Attic vases (1980, 34).

[10] Jeffery (1961) 241, 246, 252, 273, but contrast 272, where she is not certain that Ionic script arrived before the fourth quarter of the century. For further inscriptions from Selinus see Dubois (2006) 37–91; Rocca (2009).

[11] So Jordan and Kotansky (2011) 54 n. 5.

Were these sheets originally two documents, or only one? *Ensemble* 1ʳ has vertical dividing-lines to the right of its column of verses (the editors' col. i); this suggests that it had a further column to the right, and was perhaps double its present width. Since the script of *ensemble* 2 seems to be the same as that of *ensemble* 1, the column on *ensemble* 2 (the editors' col. ii) was surely the column which is now lost to the right of *ensemble* 1ʳ; one segment, with diagonal edges approximately parallel to each other and wide enough to accommodate the letters that are missing down the left side of col. ii, would be lost. According to this reconstruction, the original single tablet is broken in two, with the break running roughly parallel to the dividing line between the two columns (i.e. at the right edge of *ensemble* 1ʳ and the left edge of the lost segment before *ensemble* 2ʳ). When the original tablet was turned over, the viewer would have seen *ensemble* 1ᵛ (the editors' col. iii) on the left, containing what seems to be the end of the text, and a completely empty column to the right (i.e. *ensemble* 2ᵛ). Thus the writing remains the same way up when the tablet as reconstructed is pivoted on its long horizontal axis. In the case of the *lex sacra*, evidence survives that it was publicly displayed in such a way that it could be pivoted on its short axis; the two columns are inscribed adjacent to one another on the same side, but are written upside down relative to each other, so that the tablet had to be turned 180° about its short axis if the viewer wished to read both columns.[12] But our tablet gives directions for its own engraving and interment as a means to ensure its magical efficacy, which suggests that it would not have been on public display, but rather, as its mention of Hecate suggests, buried in her precinct west of the city itself.

2.3. THE NATURE OF THE TEXT

This physical reconstruction confirms the editors' numbering of the columns. Col. i starts with a proclamation by the author that his spells have force, and that anyone who carves them on lead and puts them in a house of stone (presumably a tomb or a chthonic shrine) will be safe from harm. The fact that it opens with ritual instructions proves that this is the start of the whole text.[13] Next, the author

---

[12] Jameson, Jordan, and Kotansky (1993) 3, 5, with frontispiece.
[13] Cf. the Orphic gold leaf from Hipponium, which also begins with instructions.

addresses the god Paean, quoting verses of his, with the first case of a refrain about φάρμακα that seems to divide the text into sections; I have labelled these sections 'preamble', 'first spell', 'second spell', and so forth in my translation (Table 2.1). Paean describes an extraordinary scene, in which the child Ossa (?) drives a she-goat, perhaps Amalthea, from Persephone's garden through Hades to milking, in obedience to Hecate, the goddess who notoriously brandishes flaming torches.[14] Paean then quotes Hecate: it is she who knows the 'paths', according to my supplement, that gods and mortals must take in the underworld. In other words, she controls the communications between the upper and lower worlds, so important for the witchcraft with which she was so notoriously connected. Since Hecate has control over witchcraft, she also has the power to prevent it. Col. i continues with someone (probably the main speaker of the text) asking a deity (Paean?) to grant a favour, presumably to prevent witchcraft and harm. At this point the text breaks off.

Col. ii begins with references to keeping away harm. Line 23 is an address to Paean, with the usual refrain about φάρμακα. He is asked to utter the words of a spell, which will keep harm from armies, ships, flocks, and the products of human skill. The spell is to be spoken by night and by day, as Paean keeps his holy oracle close to his lips: it is to be restored as [βέλτιόν ἐ]στι πόλει· τὰ γὰρ ἀρχῆς ἐστιν ἄριστα, 'it is better for the city, for order is best' (line 31). One is reminded of the popularity in the 1930s of self-hypnosis with the mantra 'every day in every way things are getting better and better', but the reference to the city lends this a more official nuance. The spell ends with the usual invocation of Paean.

The very different verses of lines 33–42 are distinct from what precedes in both form and content. They start with the largely unintelligible *Ephesia Grammata*, which, as the numerous parallels suggest, should be reconstructed as a dactylic hexameter with no third-foot caesura and at least one hiatus: ασκι κατασκι αασσια⟨ν⟩ ενδασιαν ἐν ἀμολγῶι.[15] Since these 'letters' were ascribed to the Idaean Dactyls,[16] as the presence of Damnameneus in the associated verses confirms,[17]

---

[14] See e.g. fig. 20 in Gager (1992) 181 (a *defixio* from Athens, first century BC).

[15] While we await full editions by Jordan and Kotansky, the evidence is brought together in the *apparatus criticus* in Janko (2014).

[16] Clem. Alex. *Strom.* I 73.1 (see Bernabé, this vol.).

[17] Damnameneus was one of the Dactyls (*Phoronis* fr. 2.3 Bernabé). Edmonds (this vol.) reverses the process, suggesting that the name arose as a distortion of the original wording, i.e. the δαμνυμένα of the older versions from Selinus. However, the latter is less correctly formed than is Δαμναμενεύς and thus appears to be secondary, since the original root is δαμνα-.

we should expect them originally to have formed a hexameter. The rest of this material was introduced by an instruction like [λέγ' ὧ]δε, 'speak as follows'. The garbled lines that then begin are indented, with a vertical guide-line down their left margin. These were still in hexameters (except for the divine names in 35–36 and 41), which are less irregular than has generally been thought;[18] but they are written in *scriptio continua* rather than verse by verse. The text breaks off at the bottom where the lead has perished, but parallels have enabled the editors to supply two further lines (41–2). These utterances surely have a different origin and textual history from the rest, forming a separate spell that is framed by the main text. As we shall see, their original dialect was distinct too.

Col. iii begins by referring to mortals and to deities who command. These are probably Paean, son of Zeus, and a grandson of Zeus, presumably Asclepius,[19] since these powers are invoked in lines 46–7 (my supplement [⊢υιω]ⱯνόςτⱯε Διός relies on letters preserved in the version from Epizephyrian Locri). Heracles is reminded that he shot the Hydra with blazing arrows from Apollo. These arrows overcame even the highly poisonous water-snake; so these are the appropriate gods who can send protective φάρμακα to overcome any other purveyor of poisons or of witchcraft, which would, of course, also include inexplicable fevers such as those associated with the malarial swamp that nursed the Lernaean Hydra. The spell concludes that, in this event, nobody, however πολυφάρμακος he might be, could do harm of this kind; the epithets πολυφάρμακος and πολύ[δειρος] (my supplement) draw an analogy between the many heads and necks of the Hydra and the many poisons that this person has. Then the spell ends, with blank space below.

This whole text was clearly a charm against witchcraft, poisoning, and disease—the province of deities who were ἀλεξίκακοι. At this time, and indeed later in antiquity, there was simply no popular distinction made between poisoning, disease, and witchcraft: all were ascribed to the effects of φάρμακα, with the difference that cases of witchcraft and disease were even harder to distinguish,

---

[18] e.g. by Rocca (2009) 31.

[19] The cult of Asclepius is first attested at Epidaurus in *c.*500 BC, and spread through the Peloponnese during the fifth century, reaching Athens in 420/19, where his worship tended to displace that of Apollo Paean (Parker, 1996, 175–7). Pindar was already recommending the god to Hiero of Syracuse in his *Pythian* 3 (datable to *c.*474–468 BC).

without knowledge of microbes and microscopes, than were those of poisoning.[20] The god Paean and his half-brother Heracles were both associated with averting evil, with arrows, and with overcoming poisons. Paean and Asclepius were both deities of healing, while Hecate Enodia, whose words Paean quotes, controlled witchcraft; Hecate is not proven to have been identified with Enodia before the mid-fifth century.[21] The work itself was a spell[22] or hymn,[23] most probably a paean in hexameters, as the refrain invoking Paean suggests.[24] It was literally what 'Longinus' at *De sublimitate* 16.2, describing Demosthenes' inspired and soothing mention of the Athenians' victory at Marathon in *De corona* 218, metaphorically called a παιώνειόν τινα καὶ ἀλεξιφάρμακον... λόγον. Since this tablet invokes Paean's power to keep evil from 'the city',[25] it was, I suggest, a semi-official text.[26] This exemplar was either displayed so that citizens could copy it and put it to private use, or, more probably, buried by magistrates in order to protect the city as a whole, as the tag 'it is better for the city, for order is best' suggests (line 31). This official aspect also recalls the prayers/curses prescribed in the famous *dirae Teiae*.[27] If this was an official document, it can hardly have been created after the Carthaginians sacked Selinus in 409 BC, since after that date Greeks no longer controlled its destiny; it would not have been easy for Greeks to call Selinus a 'city' after the Punic sack of 409, even though a camp of a thousand mercenaries was established among the remains in 408/7. If so, we may assign the tablet a date between *c.*450 and 410, with a preference for 430–410, while the Athenians and their Ionian allies were active in the region.

---

[20] Collins (2008) 133–5.
[21] Johnston (1999) 208.
[22] Cf. F. van Straten's restoration ἐπᾳείδω in line 1.
[23] Cf. fr. 2ʳ, line 24, where I have supplied γλυκὺν ⊦[ὕμνον]; the same phrase is found in Pi. *Nem.* 5.48, but could well be a pre-existing epic formula that happens not to be attested elsewhere.
[24] On its generic nature cf. Rutherford (this vol.), and on the refrains see Faraone (this vol.). Edmonds (this vol.) reached independently the same conclusion about its purpose.
[25] Line 31.
[26] The official aspect of this text is paralleled in the new tablets from Selinus, which both have τύχα above the first line of the 'Ephesian letters' (tablets A recto and N recto in Rocca, 2009). Since both tablets are broken off before this word, there is space for a heading such as [θεοί·] τύχα, such as we sometimes see in the prescripts of official inscriptions from later in the fifth century onwards, such as θεοί: Ἀθένα: Τύχη in *IG* i.² 355, 355a: see Meiggs and Lewis (1969) no. 54, 440/39 BC.
[27] Meiggs and Lewis (1969) 62–6 (no. 30, *c.*470 BC).

As the editors of the Selinuntine *lex sacra* suggest, specialists must have been involved in composing such texts: 'the development of ritual and religious theory in the Archaic period was in the hands of specialists who were in demand for their expertise and who travelled widely, propagating their ideas and furthering the spread of certain practices'.[28] The same is probably true of this poem. Such specialists need not have been local, and very probably were not, since neither the underlying epic language nor the Ionic script of the text are local to Selinus or even to Sicily, although epigraphic details link its transmission with nearby Himera[29] and the scribe's error αγλι (αγαι) for ἄγει at line 9 shows that he was from Selinus.[30] Several of the themes that appear in it—Apollo's concern for cities and for rulers, his power to dispel evil, the killing of serpents—are also in Callimachus' *Hymn to Apollo*,[31] which I think can now be seen more clearly to have a background in hexameters that were employed for official cult. The hexameters and spells that the tablet includes resemble the kinds of oracles and prayers that were disseminated by religious experts such as Musaeus, Epimenides, Empedocles, and the oracle-mongers whom Aristophanes caricatures in his *Knights* and *Birds*.[32] It is even possible that, rather than claiming it to be a merely local composition, the Selinuntines ascribed these verses to an itinerant religious expert whose name we know but cannot link to this particular text.

2.4. RECONSTRUCTING A NORMALIZED ARCHETYPE

The spells on the tablet resemble the Orphic gold leaves not only in chronology and geographical distribution, but also in two other ways.

---

[28] Jameson, Jordan, and Kotansky (1993) 59; cf. Burkert (1983).

[29] So Jordan and Kotansky (2011) 55.

[30] So David Jordan in a letter to me, Athens, 9 Jan. 1984. The corruption of E to A could well occur to a Selinuntine copying in his Megarian script a Himeraean text in its Euboean script.

[31] Healing: *Hy. Ap.* 40–6. Cities: *Hy. Ap.* 55–7. Killing of serpents: *Hy. Ap.* 99–104. Of course, our tablet is very different from Callimachus' *Hymn*, or indeed any other known text: above all, although it is addressed to Paean, it does not contain the refrain ἰὴ ἰὴ παιάν or the like, which we would expect to characterize any paean, whereas Callimachus' *Hymn* is addressed to Apollo, yet often incorporates or alludes to that refrain.

[32] See above, n. 5.

The Hexametric Incantations against Witchcraft 39

First, I am certain we should posit that the original texts, except for some utterances of divine names in the embedded spell (lines 33, 35-6), were in hexameters. Second, we should assume that these, except the divine names, were coherent in meaning. By a comparison of variants we can hope in many places to recover the original words with a high degree of probability. As in the case of series B of the Orphic leaves, it is not only legitimate, but actually essential to compare the versions so as to reconstruct an archetype, which can then be studied in its own right.[33] Secondly, the variants are themselves potentially of great interest: they reflect the geographical diffusion of the text in dialectal terms, and shed light on its modes of transmission, whether oral, written, or a combination of both.

My normalized text in Table 2.1 supplies what I take to have been the archetype, and my verse translation attempts to replicate its finer qualities. Since not every feature of the Getty tablet is explicable without reference to the parallels, we must posit an archetype that precedes it.[34] I have restored the second half of line 35, omitted on the tablet, from the parallel texts. I have suppressed obvious dittographies, errors in the use of the initial aspirate, and the double writing of sibilants as in ἐσστι and τόξξων.[35] Different parallel sources exist for the various parts of the text, but the format of this volume did not permit their inclusion in a full *apparatus criticus*; instead, I have simply printed the letters that are derived from them outside square brackets, and the reader will have to refer to my edition for their

---

[33] For the application of this method to the Orphic gold leaves see Janko (1984). Although I agree with Graf and Johnston (2007) 1 that the original texts also need to be edited separately, only by combining them into a reconstructed archetype can one hope to make sense of all the details that they contain.

[34] Differently J. Bremmer (this vol.), who thinks it was composed at Selinus and that this copy may itself be the archetype.

[35] This phenomenon reflects Greek ambivalence over the syllabification of words containing sibilants combined with another consonant. There was disagreement in the grammarians as to whether words such as Ἀριστίων or ἀσθενής should be divided Ἀρισ|τίων and ἀσ|θενής or Ἀρι|στίων and ἀ|σθενής (S.E. *Adv. math.* I 169-74, *Anecd. Ox.* iv. 331.21 Cramer), and this is reflected by scribes at Thurii and elsewhere (Graf and Johnston, 2007, 1); the phenomenon goes back a long way (e.g. *CEG* 112, Thisba, *c*.500), and is familiar in the west, too: thus the Paestan vase-painter Asteas (*c*.340 BC) signs himself ΑΣΣΤΕΑΣ (Berlin, Antikenmuseum F 3044). Cf. Lejeune (1972) 285-6; Threatte (1980) 527-32; Wachter (1998) 233. To suggest that no editor should normalize this phenomenon (Graf and Johnston, 2007, 1) is to overlook the difference between graphemes and phonemes, and between diplomatic versus normalized transcriptions. The doubling of *xi* is unparalleled, but evidently reflects the similar syllabification *toks-sōn*.

Table 2.1 A reconstruction of the archetype of the Getty tablet, with facing translation

Archetype of Getty tablet

Col. i

1   ...]ταισ[.]... καὶ οὐκ ἀτέλεστ' ἐπαειδω.
    ὅστις τῶνδ' ἱερῶν ἐπέων ἀρίσημα καλύψει
    γράμματα κασσιτέρωι κεκολαμμένα[36] λᾶος ἐν οἴκωι,
    οὔ νιν πημανέουσιν ὅσα τρέφει εὐρεῖα χθών,
5   οὐδ' ὅσα πόντωι βόσκει ἀγάστονος Ἀμφιτρίτη.

    Παιήων—σὺ δὲ πάντοσ' ἀλέξιμα φάρμακα πέμπεις—
    καὶ τάδ' ἐφώνησας ἔπε' ἀθάνατα θνητοῖσιν·
    "{h}Ὅσσα[37] κατὰ σκιερῶν ὀρέων μελαναυγέϊ χώρωι
    Περσεφόνης[38] ἐκ κήπου ἄγει πρὸς ἀμολγὸν ἀνάγκη[ι
10 τὴν τετραβάμονα[39] παῖς ἁγνῆς[40] Δημητρὸς ὀπηδόν,
    αἶγ' ἀκαμαντορόα νασμοῦ θαλεροῖο γάλακτος
    βριθομένην· ἕπεται δὲ θεαῖς πεπιθοῦσα φαειναῖς
    λαμπάδας· Εἰνοδία δ' Ἑκάτη φρικώδεϊ φωνῆι
    βάρβαρον ἐκκλάζουσα θεὰ θεῶι ἡγεμονεύει·
15 'ἔρχομα]ι αὐτοκέλευστος ἐγὼ διὰ νύκτα β[αθεῖαν
    ἐκ μεγάρω]ν προμολοῦσα· λέγω [θ]εόφρασ[τα κέλευθα
    ἀθανάτοις] θνητοῖσί τε δαίμο[ν]ος ἀγλα[οκάρπου.'"
    ....(.)]ος, τέλεσ[ο]ν χά[ριν] ὧι κε θ[ελήσηις
    ....(.)]ι καὶ [.].[............]σ[
20 ....(.) κα]τὰ δῶ[μα ⏑ – ⏑⏑ – –
    desunt versus fere ii v.v.

Col. ii

21 ....]ομ[
    ἀνθρώπ]ων τ' ἀνόμων ο[ἴκ]ων ἄπο χεῖ[ρας ἐρύκοις.

    Παιήων]—σὺ γὰρ αὐτὸς ἀλέξιμα φάρμα[κα πέμπεις—
    κηληθ]μοῦ κατάκουε φ[ρ]ασὶν γλυκὺν ὕ[μνον ἐΰφρων.
25 πᾶσιν δ' ἀ]νθρώποισιν ἐπιφθέγγεσθαι ἄν[ωγα,
26 ὡς δήμ]ωι κἀν εὐπολέμωι καὶ ναυσίν, ὅτα[ν κῆρ

(*Continued*)

---

[36] Or κολάψει ... κεκαλυμμένα.
[37] The interpretation of this word is very doubtful.
[38] The archetype may instead have had Φερσεφόνης.
[39] This seems more likely than τετραβήμονα.
[40] The emendation is conjectural; the archetype may indeed have had ἀγίην 'holy', describing the goat rather than the goddess.

The Hexametric Incantations against Witchcraft

Translation

Col. i

Preamble:[41]
1 ...., and the spells that I sing are not unfulfilled.
  If a man graves on tin the meaning-filled letters
  of these sacred verses and hides them in a stone house,
  no creature that the broad earth rears shall cause him harm,
5 no creature in the sea that roaring Amphitrite feeds.
  First spell:
  Paean—to every place you send protecting drugs—
  you uttered for mortals these verses immortal:[42]
  "Ossa (?) the child, from the shadowy mountains in the black-lit place,
  leads from Persephone's garden by force to its milking
10 the four-footed attendant of holy Demeter,
  the goat[43] that weighs heavy with rich milk's tireless flow.
  She (?)[44] follows, obeying goddesses[45] with torches ablaze.
  Hecate of the crossroads, screaming obscurely
  in hair-raising voice, a goddess, leads the god:[46]
15 'Self-commanded [go] I through the depth of the night
  coming forth [from the halls]. To [immortals] and mortals tell I
  the divinely shown [paths] of the bright harvest spirit.'"[47]
  [O ... ...],[48] grant favour to whomever [you] wish,
  ... ... and ... ...
20 ... ... in the house ... ...
  [lacuna of two (?)lines]

Col. ii

21 ... ... [grant] that [you keep] ... ...
  and lawless [men's] hands from our homes.
  Second spell:
  [Paean]—you send protecting drugs yourself—
  [kindly] hear in your mind the incantation's sweet song.
25 [I bid you] intone [it] for [all of the] people,
26 as in [folk] good at war and in ships, when [some doom]

(Continued)

---

[41] The italicized headings are mine.
[42] This introduces the speech of Paean (the healing aspect of Apollo), which seems to end at l. 17, including the words spoken by Hecate.
[43] Amalthea?
[44] Or 'he'; the child who drives the goat is meant.
[45] Persephone and Hecate?
[46] i.e. the child, who must therefore be divine. Johnston (this vol.) takes the subject to be Paean.
[47] i.e. the goddess Demeter. Hecate acts as intermediary between the upper and lower worlds.
[48] Paean, apparently. Johnston (this vol.) suggests that there was another *historiola* here, but my supplements contradict her theory.

Col. ii

27 ἄφνω ἐπ' ἀ]νθρώποις θανατηφόρος ἐγγύ[θεν ἔλθηι,
ὡς καὶ ἐπ]ὶ προβάτοις καὶ ἐπὶ τέχναισι βροτ[είαις.
οὕτω δὴ φ]θέγγεσθαι ἐν εὐφρόνηι ἠδὲ κατ' [ἦμαρ,
30 χρησμὸ]ν ἔχων ὅσιον στόματος θυ[ρέτροισιν ἐν αὐτοῖς·
"βέλτιόν ἐ]στι πόλει· τὰ γὰρ ἀρχῆς ἐστιν ἄριστα."
Παιήων, σὺ δ]ὲ πάντοσ' ἀκεσφόρος ἐσσὶ καὶ ἐσθ[λός.

ασκι κατασκι αασσιαν ενδασιαν ἐν ἀμολγῶι.
λέγ' ὧ]δε· ἀμολγόν⟨δ⟩' αἶξ αἶγα βίαι ἐκ κάπου ἐλαύνει·
35 τῶι δ' ὄνομα Τετραγος· σοὶ δ' ὄνομα Τραξ.
ἤδι[]τετροαναραγε Τετραγ[ος.
.........] ἀνεμώλιος ἀκτά,
⟨   ⟩ ὑδάτων ιο
[ὄλβιος ὧι κε τάδε σκεδαθῆι κατ' ἀμαξιτὸν αἰῶ,[49]
40 καὶ φρασὶν αὐτὸς ἔχηι μακάρων κατ' ἀμαξιτὸν αὐδάν·[50]
"Τραξ Τετραξ Τετραγος.
42 Δαμναμενεῦ, δάμασον δὲ κακῶς ἀέκοντας ἀνάγκαι.'

Col. iii

43 ....]κηι θν[ητ ⌣⌣— ⌣⌣ — ⌣⌣ — —
.........]ο κέλεσ[θ]ε [⌣ — ⌣⌣ — ⌣⌣ —
45 ....]ωσεισκ[..]οκ
['Ηρακλῆς] Διὸς υἱός, [.]ιστει[. π]αγκακ[⌣ — —,
υἱω]νός τε Διός· μνῆσαι δ' Ἑκάτοιο φ[αεινῶν
οἷς π]α[ί]ε[ι]ς τόξων καὶ ὕδρης πολύ[δειρα κάρηνα.
Παι]ήων —ὁ γὰρ αὐτὸς ἀλέξιμα φάρμακα πέ[μπει—
50 οὐ]κ ἂν δηλήσαιτ' οὐδεὶς πολυφάρ[μακος ἄλλος.
vacat

sources.[51] Those tempted to try their own hand at restoring the lacunae should remember that the sign for the aspirate, which is not always used, takes up a full letter-space.

The text presented here, and indeed that of my full edition, is rather different from the *editio princeps*.[52] Its editors' achievement reflects an immense and admirable labour of decipherment on their part, not just of the Getty tablet itself, but of the badly damaged parallel texts which do so much to elucidate its text. Jordan has also done the hard work of comparison between the tablet and the remarkably difficult parallel texts that he has identified. However, the *editio princeps* still needs improvement in three ways.

---

[49] The Phalasarnan version has the holy shout ἰώ, but the agreement of several texts suggests instead αιω, perhaps the rare accusative αἰῶ from αἰών, apparently meaning 'forever'.

[50] The older Seliuntine versions have instead μακάρων ἄπο κήδεα εἰδώς.

[51] Janko (2014).   [52] Jordan and Kotansky (2011).

The Hexametric Incantations against Witchcraft 43

Col. ii

27 [comes suddenly] nigh bringing men to their deaths,
[as too both] for flocks and for mortal men's crafts.
Utter [what follows] by night and by day,
30 keeping holy your [oracle in][53] the doors of your mouth:
'[better] so for the city: for order is best.'
[Paean]—to every place you bring cures and are good.
Spell of the Idaean Dactyls (in Doric dialect):
aski kataski aassian endasiân en amolgôi.[54]
[Speak thus]: Goat drives goat by force from the garden to milking.
35 His name is Tetrâgos; your name is Trâx.
 ⋯ ⋯ ⋯ *tetroanarage* Tetrâgos
 ⋯ ⋯ ⋯ ⋯ windy shore,
 ⋯ ⋯ ⋯ of the waters ⋯ ⋯ ⋯
Happy is he for whom these words(?) are always(?) spread along the road,
40 who keeps in mind along the road the saying of the blessed gods:[55]
'Trâx Tetrâx Tetrâgos.
42 Damnameneus, subdue by force those who are resistant in evil.'[56]

Col. iii

Concluding spell:
43 ⋯ ⋯ ⋯ ⋯ ⋯ ⋯ mortal ⋯ ⋯ ⋯ ⋯ you[57]
command ⋯ ⋯ ⋯ ⋯
45 ⋯ ⋯ ⋯ ⋯ ⋯ ⋯ ⋯ ⋯ ⋯ ⋯
Heracles, son of Zeus, [you repel?] completely evil [deeds?],
and grandson of Zeus:[58] remember the Far-shooter's blazing arrows,
with which you smite the many-necked heads of the Hydra.[59]
Paean—for he sends protective drugs himself—
50 no one else with many drugs could inflict harm.

First, small pieces have fallen off the tablet along the breaks between its separate fragments since it was first studied. Early tracings of it, which were distributed as handouts at seminars and which are still in my possession, show parts of letters that the editors do not

---

[53] Or 'sceptre by'? A long noun is needed to fill the wide lacuna, and few are available.

[54] Magic words (the 'Ephesian letters', ascribed to the Idaean Dactyls), which seem to scan as a rough hexameter. The verses that follow down to l. 42 are in a different dialect from the rest.

[55] Or 'and keeps it in mind, though he has troubles from the gods' (the version of the earlier Selinuntine tablets).

[56] These two lines, restored from parallels, seem to be the 'saying of the gods'. Damnameneus was one of the Idaean Dactyls. The name is given as Damnymena in the earlier Selinuntine version.

[57] Plural.

[58] Asclepius is the only grandson of Zeus who belongs in this context of healing.

[59] Heracles killed the Hydra in the swamp at Lerna, which apparently symbolizes recurrent fevers such as those of malaria. Apollo's burning arrows that Heracles uses perhaps relate to the cure of such fevers.

print and that do not appear on the tracings that they have reproduced.[60] Likewise, early transcripts record letters that have since disappeared. This is reminiscent of the editing of carbonized papyri such as those from Herculaneum: an accurate representation of the current state of the text is not necessarily the best edition. Further unrecognized traces can also be seen on the new high-resolution images of the original.

Secondly, over the many years while the publication of this text was in progress, the editors rarely succeeded in keeping track of which scholars first contributed ideas for readings or restorations. I well know from my own experience how hard it is, when one is leading a seminar on a difficult text, simultaneously to record who suggests what amidst the give and take of excited discussion. The mass of information that I have gathered, derived from two decades of notes and correspondence with the editors, as to which particular scholars first advanced each of the proposed supplements to the text (and indeed the alternatives that are not printed), forms the basis of the apparatus to my full text.[61]

Lastly, the editors' *Sprachgefühl* for the idioms and metrical features of early hexametric poetry can be improved, and they have not always printed the better of two interpretations that they had themselves advanced.

2.5. THE LANGUAGE OF THE TEXT

The dialectally interesting features of the Getty text must be divided into two groups, those that relate to the scribe and those that relate to the archetype.

Features attributable to the scribe

1. The scribe is unsure of the correct use of the aspirate, which was present in his own Selinuntine dialect. He supplies it rightly most of the time, as in standard Homeric verse, with its Attic (or, as some claim, Euboean) veneer over the psilosis that was standard in the

[60] Jordan and Kotansky (2011) figs. 1–3.   [61] Janko (2014).

original East Ionic version of the Homeric epics. However, he puts the aspirate falsely thrice: in {h}ἔπε' at line 7 (where ϝέπε' must not be read—there is no trace of digamma in these texts, any more than there is in Homer), {h}ὀπηδόν at line 10, and {h}ἀλέξιμα at line 23. Often he leaves it out.[62] Evidently he was not sure where, in this poetic text, he should supply the aspirate and where not. This feature proves that the exemplar from which the scribe copied did not have a graph for the aspirate, i.e. that it was in East Ionic script. Hence at least the hyparchetype of the text, if not also the archetype itself, was in that script.

2. In the preamble at line 4 the Getty text has νιμ, i.e. νιν with assimilation before the following consonant. At line 9 the reading ἐγ κήπου in the Getty text is another such assimilation, usual in fourth-century texts such as the Derveni papyrus; it is remarkable that it survives in the Duke tablet. The Cologne tablet has normalized to ἐκ. Whether this system goes back to the archetype or not, it is a *sandhi* phenomenon that has been removed from our literary texts by a process of normalization.[63]

3. In line 50, Ruth Scodel and I once suggested that the Doric form αἰ 'if' is used instead of Homeric εἰ. However, as Roy Kotansky understood, the simplest correction of the corrupt text is surely to delete {ουδαι} after οὐδείς: the scribe started to write ουδεις a second time by dittography, lapsing into Selinuntine script in which ε looks like α, just as in his error αγαι for ἄγει at line 9. However, the Locrian parallel is reported to have ουδ followed by the lower end of a diagonal rising to the right.[64]

4. The scribe writes σκιαρῶν at line 8. The parallel texts show that the original form was Homeric σκιερῶν, since the Cologne tablet has σκιε̣ι̣ρων⌋, the Michigan papyrus σκιερων,[65] and the Duke tablet reflects the vocalism in -e-. The dialectal distribution of the two forms is unclear; there is comparable variation in μιαρός/μιερός, πιαρός/πιερός, and χλιαρός/χλιερός. The form σκιαρός may contain the normal West Greek reflex of the laryngeals where they were in contact with /r/, as in Doric ἰαρός instead of ἱερός and in Cretan

---

[62] Line 5; 10, where he wrote ι instead; 12; 13; 38; 47.
[63] It survives in Homeric papyri in such readings as ἐμ μεγάροισι.
[64] Jordan (2000a) 98, on fr. 4.7.
[65] This is wrongly transcribed and misdivided KATASKEI ERŌN in Betz (1992) 297, as autopsy reveals; also, σεμνυηρ is given as SAMNYĒR.

ἄρατρον instead of ἄροτρον.⁶⁶ In any case, ἱαρός and μιαρός were the forms current at Selinus, and the parallel texts prove that this relates to the transmission and not the archetype.

5. In line 9, the Getty text has the Attic form Φερσεφόνης rather than the Homeric form Περσεφόνη, but the name appears with an initial pi in the Duke tablet; other sources are lacunose. Φερσεφόνη also occurs in the *Descent of Pirithous (Minyas)* by Prodicus of Phocaea,⁶⁷ Sappho, choral lyric (with Doric endings), tragedy, Empedocles, and the *Orphica*. With only one parallel, it is hard to be sure which form the archetype had.

Features attributable to the archetype

The language is discussed following the order of the text.

Lines 3–4: the formulae contrasting the progeny of land and sea have good parallels in post-Homeric epic,⁶⁸ and the hiatus at the main caesura in line 4 marks the junction between established formulae. However, the 'violent' enjambment by which the adjective ἀρίσημα governs its noun γράμματα in the next verse is very rare indeed in early epic.⁶⁹ Hence the preamble seems unlikely to antedate the sixth century.

Line 4: νιν is the standard Doric form of the pronoun for Ionic μιν, which is the invariable form in Homer. νιν occurs a few times in post-Homeric epic and elegy,⁷⁰ as well as in choral lyric and tragedy. It is unclear here, for lack of parallels, whether this is an accident of transmission or a fact about the dialect of the archetype. If the latter, this suggests a Doric author who was well used to the epic language.

Lines 8–10: the separation of Ὄσσα (if that is indeed the child's name) from παῖς by a whole verse would be another mark of sophisticated and non-traditional composition.

Line 9: ἀμολγός means 'milking(-time)' rather than 'dark' or ἀκμή, which may have been its original sense.⁷¹ The same sense may occur

---

⁶⁶ I will make the argument for this sound-change in Doric dialects in a forthcoming paper.
⁶⁷ See Janko (2000) 336–7; West (2003) 268–74.
⁶⁸ Cf. Janko (1982) 28, on Hes. *Th.* 582, *Hy. Ap.* 21, *Hy. Aphr.* 4–5, *Hy.* 30.3, and *Cypria* fr. 7.12.
⁶⁹ Janko (1992) 121–2.
⁷⁰ *Cypria* fr. 9.12, *Hy. Aphr.* 280, Theogn. 364, Choerilus of Samos fr. 22.30 Bernabé.
⁷¹ Beekes (2009) s.v.

in the embedded spell at lines 33–34, where the word needs to be restored twice, not once. This word was later understood as 'milking-time'.[72] Such a reuse of obscure oral-traditional terms smacks of a date in the sixth or fifth century; it may also indicate that this spell and the embedded one share a common origin. The non-traditional word μελαναυγής is first attested in Euripides' *Hecuba* 152, νασμῶι μελαναυγεῖ. It is very striking indeed that νασμός occurs here in the very next line, as if its composer knew this passage of Euripides (the word does indeed seem like one of the latter's creations)[73]—unless of course Euripides is creating a tragic variation on the phrasing of this very poem, a stream of blood instead of a stream of milk; for μελαναυγής seems more obviously applicable to a place in the underworld than to blood.

Line 10: τετραβήμονα contrasts with the Doric vocalism τετραβάμονα in the Cologne tablet. I suspect that the archetype had Doric ᾱ, not Attic–Ionic η. τετραβάμων is first found in Euripides, who was fond of this word,[74] and compounds in -βάμον- are first seen in the trimeters and lyrics of Aeschylus; but the Ionic vocalism is nowhere attested in such compounds, except that Aeschylus is said to have used the *hapax legomenon* ταχυβήμων in his *Psychostasia*.[75] Yet Aeschylus strongly favours compounds in -βάμων elsewhere, namely ἱπποβάμων, λεοντοβάμων and πεδοβάμων. Forms in -βάμον- are also known in elegiacs by Ion of Chios (fr. 5.5) and in the Strasbourg papyrus of Empedocles' *On nature* I line 298, in the phrase ἀμπελοβάμ[ονα βότρυν] 'climbing vine'. The fact that Aeschylus, Empedocles, and Ion use Doric ᾱ in such compounds, even though the rest of their diction adheres closely to the Homeric or Attic *Kunstsprache*, shows that it was standard in the fifth century. The phrase of unknown authorship ταχυβάμονας ὅρκους, on which Aristarchus commented,[76] might seem, as its dactylic metre suggests, to

---

[72] Philox. fr. 7.21 Theodoridis; Ap. Soph. *Lex.* 28.24–5 Bekker.
[73] So J. Bremmer (this vol.).
[74] *El.* 476 (τετραβάμονες ἵπποι), *Tro.* 516 (τετραβάμονος... ἀπήνας), *Hel.* 376b (τετραβάμοσι γυίοις), *Pho.* 792 (ἅρμασι... τετραβάμοσι), *Pho.* 808 (τετραβάμοσι χαλαῖς).
[75] Hsch. *Lex.* α 8335 Latte = *TrGF* fr. 280 Radt.
[76] "ταχυβάμονας ὅρκους"· Ἀρίσταρχος κατ' ἀντίφρασιν ἀκούει ἀντὶ τοῦ "βραδεῖς" (Pausanias, Ἀττικῶν ὀνομάτων συναγωγή τ 17 Erbse). Pausanias' entry is abbreviated, with no mention of Aristarchus, in Hsch. *Lex.* τ 287 and related sources. ὅρκοι are those things upon which one swears that will enforce oaths if they are broken.

derive from epic or elegy (one thinks of Archilochus and Lycambes' broken oaths). Yet this *hapax legomenon* is surely from an anapaestic passage of Aeschylus' *Psychostasia*, since the latter play contained ταχυβήμων, the Ionic form of this otherwise unknown word;[77] this was surely the same phrase, which Aeschylus would have used with the spelling in alpha.[78] We already knew that Aristarchus wrote a commentary on Aeschylus' *Lycurgus*;[79] this is the first evidence that he also wrote on the *Psychostasia*.[80]

In the same verse the Getty text has ιαγιην, i.e. hαγίην, which is confirmed by ἁγίην on the Cologne tablet; that at Duke has a corruption of *agian* with the Doric vocalism ā. But the epithet ought originally to have been ἁγνήν, since ἅγιος is not Homeric but is first attested in Herodotus, or even ἁγνῆς, since in epic usage ἁγνός was a traditional epithet of Demeter, Δημήτερος ἁγνῆς,[81] and not of her attendant. If in the archetype it belonged to Demeter, the text would have run ἁγνῆς Δήμητρος ὀπηδόν, 'attendant of holy Demeter', with the traditional noun–epithet formula transposed. If this is so, corruption to ἁγίην had already taken place by the end of the fifth century; but perhaps the poet, rather than the copyist, replaced the traditional epithet with a more current alternative of the same meaning.

Line 11: ἀκαμαντορόα is the Doric genitive of ἀκαμαντορόης. In Attic, the genitive would be -ρόου, and in Ionic -ρόεω. However, the parallel texts seem to support the ending in -ā, contracted from the

---

[77] W. Headlam emended to ταχυβάμων (*CR* 13, 1899, 3), without making this connection.

[78] The proof is Hesychius' curious entry (*Lex.* α 8335 Latte) "αὐριβάτας" (fr. 280 Radt)· Αἰσχύλος τὸ "αὐρι-" (fr. 420 Radt) (αυριον cod.: corr. Pauw) ἐπὶ τοῦ "ταχέως" τίθησι· καὶ ὁ αὐτὸς Ψυχοστασίᾳ οὕτως φησὶ τὸ ὄνομα "ταχυβήμων". ταχυβήμων is Salmasius' palmary correction for the ταχυβηλων of the MS. Radt refers αὐριβάτας to the *Psychostasia*, clearly wrongly, and αὐρί, which he takes to be a whole word rather than a prefix (which, with Mette fr. 207b, I think it must be), to an unidentified play. Both entries clearly belong to the same discussion by Aristarchus of odd words for 'swift' in Aeschylus.

[79] Schol. Theoc. 10.18e with Pfeiffer (1968) 222 and Schironi (2004) 40.

[80] Snell and Kannicht included the phrase among the fragments of tragedy as fr. adesp. 333a, but it can now be assigned to Aeschylus' *Psychostasia*. Aristarchus refers to the play in schol. Hom. *Il.* VIII 70 (Aristonicus in codex Venetus A).

[81] *Hy. Dem.* 439. This is the original formula, and not (*pace* Richardson, 1974, 47) an adaptation of the Hesiodic formula Δημήτερι θ' ἁγνῆι (Hes. *OD* 465), where the formula is declined and split (in the dative it would otherwise have a hiatus); cf. Archil. fr. 322 West, Δήμητρος ἁγνῆς καὶ Κόρης / τὴν πανήγυριν σέβων, where the genitive remains but the form of the name is modified.

The Hexametric Incantations against Witchcraft 49

inherited morpheme in -āo: the Cologne text has ακαμαντοργηας, and the Duke tablet has a word ending in -rea. This riverine epithet was known only from Bacchylides 5.180, ἀκαμαντορόαν Ἀλφεόν; there is a parallel for the ending in Panyassis fr. 28 Matthews, Ἀχελωΐου ἀργυροδίνᾱ, although the same formula in the Orphic cosmogony that is quoted in the Derveni papyrus has ἀργυροδίνεω.[82] In the epic of the sixth and fifth centuries the termination -εω became increasingly unstable and liable to replacement by ᾱ in poets whose own dialect was Doric, like Panyassis. It seems that the composer of the archetype of this spell belonged to this group. The epithet agrees with νασμοῦ, where the contracted genitive singular in arsis confirms that the phrase cannot be very old.

The application of φαειναῖς to θεαῖς is not traditional either, and entailed the rather forced accusative of respect λαμπάδας.[83]

Line 11: [Ε]ἰνοδία{ι} δ' Ἑκάτε{ι} must be corrected to the nominative case, as the Duke tablet confirms (the Cologne tablet has final vowel in ⟨Ε⟩ἰνωδι[missing).[84] This usage of alpha and eta in the a-stem declension is consistent only with Attic dialect. The vocalism is not consistent with Ionic or Doric, although of course this could be a stray Doric ᾱ; the sole parallel in early epic is the securely transmitted Attic formula λαμπράν τε σελήνην in Hesiod.[85] This is another case where the usage of Ionic η for inherited ᾱ even after ι is not consistent. Moreover, the phrase Εἰνοδίας Ἑκάτης occurs not only in the *Orphic Hymns*[86] but also in an anapaestic passage of Sophocles' *Rhizotomoi*, a play about Medea.[87] The fragment runs:

Ἥλιε δέσποτα καὶ πῦρ ἱερόν,
τῆς Εἰνοδίας Ἑκάτης ἔγχος,
τὸ δι' Οὐλύμπου ⟨προ⟩πολοῦσα φέρει
καὶ γῆς ἀνιοῦσ' ἱερὰς τριόδους.[88]

---

[82] Col. 23.11; the same Orphic verse is cited in the papyrus commentary of 'Ammonius' on *Il.* XXI 195 = *P. Oxy.* 221 col. ix 1–2.

[83] λαμπάσιν should not be introduced into the text, since it would create even greater obscurity.

[84] For the epithet cf. Hes. *Cat.* fr. 23a.6, Ἄρτεμιν Εἰνοδί[ην, πρόπολον κλυ]τοῦ ἰ[ο]χ-[ε]αίρ[ης]; Ϝαστικᾶι Ἐνοδίαι (*CEG* 342, Larissa, *c.* 450–425 [?], second half of a pentameter); Eur. *Ion* 1048–50 Εἰνοδία θύγατερ Δάματρος, ἃ τῶν νυκτιπόλων ἐφόδων ἀνάσσεις; Eur. *TrGF* fr. 308. None of these parallels is close.

[85] *Th.* 19, 371. [86] *Hymn* 1.1 (accusative).

[87] This parallel was noted by J. Bremmer (this vol.). [88] Fr. 535 Radt.

Pearson restored ⟨προ⟩πολοῦσα, a very rare word, after the exact parallel Εἰνοδίας Ἑκάτης in a passage where Hecate 'comes forth' with her torch, here called her 'spear'; this is as striking as the parallel with Euripides' *Hecuba* discussed above. Should we instead restore ⟨προ⟩μολοῦσα?

Line 13: φρικώδης is not attested in the early epic, but first occurs in Euripides (*Andr.* 1148, *Hipp.* 1202, 1216), each time describing a terrifying divine utterance exactly as here, as it also does in Andocides (*De myst.* 29).

Line 14: βάρβαρον ἐκκλάζουσα evokes another possible parallel in Sophocles: birds of ill omen κακῷ / κλάζοντας οἴστρῳ καὶ βεβαρβαρωμένῳ (*Ant.* 1001–2). The compound verb is first in Euripides (*Ion* 1204).[89] The Cologne variant βαρβάρεον κλάζουσα contains an adjective that is otherwise unknown.

Lines 15–16: αὐτοκέλευστος is first in Xenophon and θεόφραστος in Pindar.[90]

Line 24: φρασίν is the inherited dative plural of φρήν, which was changed to φρεσίν by analogy. φρασίν persisted in the Dorian language of choral lyric in Stesichorus and Pindar; it was no doubt retained as an archaism in Doric dialects such as those of Selinus and Locri. Standard epic diction uses φρεσίν. However, at line 39, although the Getty and the Locrian tablets both have φρασίν, that from Phalasarna in Crete has φρεσίν, which may suggest that the archetype had the standard epic form (we might expect φρασίν to have survived in Cretan, a conservative dialect). Thus the archetypal reading here is not entirely certain.

κατακούω is not attested before the late fifth century. The restored phrase γλυκὺν ὕ[μνον], where only the aspirate of ὕ[μνον] survives, is paralleled in Pindar.[91] ἐπιφθέγγομαι is first in Aeschylus.

Line 26: the crasis κἀν for καὶ ἐν is a post-Homeric, indeed sixth-century feature: it first appears in Sappho (fr. 55.3) and then in Hipponax, Pindar, and Aeschylus. εὐπόλεμος is first attested still later, in Attic inscribed epigrams of 432 and c.400 BC,[92] in

---

[89] This was pointed out by J. Bremmer (this vol.).   [90] Fr. 165 Maehler.

[91] *Nem.* 9. 3, a poem for Chromius of Sicilian Aetna. The only other parallel is a fragment of an unidentified lyric poet (again Pindar?) quoted at Athen. XIV 633a–b, γλυκυτάτων πρύτανιν ὕμνων (= *PMG lyrica adespota* fr. 36b1 Page), unless one were to count ὕμνει, γλυκύδωρε Κλεοῖ (Bacch. 3.3).

[92] νίκεν εὐπόλεμομ (*CEG* 10 [iii].4, first half of a pentameter); εὐπόλεμόν τ(ε) ἀρετήν (*CEG* 102.2, second half of a pentameter).

Hippocrates (as a name) and in Xenophon.[93] The vocalism ναυσίν is, of course, Attic, Aeolic (in Sappho), or Doric (in Pindar) rather than Ionic.

Line 27: ἄφνω, if correctly restored, is first found in Aeschylus, as is θανατήφορος.[94]

Line 28: this verse contains two short dative plurals, προβάτοις and βροτ[είαις] or -οις, and a long dative plural with a vocalism in alpha τέχναισι, where we might have expected τέχνηισι. Datives in -οις before a consonant, rare in Homer, increase in frequency after his time.[95] Datives in -αισι enter the epic only at Hy. Dem. 368 (θυσίαισι), where this morph is probably owed to Attic influence, and in the Dorian Meropis fr. 4.3 ([ἀ]θάναται θνηταῖσι);[96] it is also in Theognis and in Doric and Aeolic lyric from Alcman onwards. Short datives in -αις are very rare in Homer (only three occurrences) but more common in post-Homeric epic, where they become at least as frequent as those in -ηις.[97] βρότειος, rather rare earlier, is common in Aeschylus, Empedocles, and Euripides.

Line 29: εὐφρόνη, never found in early hexameters or elegy, first occurs in Archilochus and is common in Heraclitus and Aeschylus.

Line 30: θυ[ρέτροισιν], if correctly restored, is scanned with 'Attic correption', like ὕδρης in line 48.

Line 32: ἀκεσφόρος occurs only in Euripides[98] and Astydamas.[99]

Line 33: the magic words to be reconstructed ασκι κατασκι αασσιαν ενδασιαν ἐν ἀμολγῶι are a variant of the 'Ephesian letters' explained by Androcydes the Pythagorean;[100] whether they were ever actually

---

[93] Not in [Hom.] Hy. 8.4 to Ares, since this is in fact by Proclus (West, 1970).
[94] Cho. 369.
[95] See Janko (1982) 54–7 for statistics. I have restored another case in line 30, where for the association of doors and mouths cf. αὐλῆς καλὰ θύρετρα καὶ ἀργαλέον στόμα λαύρης (Hom. Od. XXII 137) and ἀθύρωτον στόμα (Aristoph. Ran. 838 v.l.).
[96] For the formula cf. μνῆμα τό[δ(ε) ἀθάνα]τον θνητ[ō] (CEG 103.1, Attica, c.400).
[97] For statistics see Janko (1982) 171–2.
[98] Ion 1005.
[99] Fr. 6.2.
[100] Ἀνδροκύδης γοῦν ὁ Πυθαγορικὸς τὰ Ἐφέσια καλούμενα γράμματα ἐν πολλοῖς δὴ πολυθρύλητα ὄντα συμβόλων ἔχειν φησὶ τάξιν, σημαίνειν δὲ "ἄσκιον" μὲν τὸ σκότος, μὴ γὰρ ἔχειν τοῦτο σκιάν· φῶς δὲ "κατάσκιον", ἐπεὶ καταυγάζει τὴν σκιάν· "λίξ" τέ ἐστιν ἡ γῆ κατὰ ἀρχαίαν ἐπωνυμίαν καὶ "τετράξ" ὁ ἐνιαυτὸς διὰ τὰς ὥρας, "δαμναμενεὺς" δὲ ὁ ἥλιος ὁ δαμάζων, τὰ "αἴσια" τε ἡ ἀληθὴς φωνή. σημαίνει δ' ἄρα τὸ σύμβολον ὡς κεκόσμηται τὰ θεῖα, οἷον σκότος πρὸς φῶς καὶ ἥλιος πρὸς ἐνιαυτὸν καὶ γῆ πρὸς παντοίαν φύσεως γένεσιν (Clem. Alex. Strom. V 45.2). The same material is in Hesychius in abbreviated form (Lex. ε 7401 Latte, s.v. Ἐφέσια γράμματα). Androcydes

meaningful in any language I leave to others to investigate.[101] I have shown in my full text how the different witnesses can be harmonized in such a way that these 'letters' can be scanned as a hexameter, albeit a rough one.[102]

ἐν ἀμολγῶι seems here to have its original sense 'in the darkness', not the adapted sense of 'milking' seen in line 9 above (where see note) and in ἀμολγόν⟨δε⟩ in line 34.

Line 34: the Selinuntine tablet has ᾱ in βίαι ἐκ κή⌊που⌋; this usage is again consistent with Attic. Since the Phalasarna text has βίαι ἐκ κήπō, this may have been in the archetype. However, since the Himeraean text has κᾱπō with a Doric vocalism (βίαι is missing or replaced by something else), βίαι may equally well come from a Doric archetype.

Line 35: τῶι δ' ὄνομ⌊α⌋ Τετραγος contains the normal epic form ὄνομα, and the Himeraean text has τῷι δ' ὄνο⟨μ⟩α Τετρα⌊γος⌋. The Lokrian text has ὄνυμα instead, with an additional phrase that repeats the word: ⌊τῷι δ'⌋ ὄνυ⌊μα τ⌋ετρακο⟨ς⟩ {-αο} σοὶ δ' ὄνυμ⌊α Τρ⌋[α]⌊ξ⌋. This additional phrase reappears on the Phalasarna tablet: τ⌊ῶι ὄ⌋νομα Τετραγ⌊ος⌋· σοὶ δ' ὄνομα Τρέξ. Here the spelling Τρέξ, taken from a hyparchetype in which η was not used, shows that the alpha in Τραξ was long,[103] and we can infer from this that the alphas in Τετραξ Τετραγος were long also. This additional phrase must have fallen out in the Getty version. Despite its preponderance in the sources, we cannot be sure that the archetype had ὄνομα; the alternative ὄνυμα is common to most, or perhaps all, dialects except Attic–Ionic.[104]

(whose Περὶ Πυθαγορικῶν συμβόλων antedates the first century BC, since it is mentioned by Tryphon the grammarian) is missing from all collections of fragments, including VS; see Burkert (1972) 166–73.

[101] See Bernabé (this vol.). However, it is hard to argue that these evolved from the intelligible Greek of line 8 (κατὰ σκιερῶν etc.); rather, knowledge of them will have interfered with the text of line 8. I doubt whether the embedded spell arose as a corrupt version of the *historiola*, since the two texts are so divergent (for this suggestion see Faraone, this vol.).

[102] For arguments against attempts to make the 'Ephesian letters' scan see Bernabé (this vol.).

[103] Hence I propose that Clement's 'Ephesian letters' λίξ τετράξ (also found at *Testamentum Salomonis* 7.4), which are given as αἶξ τετράξ in Hesychius and as αιξ τετροξ on the Southesk gemstone, are actually a mistake for ⟨Τρ⟩αξ τετραξ (line 41) with an *iota mutum* falsely supplied.

[104] Buck (1955) 27.

Lines 36-37: ἀνεμώλιος is used untraditionally to mean 'windy' rather than 'vain'. The meaning 'windy' is recognized by Apollonius Sophista[105] at Hom. *Il.* V 216, but Homer is unlikely to have intended it there. ἀνεμώλιος might originally be derived from ἄνεμος,[106] but nowhere in Greek is this sense securely attested, whereas it can always be taken as 'vain'. We may compare the use of ἀμολγός to mean 'milking' rather than its apparent original sense 'dark' or ἀκμή.[107] Both times, the etymologically obvious sense of the word is applied rather than the obscure meaning that was current in traditional poetry; but in neither case is it credible that the original etymological meaning, if such it is, survives only in our text rather than in Homer. Such reinterpretations of oral-traditional terms suggest a date in the sixth or fifth century. It is particularly apt to find this in a magical text: for much of the effect of magic depends on recovering the supposed original sense of words imposed by the primal ὀνοματοθέτης, as we can see from Androcydes' discussion of the 'Ephesian letters'.[108]

Line 39: the older Selinuntine versions have the unintelligible κατασικον for κατ' ἀμαξιτόν: perhaps there was a confusion between Σ and the letter san (Μ), or this is a confused reminiscence of κατασκι. Most sources, including the Getty tablet, have αιω at the end of the verse. The Phalasarnan version has the holy shout ἰώ; αιω must be the rare accusative αἰῶ 'life' from αἰών, apparently meaning 'forever' in this context, like ἐς αἰῶ in a later epigram.[109] This form appears once in Aeschylus[110] and at the end of a hexameter in an oracle of Apollo quoted by Eusebius.[111] It reflects the ancient *s*-stem declension also seen in αἰεί and αἰές rather than the *n*-stem declension seen in αἰέν; both are inherited from Indo-European.[112]

Lines 39-40: the Getty tablet may have had the Doric form αὐδάν for αὐδήν (it is lacunose here), since the parallel text from Phalasarna has αὐδάν and that from Locri ⌊αὐδ⌋ά⟨ν⟩. This is not the only feature of the 'embedded spell' of lines 33-42 that seems to reflect an originally Doric dialect for the archetype of this portion of the text. However, the earlier Selinuntine versions have a different half-line entirely.

---

[105] p. 35.18 Bekker.   [106] Beekes (2009) s.v.   [107] Beekes (2009) s.v.
[108] See n. 100.   [109] *Anth. gr. appendix* 200.7.
[110] *Cho.* 350, where it is a metrically necessary emendation by H. Ahrens.
[111] εὐχαίτης ἐπίκειται Κρόνος, στυγεροῖσι δὲ κέντροις / ἀλγύνει παιδὸς ταλαοῦ δυσπέμφελον αἰῶ (*Praep. Ev.* VI 2.1).
[112] Beekes (2009) i. 35, 46-7.

Line 48: the scansion of ὕδρης as an iamb is a relatively recent phenomenon, since this treatment of a plosive followed by a liquid within a word is rare until the poetry of Solon, Theognis, and Pindar;[113] thus such 'Attic correption' occurs only once in the Homeric *Hymn to Demeter*, which I date to the later seventh century.[114] The 'violent' enjambment by which φ[αεινῶν], if I have restored it correctly, agrees with τόξων in the next verse is another recent phenomenon; such enjambments are hardly known in early epic, where they usually adapt an existing formula.[115] These two features suggest that the spell in lines 43–50, in its present form, is no earlier than the sixth century in origin.

Line 50: the Getty text has ⌊οὐ⌋κ ἄν, but the Locrian parallel has οὔ κᾱ, with the Doric enclitic modal particle κᾱ, as in Theocritus, instead of Homeric ἄν. It is, of course, possible that the Locrian engraver simply omitted the ν, and that we should read οὐκ ἄ⟨ν⟩. But in any case, given its thorough-going Homeric colouration, the Getty text seems likely to have the original reading, whereas the Locrian text is heavily Doricized. Thus in the same line, where the Getty tablet has δέ{ι}λησαιτ(ο), Scodel recognized this as δηλήσαιτο, the standard epic form, but the Locrian tablet has δᾱλέσαιτο, again with a Doric form. Jordan rightly compares the Homeric *Hymn to Demeter* 228, οὔτ' ἄρ' ἐπηλυσίη δηλήσεται οὔθ' ὑποτάμνον, where the same verb is used of witchcraft. Compare also the Phalasarna tablet lines S–T,[116] which read ο⟨ὔ⟩ με καταχρίστ[ωι δ]ηλήσετοι[117] οὔτ' ἐπενίκτωι / οὔτε ποτῶι ...

2.6. CONCLUSION

In conclusion, the main text is a series of prayers to Paean, Heracles, and Asclepius to avert harm from individuals and protect the whole

---

[113] West (1982) 17.   [114] Janko (1982) 181–3; (2011) 31–2.
[115] See above, n. 69. The closest parallel is φαίδιμα τόξα (*Hy. Ap.* 4), but this is not a traditional phrase (Janko, 1982, 101).
[116] Jordan (1992).
[117] [δ]ηλήσετοι has not yet been recognized as the first instance in a Cretan text of the original Indo-European third-person primary ending in -τοι, which otherwise survives only in Arcadian dialect (Buck, 1955, 113) and of course in Mycenaean (Ruipérez, 1952). However, finding such a form in Cretan is not surprising, since the dialect of west-central Crete shares several important features with Arcadian (Duhoux, 1988, 57–61).

city from disease, poison, and witchcraft, which were not clearly distinguished in the popular thought of antiquity. These prayers would have been performed by priests on behalf of the city, and remind one of the μαντοσύναι and 'speech that heals diseases of all sorts' that Empedocles professed to the citizens of Acragas.[118] Its author was drawn from the ranks of the μάντεις τε καὶ ὑμνοπόλοι καὶ ἰητροί whom Empedocles groups together, since the work of seers, poets, and doctors still overlapped during his time.[119] Its archetype was in a post-Homeric form of the epic dialect, but with occasional Dorisms that were typical of epic poets of the fifth century such as Panyassis; there are also some Attic uses of ᾱ. It was apparently written in East Ionic script, like contemporary texts of Homer, but our copy was made by a Selinuntine scribe. The numerous lexemes shared with tragedy are not particularly significant, since the vagaries of preservation of Greek poetry and of Greek in general are such that this situation is normal in post-Homeric poetry.[120] But the striking parallels with Sophocles' *Rhizotomoi* and Euripides' *Hecuba* strongly suggest that the poet who composed these spells was familiar with some Attic tragedies of the latter half of the fifth century.[121] His diction also reveals the Athenian Empire's influence, which of course extended to western Sicily from 427 onwards. The vagaries in the paradosis suggest that the text was disseminated by both memorization and written transmission. It circulated widely in the Greek world, and would have been spread by wandering ἰατρομάντεις such as the Cretan Epimenides; indeed, the location of the copies shows that the major trade route between Crete and western Sicily played a part in its early diffusion.

The 'embedded spell' at lines 33–42 was mainly in hexameters also.[122] This was the *Ephesia Grammata*, a charm against witchcraft

---

[118] Fr. 115.10–11 VS.
[119] Fr. 146.1 VS. On seers as healers see most recently Flower (2008) 27–9.
[120] Janko (1982) 102–5.
[121] So too Bremmer (this vol.).
[122] The only part of the text that could possibly bear any relation to rites of initiation into the mysteries of Demeter and Persephone is the *historiola* in lines 8–17, pace Jordan and Kotansky (2011) 54; my scepticism is shared by Bremmer and Edmonds (both in this vol.). On this passage see further Johnston (this vol.).

that had long been popular[123] and was ascribed to the Idaean Dactyls.[124] The archetype was in Doric dialect, and may well go back to an older original than the main spell, as the earlier Selinuntine parallels and its association with Croesus confirm.[125] Epigraphy makes clear that there were epichoric traditions of Doric hexameter poetry,[126] and these may even have survived among rustics in Sicily, eventually to be adapted by Theocritus. Yet even here the apparent reinterpretations of $ἀμολγός$ and $ἀνεμώλιος$, if such they are, would be anti-traditional, and might point to a date of composition no earlier than the sixth century. This spell was transmitted by memorization as well as in writing, as the sometimes garbled versions and ancient references to memorizing the *Ephesia Grammata* confirm.[127]

---

[123] One story, cited by Bernabé (this vol.), held that Croesus was saved by reciting it on the pyre (Ael. Dion. ε 79 = Apostol. *Paroem.* 11.29, with Phot. *Lex.* ε 2403 Theodoridis and other sources). Although it is likely to be historically false, such a tale is likely to have arisen in the century after his alleged immolation, which fascinated Greeks of the time, as we know from vase-painting and Bacchylides (Maehler, 2004, 80–3).
[124] Bernabé (this vol.).
[125] Rocca (2009).
[126] Cf. Wachter (1998) 330–42.
[127] Plut. *Mor.* 85 b.

3

Spoken and Written Boasts in the Getty Hexameters: From Oral Composition to Inscribed Amulet

Christopher A. Faraone

The Getty Hexameters are marked by an astounding array of boasts not only about the power of song and speech, but also about the efficacy of writing. The far more numerous allusions to speech undoubtedly stem from the origin of the text as an oral composition, as Richard Janko has demonstrated in his essay in this volume. As a result, these boasts frequently stress both the skill and the knowledge of the inventor or performer. The one long boast about the efficacy of written text, on the other hand, emphasizes the automatic power of the inscribed object, with no mention of the skill or knowledge of the maker. In what follows, I first describe these boasts to give a sense of their density and position, and then show how other early Greek incantations (or the earliest literary references to them) can broaden our understanding of the different kinds of claims made for speech and text in the Getty Hexameters. The chapter concludes by speculating about the historical position of the Getty tablet on the cusp between an orally composed charm and an inscribed text.

BOASTFUL SPEECH AND TEXT IN THE GETTY HEXAMETERS

The comprehensible text begins in mid-verse with someone speaking in the first-person voice: 'I sing incantations that are not ineffective' (καὶ οὐκ ἀτέλεστ' ἐπ[α]ϵίδω). If this verse stands at or very near the start of the amulet, then we must think about the traditional opening of other kinds of hexametrical texts, for example, epic or hymnic narrative, where poets often use the simplex form of the same verb in the first-person singular to describe a performance that is about to begin. Similar preludes from non-magical hexametrical genres do not, however, usually include self-advertising boasts about efficacy (e.g. οὐκ ἀτέλεστ') or the singer's skill, but focus rather on the content of his narrative (e.g. the anger of Achilles) and his dependency upon the supernatural help of the Muses. But as we shall see, such boasts of the singer's skill or the efficacy of his incantatory words are not uncommon in the earliest Greek charms or in the literary texts that allude to them.

The Getty Hexameters shift abruptly in line 2 to a conditional sentence that also makes a boast about their efficacy, but here it is about the materiality and efficacy of inscribed letters (lines 2–5):

> ὅστις τῶν[δ]' ἱερῶν ἐπέων ἀρίσημα καλ⟨ύ⟩ψει
> γράμματα κασσιτέρωι κεκολαμμένα λᾶος ἐν οἴκωι,
> οὔ νιμ πημανέουσι ὅσα τρέφει εὐρεῖα χθών
> οὐδ' ὅσα πόντωι βόσκει ἀγάστονος Ἀμφιτρίτη

Whoever hides in a house of stone the notable letters of these sacred verses inscribed on tin, as many things as broad Earth nourishes shall not harm him nor as many things as much-groaning Amphitrite nourishes in the sea....

The switch from the first person ('I sing....') in the first line to the anonymous 'whoever' in the second is at first glance surprising. This conditional sentence, however, serves the same purpose as a recipe, e.g. (to paraphrase it in the imperative mode) 'inscribe these letters... and afterwards nothing will harm you.' Here the phrase 'the notable letters of *these* sacred verses' refers, of course, to the letters on the lead tablet (lead and tin were often confused in antiquity), but it can also refer to the words that follow on the tablet.

There is another abrupt shift in lines 6–7, where the poet addresses the healing god Paean:

> Παιήων—σὺ δὲ παντόσ' ἀλέξιμα φάρμακα πέμπεις
> καὶ τάδ' ἐφώνησας ἔπε' ἀθάνατα θνητοῖσιν·

Paean (I invoke you) for in every direction you send averting charms (*pharmaka*), and you (once?) spoke these immortal verses to mortal men.

Here we might have expected a prayer (e.g. 'Would that you, O Paean, send healing *pharmaka* to me!'), but instead we first get a generalized description in the present tense of Paean's ability to send healing *pharmaka* everywhere, followed by the boast that it was he who (presumably first) uttered 'these hexametrical verses'. Here the deictic pronoun τάδε (line 7) must refer to the long descriptive passage that follows in lines 8–14 of the *pais* leading the four-footed servant of Demeter from the garden of Persephone. This second boast, then, is that the inscribed words on the tablet quote hexametrical verses that were once (and probably originally) uttered by the god Paean.

The introduction of Paean here is abrupt and oddly devoid of syntax, but since he appears three other times in similar fashion (once with γάρ replacing δέ), we should probably understand the syntax as a vocative followed by explanatory δέ (as I have translated above). We find a similar construction on the similar lead amulet from Phalasarna (line G):

Δαμναμενεῦ, δάμασον δὲ κακῶς [ἀ]έκοντας ἀνάγκα[ι].

'O Damnameneus (= "Tamer")! (I invoke you for this reason): tame by force the wickedly unwilling!'

All of these lines seem to mimic the explanatory δέ used in epic verse,[1] with one important difference: in epic, the first word in the line is usually enjambed from a longer sentence that precedes and the δέ clause that follows usually provides an explanation for the name or epithet isolated at the start of the verse, sometimes with a *figura etymologica*, as we see above with Damnameneus ('Tamer') who is invoked 'to tame'. If we take our lead from this example, then, we might perhaps understand that the name Παιήων somehow invokes him and that the words that follow explain the invocation, e.g. 'Paean ⟨I invoke you⟩ because you send...'

Within this first set of verses quoted from Paean (lines 8–14) we find yet another level of embedded speech: Hecate Enodia 'cries out in a horrible barbarian voice' (φρικώδει φωνῆι | [β]αρβάρ⟨ω⟩ι ἐκκλάζουσα) and makes a heavily emphatic boast: 'self-commanded I myself... approach and speak divinely, (αὐτοκέλευστος ἐγὼ διὰ νύκτα...

---

[1] Race (2000).

προμολοῦσα λέγω [θ]εόφρασ[τα].'[2] Here presumably Hecate's own claim to speak (note: not 'sing') 'divinely uttered things' (*theophrasta*) is similar to the poet's claim that Paean once spoke 'immortal verses', but Hecate speaks within the narrative and there is not the additional claim that she can heal. In fact, her intervention here—crying out in a horrible voice—suggests that her words are threatening. Unfortunately, we do not know how much longer her speech continued or whether there was any response.

If, then, lines 1–7 of the Getty Hexameters are meant to be continuous text, we have three boasts about the narrative that eventually follows: (i) the claim of the power of the 'not inefficacious verses' of a presumably human singer ('I sing'); (ii) the power of these same 'sacred verses' when inscribed; and (iii) the earlier invention of these 'immortal verses' by the healer god Paean, who once uttered them for the benefit of mortal men. This final claim, as we shall see, fits the pattern of assigning to the gods the invention of various human technologies, for example, the *iunx*-spell to Aphrodite or the binding spell to the Furies.

In column ii of the Getty Hexameters, after two somewhat lacunose lines, we find the second iteration of the verse describing Paean as the sender of *pharmaka* (line 23), followed by a command to someone with a singular imperative to 'listen carefully' (κατάκουε), and then a set of instructions about when and in what ritual state one should make an utterance. These verses seem, in fact, to be arranged in a somewhat elaborate ring construction framed by the repetition of the infinitive ἐπιφθέγγεσθαι (lines 25–30):

A: ...ἀ]νθρώποισιν ἐπιφθέγγεσθαι ἀν[ωγα
B: ...λα]ῶι κἂν εὐπολέμωι καὶ ναυσὶν,
C: ὅτα[ν κὴρ
...ἐπ' ἀ]νθρώποις θανατηφόρος ἐγγύ[θεν ἔλθηι,
B: ...τ' ἐπ]ὶ προβάτοις καὶ ἐπὶ τέχναισι βροτ[είαις,
A: ...ἐπιφ]θέγγεσθαι ἐν ἐϋφρόνηι ἠδὲ κατ' [ἦμαρ
      θυμὸ]ν ἔχων ὅσιον...

A: ...I command you to utter for mortals...,
B: ...both for [an army] good at war and for ships
C: whenever [doom comes] near bringing death to mortals

---

[2] I prefer the emendation of *Einodia Hecate* in the nominative suggested in the notes to the translation in this volume.

B: .... both for the flocks-and-herds and for the handiworks of mo[rtals],
A: ... utter [it] by night and by [day],
... keeping pure your [heart?]

Since we are missing text in this column at the start and end of lines, it is difficult to make out the precise syntax of the two infinitives, but if the restoration 'I command' (ἄν[ωγα) at the end of line 25 is correct, we have instructions to human users on how and when to make their utterance: they must be ritually pure (line 30), they must speak day and night (line 29), and they must do so in response to a 'death-bringing' danger that is approaching mortals (lines 26–27). Thus, whereas the first column began with a boast that the inscribed letters would protect a single 'house of stone', here the protection seems more widely understood to include the military forces (the army and the navy) as well as the flocks and handicrafts of a larger group of people, presumably a whole city. And, indeed, the word *polis* does appear in the final line of this section (31).

This whole section is, in fact, oracular in tone and content: like many Apolline oracles it seems to imagine a city in a time of great plague or disaster and it offers a ritual solution. Extant oracles do, moreover, sometimes contain direct commands from Apollo himself, usually in the first person (κελεύω: Parke and Wormell, 1961, nos. 17.1, 173.1, 230.1), but occasionally in the third person (43.1–2: Ἀπόλλων ... κελεύει and no. 363.1: Φοῖβος ἄνωγεν). When Sophocles has Creon report that 'Phoebus commands us (ἄνωγεν ἡμᾶς Φοῖβος) ... to drive out the pollution' (*Oedipus Rex* 90), he undoubtedly has this convention in mind.[3] And as in the case of the Getty Hexameters, the verbs of command nearly always appear at the end of the first hexameter line of the oracle. Here, then, the *alexima pharmaka* sent by Paean may, in fact, be (or at least claim to be) a quotation of an Apolline oracle, which would not, of course, be so surprising, given the fact that in the late Archaic period Paean becomes an epithet of Apollo and the paean one of his favourite types of hymns. The difficulty here, of course, is that these

---

[3] The verb κελεύειν also shows up in magical texts; see, e.g., a pair of identical Roman-era bronze amulets from southern France (*GMA* 11A and B), which ask a supernatural power named Thôsouderkou to turn away various evils from a vineyard 'because the god Ôamoutha commands ⟨it⟩' (κελεύει θεὸς Ὠαμουθα), and a Latin incantation preserved in Pliny that seems to be a translation of a Greek incantation in which Apollo or Phoebus commands that the plague (*pestis*) not increase. See Faraone (2009a).

verses seem to be a prelude directing us how and when to recite some special text, but it is not clear what that text is. Since Apolline oracles (especially in Ionia) often command choral performances in times of crisis, perhaps we should imagine that the song to be sung is a paean.

Line 32 (the very next verse after the end of the instructions) contains a somewhat different refrain about Paean, which emphasizes who he is rather than what he does: 'Paean, because in every direction you are a bringer of healing and excellent' (Παιήων, σὺ δ]ὲ παντόσ' ἀκεσσφόρος ἐσσὶ καὶ ἐσθ[λός). Here, as Ian Rutherford suggests in his essay in this volume, we see some slippage between Paean—the god who invents or sends the hexametrical verses and *paieôn*, the hexametrical song that is recorded on the tablet. This refrain ('*Paean*, [I invoke you] because you are [i.e. as a song] bringing healing in all directions and are excellent') is, of course, the semantic equivalent to the previous refrain ('Paean, for you [i.e. as a god] send in every direction healing *pharmaka*'), but it may have been placed here to identify the next section of verse (an abbreviated version of the *Ephesia Grammata*) as the paean to be uttered when doom comes near.

Column ii differs in some important ways from column i. There are, for example, no deictic words here to indicate precisely which verses or words are to be 'uttered' at this dangerous time (cf. line 2 '*these* sacred verses' or line 7 '*these* immortal verses') and very little boastful language, outside of the refrain about the 'cure-carrying and excellent' Paean or paean (32) and his 'healing *pharmaka*' (23). The final lines in side B, column i reiterate the verse (line 49) about Paean and his *pharmaka,* and our text ends with a final boast presumably about the protective value of these same *pharmaka* (line 50): 'no one powerful in drugs could [come and] do any harm' (οὐ]κ ἂν δηλήσαιτ' οὐδεὶς πολυφάρ[μακος ἐλθών).

BOASTS IN OTHER EARLY GREEK INCANTATIONS

Let me begin by recalling that there are a number of references to the practical use of sung incantations in the earliest strata of Greek literature. In the *Odyssey*, for example (XIX.455–58), the sons of Autolykos use an incantation to stop the wounded thigh of Odysseus from bleeding (ἐπαοιδῇ δ' αἷμα ... ἔσχεθον),[4] and Pindar tells us that Aphrodite taught Jason how to use the *iunx*-wheel and 'prayer-incantations' (λιτάς τ' ἐπαοιδάς) to seduce Medea (*Pythian* 4.213-19).[5] In Aeschylus' *Eumenides* we even see a spell enacted on stage as the chorus of Furies casts their pre-trial 'binding spell' (*hymnos desmios*) on Orestes—a scene which provides an *aition* for the well-documented use of the same kinds of binding spells by litigants arguing cases in Athenian courts of law.[6] Perhaps most importantly, according to the reported results in each of these narratives, the incantation is always efficacious: Odysseus' leg stops bleeding, Medea falls in love and runs off with Jason, and Orestes is unable to defend himself at trial and must call on Apollo to speak on his behalf.[7] The earliest Greek poets, in short, tell us or show us plainly that incantations were being sung in the days of the heroes and that they were invariably successful.[8]

We do have, moreover, one instance in which a hexametrical poet quotes or alludes to a charm in the same meter in which charms were traditionally composed: dactylic hexameters. Near the beginning of the *Homeric Hymn to Demeter*, the goddess disguises herself as an old woman looking for employment as a nurse for a young child and boasts about her knowledge of protective magic (227-30):[9]

> θρέψω, κοὔ μιν ἔολπα κακοφραδίῃσι τιθήνης
> οὔτ' ἄρ' ἐπηλυσίη δηλήσεται οὔθ' ὑποταμνόν·
> οἶδα γὰρ ἀντίτομον μέγα φέρτερον ὑλοτόμοιο,
> οἶδα δ' ἐπηλυσίης πολυπήμονος ἐσθλὸν ἐρυσμόν·

228 ὑποταμνόν M: ὑπόταμνον Allen *et alii*: ὑποτάμνων Ignarra, Delatte

I will nurse him, and I do not expect—through any weak-mindedness of his nurse—that witchcraft or an 'undercutter' will harm him, for I know an antidote far stronger than a 'woodcutter' and I know an excellent defence against woeful witchcraft.

---

[4] Renehan (1992) provides bibliography and the most recent discussion. He rightly questions (pp. 2-3) the popular interpretation of e.g. Lián-Entralgo (1970) 21-3 that the incantation also bound up the wound, pointing out that there are two actions: the physical binding of the wound and then the singing of the spell to make the bleeding stop.
[5] Faraone (1999a) 56-8 and (1999b) 113-15.
[6] Faraone (1985).
[7] Faraone (1999b).
[8] Faraone (1999a) 57-8.
[9] *Homeric Hymn to Demeter* 227-30. For the significance of Demeter's claim to knowledge of healing magic, see Richardson (1974) 229-31 and Scarpi (1976) 159-73.

Scholars have shown that in her boast Demeter imitates a popular magical charm, both in its form and in its content. The words 'under-cutter' (ὑποταμνόν) and 'woodcutter' (ὑλοτόμος), for instance, seem to be the folk-names of demons that cause teething pains in babies,[10] and the word ἐπηλυσίη is a term used elsewhere in hexameters for the 'attack' or 'assault' of a demon, sickness, or spell.[11]

There are formal parallels as well. More than a half-century ago Paul Maas showed that the second line of Demeter's boast is strikingly similar in structure to the penultimate line of the incantation inscribed on the lead amulet from Phalasarna,[12] and there are similar boasts on a recently published lead amulet from Locri and in the final verse of our Getty text:[13]

οὔ με καταχρίστ[ωι δ]ηλήσεται οὔτ' ἐπενίκτ[ωι]
οὔτε πατῶι [οὔ]τ' ἐπατωγῆι.   (Phalasarna, Crete)

'. . . shall harm me neither with ointment nor application, nor drink nor spell'

[οὐ]κ ἂν δ⟨η⟩λήσαιτ' οὐδείς {ουδαι} πολυφάρ[μακος? (Getty Hexameters 50)

οὔ κα δαλήσαιτο οὐδ α[ἰ πολυφάρμακος? (Locri)

'No one could harm (you?), not even one armed with powerful drugs'

These similarities were probably not the result of a written handbook, but rather arise from a more fluid oral tradition, as we can see from the different sources of danger:

Demeter	'undercutter', 'woodcutter', witchcraft (attacks against the baby prince)
Crete	unguent, application, potion, incantation (attacks against 'me')
Getty/Locri	a *polypharmakos* (sorcerer?) (object of attacks not given)

---

[10] Allen (1895) 13 in a brief note and then again in Allen, Halliday, and Sikes (1936) 155–6. See Faraone (2001a) for a detailed defence of Allen's thesis against Richardson and others.
[11] Faraone (2001a).
[12] Of the earlier work, much valuable information can still be got from the discussions of Wünsch (1900) 73–85, but for the best text, see Jordan (1992) 191–4, whose text and translation I give here; the uncorrected text is: ὅ με καταχρίστ[ωι δ]ηλήσετοι οὔτε ἐπηνίκτ[ωι] / οὔτε πατῶι [οὔ]τ' ἐπατωγῆι. For full text and commentary see the Appendix to this volume.
[13] Jordan (2000a). These texts also carry versions of the *Ephesia Grammata*, for which see Jordan (2000b) and the essays of Bernabé and Janko in this volume.

There are also obvious differences in syntax, in verbal modes, and in the structure of the hexametrical verse. The Cretan amulet and the *Hymn to Demeter*, for example, make their boasts more concrete by using the future tense and naming a single individual ('me' and 'him', i.e. the son of Celeus) to be protected from various dangers, while the West Greek texts use the optative and do not limit the protective power of the boast to any single individual. In the West Greek amulets, moreover, the verb stands at the beginning of the second foot and ends before a masculine caesura, whereas in the *Hymn to Demeter* and on the Getty amulet the verb begins after the feminine caesura. The close parallels between the boasts in the *Hymn* and the Cretan tablet are interesting, not least because the disguised Demeter claims fictitiously to have been kidnapped from her home in Crete.

In fact, we even find a variant of this boast about protection from future harm in a passage at the start of the Getty tablet (lines 2–5) that was discussed earlier: 'Whoever hides in a house of stone the notable letters of these holy words inscribed in tin, the beasts (or demons?) shall not harm him....' Here, too, the future verb for harming (οὔ νιν πημανέουσι) falls before the caesura, but the boast is not (as in the case of Demeter) about an oral performer's claim to expert knowledge of incantations, but rather (as was discussed above) about the efficacy of the verses as an inscribed text, a point that the text emphasizes by devoting nearly all of the first two verses to a detailed description of the letters, the act of inscription, and the specific medium of the tablet.

Comedy and satyr plays supply good information about the form and use of magical incantations in Classical times. In Euripides' *Cyclops*, for example, the frightened satyr-chorus refuses to follow Odysseus' commands to take up the firebrand and twist it into the eye of the sleeping Cyclops (630–1)—instead they offer this alternative (646–8):

> ἀλλ' οἶδς' ἐπῳδὴν Ὀρφέως ἀγαθὴν πάνυ,
> ὥστ' αὐτόματον τὸν δαλὸν ἐς τὸ κρανίον
> στείχονθ' ὑφάπτειν τὸν μονῶπα παῖδα γῆς.

But I know an entirely excellent incantation of Orpheus, so that of its own accord the burning brand moves towards his skull and sets afire the one-eyed child of earth.

Here the satyrs appear as oral performers who, like Demeter, boast of the efficacy of their 'excellent incantation' and emphasize their special knowledge by placing (again like Demeter) the verb οἶδα at the start of a verse and phrase (*Hymn to Dem.* 228–29):

> οἶδα γὰρ ἀντίτομον μέγα φέρτερον ὑλοτόμοιο,
> οἶδα δ' ἐπηλυσίης πολυπήμονος ἐσθλὸν ἐρυσμόν.

... for *I know* an antidote far stronger than a 'woodcutter' and *I know* an excellent defence against woeful witchcraft.

The satyrs, moreover, refer to their charm as an *epôidê*, a term which (as we saw earlier) appears in Homeric and Pindaric descriptions of magical incantations.

As it turns out, we find the uncontracted version of this same term (*epaoidê*) at the end of a short hexametrical fragment from a lost play of Aristophanes:[14]

> ὀσφὺν δ' ἐξ ἄκρων διακίγκλισον ἠΰτε κίγκλου
> ἀνδρὸς πρεσβύτου· τελέειν δ' ἀγαθὴν ἐπαοιδήν

Jiggle from its foundations the rear end of the old man just like a jigglebird and *make efficacious an excellent incantation*.

I have shown elsewhere that this fragment was most probably the closing couplet of a parodic love-charm that ended with a coda (these are the words above in italics) well known in later magical texts,[15] for example, the following verses that also appear at the end of hexametrical erotic spells preserved in a papyrus handbook (*PGM* XX; 1st century BCE):

> πότνια θεά, ... τέλεσόν μ[οι] τελέαν ἐπαοιδήν (col. i.26–7)
> πότνια Κυπρογένεια τέλει τελέαν ἐπαοιδήν (col. ii.25)

'Lady goddess ... *make efficacious* for me *an efficacious incantation*'
'Lady Cyprogeneia, *make efficacious an efficacious incantation*'

There is one subtle, but important, difference here: in these papyrus spells and in the Aristophanic parody, some god is invoked to bring to perfection the incantation, whereas in the two literary texts Demeter (disguised as a wet-nurse) and the satyrs claim their own special knowledge of the incantation, apparently without any debt to the divine.

---

[14] Ael. *N.A.* XII.9 = Aristophanes *Amphiaraus* fr. 29 (K–A).
[15] Faraone (1992).

I suggest, then, that when the satyr-chorus uses the phrase 'an entirely excellent incantation of Orpheus' they, too, are echoing or alluding specifically to this popular coda to hexametrical incantations. This allusion would make sense, of course, to an audience who believed that Orpheus was a hexametrical poet extraordinaire. It is interesting to note other important variations because they suggest an older and relatively malleable oral tradition. The later versions of the coda in the magical papyri from Egypt refer to a *teleios* ('efficacious') incantation, but the earlier Attic versions use a different adjective to describe the charm: both Aristophanes and Euripides use the word *agathos* ('excellent'), while Demeter uses an adjective with a similar meaning, *esthlos*. In an earlier publication I suggested that we could explain this difference in one of two ways: either as a chronological variation (e.g. the Greeks used 'excellent incantations' in the Classical period and then switched to the 'efficacious incantations' in late Hellenistic times), or as a regional change (the Greeks in Attica used 'excellent' and those elsewhere used 'efficacious').[16]

The first fragmentary line of the Getty Hexameters now offers us evidence that it was, in fact, a regional variation, when it boasts: 'I incant not inefficacious things:'

Getty (line 1):   καὶ οὐκ ἀτέλεστ' ἐπ[α]είδω
PGM XX: τέλεσόν μ[οι] τελέαν ἐπαοιδήν
                  τέλει τελέαν ἐπαοιδήν

Here we can see clearly that the boast on the Getty tablet is a negative formulation of the same claim that we find in the later non-Attic versions of the coda, which—as the underlined words above reveal—use the same sounds and syllables in the same line positions.

CONCLUSION

Let me close by noting that the mixture of or tension between the spoken and written word that we find in the Getty Hexameters is not unique. This late Classical self-consciousness about writing has an instructive parallel in the contemporary Orphic gold tablets. Since

[16] Faraone (1992).

Zuntz' B-tablets themselves tell us to recite a crucial portion of the text to the gatekeepers of the underworld,[17] scholars have usually thought that the surviving inscribed tablets were designed to jog the memory of the person once he or she had descended into Hades. But in recent years scholars have begun to realize that some of these 'Gold Leaves' may have also served as amulets that protected people while they were still alive.[18] This novel focus on the inscription of these originally oral compositions is clearest in the two fragmentary verses that appear at the start or end of the two earliest and longest Orphic gold tablets, the one from Petelia and another from Hipponium in southern Italy. Martin West has restored them as follows:[19]

>   Μνημοσύνης τόδε (?)θρῖον·[20] ἐπεὶ ἂν μέλλῃσι θανεῖσθαι
>   [ἐν πίνακι χρυσέῳ] τόδε γρα[ψάτω ἠδὲ φορείτω].

This is the (?)leaf of Memory. Whenever he (i.e. the initiate) is about to die, let him write this [on a golden tablet and carry it].

This instruction is, of course, quite similar in its formulation to the reiterated commands in column ii of the Getty Hexameters to 'utter' something 'whenever [doom comes] near, bringing death to mortals....'

We see again, however, the all-important difference between spoken and written speech: in the Getty Hexameters we are to *speak* the incantation, when doom comes near, but here on the two oldest and longest of the Orphic tablets we are told to *inscribe* the text 'whenever someone is about to die', a phrase that commentators understand to mean that at this point death is inescapable and the owner will carry the verses on the tablet into the underworld. This is undoubtedly one meaning and probably their original meaning, but, just as we saw in the four verses about the 'house of stone' quoted at

---

[17] Zuntz (1971).
[18] See Kotansky (1991) 114–15 and (1994) 107–22 no. 27; Faraone (2008) and (2009b).
[19] I give the text and translation of Janko (1984), with the addition of the supplements to the second line by West (1975).
[20] The tablet has ϝριον; other suggestions include ἠρίον ('tomb') or σρίον (Laconian dialect for θρῖον). A related gold tablet—inscribed some seven centuries later for a Roman noblewoman named Caecilia Secundina—reads: Μνημοσύνας τόδε δῶρον, ἀοίδιμον ἀνθρώποισιν. See Janko (1984) 91–2 and Kotansky (1994) 107–22 for general discussion and Faraone (2009b) for defence of θρῖον ('leaf').

the start of the Getty Hexameters, the new epigraphic habit of inscribing these orally composed or memorized texts on gold tablets seems to have led to a novel consideration of these verses as a palpable and powerful written text that could also be used as an amulet to ward off death.[21] The Petelia tablet, moreover, although inscribed in the fourth century BCE, was discovered rolled up in a Roman-period amulet case, suggesting that the final owner of it wore it around his neck and that he, at least—and presumably a long line of ancestors before him—interpreted the Greek text differently to mean that the verses would protect him whenever it seemed that death was threatening, for example, in the form of a serious illness or a difficult situation on a battlefield. Otherwise it is hard to explain why the Petelia tablet was not found unrolled in a fourth-century BCE grave, where it would have been the most useful as a passport for its original owner.[22]

Let me sum up, then, the similarities and differences between the boasts that we find on the Getty tablet and those in the literary testimonia discussed in the second half of this chapter. In the latter, claims about the efficacy of oral incantations seem to focus on the expertise of the performers themselves, for example, the claim of the disguised Demeter or Euripides' satyrs that they *know* excellent incantations that can protect babies and save one's own self from danger. The satyrs, moreover, cite an author for their excellent spell (Orpheus), as do the Furies, who in their refrain boast about the 'binding spell of the Furies'. In the Getty Hexameters, we find this kind of forceful first-person claim only once, in what appears to be the boast of a poet-sorcerer that 'I sing not inefficacious things', a phrase that expresses through *litotes* the same claim as the other hexametrical incantations that boast about their 'efficacious' or 'excellent' incantations. Similar language also appears, however, in the repeated third-person boasts about Paean himself, who 'sends in every direction protective charms (*alexima pharmaka*)', especially

---

[21] Faraone (2008) and (2009b).
[22] Because one edge of the tablet was torn away to fit it in the Roman-period capsule, some scholars (e.g. Bernabé and Jimenez, 2008) think that someone discovered the tablet in the Roman period (perhaps in a grave) and then reused it in a new amulet case, but they offer no parallels for this, whereas we do have a good parallel for a powerful migraine amulet kept in the family for over a century (see Kotansky's comments on *GMA* no. 13).

in the one variant that seems to address *paean* the song, rather than the god:

[Παιήων· σὺ δ]ὲ πάντοσ' ἀκεσσφόρος ἐσσὶ καὶ ἐσθ[λός] (32)
'[Paean, for you] in every direction are cure-bringing and excellent.'

The claim of excellence at the end of the line recalls the language of Demeter, who boasts that she knows an 'excellent defence' (ἐσθλὸν ἐρυσμόν) against disease.

In the end, then, the knowledge of hexametrical song, which hymns and epic narrative attribute to the Muses, the composers of early Greek incantations seem to claim either for themselves or (in the Getty Hexameters alone) for the god Paean. The power of inscribed verses is, however, alluded to only once in all of the late Classical lead amulets—near the start of the Getty tablet (lines 2–5). The absence, in fact, of any self-consciousness about the act of writing on any of the other late Classical lead amulets from Selinus, Himera, Locri, and Crete and anywhere else in the Getty Hexameters suggests that the practice of inscribing magical charms was still in its infancy and that the Getty tablet stands out as an early experiment when it boasts of the special power of these sacred words inscribed in tin and hidden in a house of stone.

4

The *Ephesia Grammata*: Genesis of a Magical Formula

Alberto Bernabé

4.1. INTRODUCTION

Different traditions talk about a magical formula of great power called the *Ephesia Grammata*[1]. Later literary sources present this formula as a prosaic list of names, with only slight variants from one to another: *aski, kataski, lix, tetrax, Damnameneus, Aisia*. In recent years, however, our knowledge of the origins of this formula has been greatly enriched by the appearance of various hexametric versions inscribed on lead tablets, which contain all the elements in the prosaic formula, but with remarkable differences and additions. The Getty Hexameters preserve the earliest and fullest versions of both the poetic and prosaic versions and allow us an unparalleled opportunity to fully reconstruct the evolution of the formula.

In this chapter I will outline some key points to determine which elements of the hexametrical versions that date to the late Classical period have been used and, in some cases, distorted, in order to create the famous prosaic *Ephesia Grammata* of Roman times. I will also offer some possible explanations for this process.

---

[1] On the Ἐφέσια γράμματα cf. Wyttenbach note to Plut. *quom. quis suos in virt. sent.* 85B; Wessely (1886); Heim (1893) 46–67; Ziebarth (1899); Wünsch (1900) 78ff.; Roscher (1901); Huvelin (1901); Audollent (1904) LXIX; Kuhnert (1905); Schultz (1909a, b); Siebourg (1915); Deissmann (1918); Picard (1922) 131, 434; Bonner (1950) 5; Preisendanz (1961); Betz (1980) 291–2; Luck (1985) 17; Arnold (1989) 14–19; Teodorsson (1989) III 84; Kotansky (1991) 110–11; Faraone (1992) 45; Gager (1992) 5–6; Kotansky (1995) 256; Versnel (1996) 233ff.; Ogden (1999) 46–7; Rocca (2009) 31–48.

4. 2. A POWERFUL FORMULA

A series of authors have talked about the power of the *Ephesia Grammata* at different times and periods. Let us have a look at the texts:

Anaxilas fr. 18.6–7 K.–A.

> ἐν σκυταρίοις ῥαπτοῖσι φορῶν
> Ἐφεσήια γράμματα καλά.

Carrying about, on little bits of stitched leather,
lovely Ephesian letters. (Trans. C. B. Gulick)

Menander fr. 274 K.–A.

> Ἐφέσια τοῖς γαμοῦσιν οὗτος περιπατεῖ
> λέγων ἀλεξιφάρμακα.

He walks (i.e. in a circle) around those getting married speaking Ephesian remedies.

Photius s. v. Ἐφέσια γράμματα (II 227 Theodoridis)

> καὶ Ἐφέσια ἀλεξιφάρμακα· ὀνόματα ἄττα καὶ φωναὶ ἀντιπάθειάν τινα
> φυσικὴν ἔχουσαι.

Also 'Ephesian remedies': some names and sounds that have a physical counteraction.

Plutarch *Quaest. conv.* VII.5.4, p. 706D

> ὥσπερ γὰρ οἱ μάγοι τοὺς δαιμονιζομένους κελεύουσι τὰ Ἐφέσια
> γράμματα πρὸς αὑτοὺς καταλέγειν καὶ ὀνομάζειν.

For just as sorcerers advise those possessed by demons to recite and name over to themselves the Ephesian letters. (Trans. by E. L. Minar Jr.)

Clement of Alexandria *Strom.* I.15.73.1

> τινὲς δὲ μυθικώτερον τῶν Ἰδαίων καλουμένων δακτύλων σοφούς τινας
> πρώτους γενέσθαι λέγουσιν, εἰς οὓς ἥ τε τῶν Ἐφεσίων λεγομένων γραμμάτων
> καὶ ἡ τῶν κατὰ μουσικὴν εὕρεσις ῥυθμῶν ἀναφέρεται.

Some more fabulously say that certain of those called the Idaean Dactyls were the first wise men, to whom are attributed the invention of what are called the 'Ephesian letters', and of numbers in music. (Trans. by Ph. Schaft *et al.*)

Clem. Alex. *Strom.* V.8.45.2

Ἀνδροκύδης[2] γοῦν ὁ Πυθαγορικὸς τὰ Ἐφέσια καλούμενα γράμματα ἐν πολλοῖς δὴ πολυθρύλητα ὄντα συμβόλων ἔχειν φησὶ τάξιν.

Androcydes the Pythagorean says the far-famed so-called Ephesian letters were of the class of symbols. (See the next part of this passage in § 3.)

Diogen. IV.78 (*Paroem. Gr.* I 244.5) Apostol. VIII.17 (*Paroem. Gr.* II 429.15)

Ἐφέσια γράμματα· ἐπωιδαί τινες ἦσαν, ἅσπερ οἱ φωνοῦντες ἐνίκων ἐν παντί.

Ephesian Letters. They were certain spells, by reciting which they won in all contests.

Ael. Dion. ε 79 Apostol. 11, 29 (*Paroem. Gr.* II 523, 1), Phot. *Lex.* II 226 Theodoridis, Suda II 483, 16 Adler, *Et. M.* 402.22

μετὰ γραμμάτων Ἐφεσίων παλαίεις· ἐπὶ τῶν ἐπωιδαῖς ἰσχυόντων. ταῦτα δὲ ἦσαν ἐπωιδαί τινες δυσπαρακολούθητοι ἃς καὶ Κροῖσος ἐπὶ τῆς πυρᾶς εἰπὼν ὠφελήθη καὶ ἐν Ὀλυμπίαι Μιλησίου καὶ Ἐφεσίου παλαιόντων, τὸν Μιλήσιον μὴ δύνασθαι παλαίειν διὰ τὸ τὸν ἕτερον παρὰ τῶι ἀστραγάλωι ἔχειν τὰ Ἐφέσια γράμματα· φανεροῦ δὲ τούτου γενομένου καὶ λυθέντων αὐτῶι τριακοντάκις τὸ ἑξῆς πεσεῖν τὸν Ἐφέσιον.

'You wrestle with Ephesian Letters'. It is applied to those who win with the help of incantations. These spells were hard to understand; by pronouncing them on his funeral pyre even Croesus saved himself. In Olympia, when a Milesian competed against an Ephesian, the Milesian could not beat him in wrestling because that other one wore the Ephesian letters on his ankle. But when this was discovered and the letters removed, the Ephesian was defeated thirty times in a row.

Eust. *in Od.* 1864.19 *ad* Hom. *Od.* XIX.247

Παυσανίας δέ φησιν ἐν τῶι κατ' αὐτὸν ῥητορικῶι λεξικῶι (ε 85 p. 183 Erbse) καὶ ὅτι φωναὶ ἦσαν τὰ Ἐφέσια γράμματα, φυσικὸν ἐμπεριέχουσαι νοῦν ἀλεξίκακον, ἃς καὶ Κροῖσον ἐπὶ πυρᾶς φησὶ καὶ αὐτὸς εἰπεῖν, καὶ ὅτι ἀσαφῶς ⟨δὲ⟩ καὶ αἰνιγματωδῶς δοκεῖ ἐπὶ ποδῶν καὶ ζώνης καὶ στεφάνης ἐπιγεγράφθαι τῆς Ἀρτέμιδος τὰ τοιαῦτα γράμματα[3].... καὶ παροιμία τὸ Ἐφέσια γράμματα, ἐπὶ τῶν ἀσαφῆ τινὰ λαλούντων καὶ δυσπαρακολούθητα.

---

[2] Fr. 2 Hölk, *de acusm. sive symb. Pyth.* p. 47, Theslleff p. 170, cf. also Diels, *Vorsokr.* I 465, 24; Burkert (1972) 167; Gordon (1999) 239.
[3] Cf. McCown (1923) 129 n. 8.

Pausanias in the *Rhetorical Lexicon* says that the Ephesian letters were words encompassing in themselves the natural sense of warding off evil. He also says that Croesus spoke these on the pyre, and that such letters seem to have been inscribed unclearly and enigmatically on the feet and girdle and crown of (i.e. the statue of Ephesian) Artemis... and there is the proverb 'Ephesian letters' which is applied to those who say unclear things that are hard to understand.

As we can see, these *Ephesia Grammata* were thought to have power either as a written text (Anaxilas and the tale of the Ephesian fighter as quoted by Aelius Dionysius) or as an oral incantation (Menander, Plutarch, Diogenianus, etc. and Croesus, according to Aelius Dionysius). They also served many purposes: to bring good luck to newly-weds (Menander), as a physical antidote (Photius), to free oneself from the possession of an evil spirit (Plutarch), to enforce a magical spell (*vid. infra*), or to succeed in competitions (Diogenianus etc.). They are connected to the magi (Plutarch), to the Dactyls of Ida (Clement), and, at a very late date, to the statue of Artemis at Ephesos (Eustathius). In any case, it is a 'far-famed' formula (Clement).

Regarding the relationship between the formula and Ephesos, we have already seen that Eustathius echoes a certain tradition transmitted by the Atticist Pausanias, according to which those letters were inscribed 'on the feet, girdle, and crown of the cult statue of Artemis'; this fact led Picard[4] to believe that the letters engraved on an idol of Artemis were a far memory of the Luwian hieroglyphics inscribed on the divine images,[5] whereas McCown[6] linked this formula to the books of magic that were burnt by the first Christians from Ephesos.[7] The magi from Ephesos are also mentioned by Xenophon, the Ephesian.[8] There is, however, the possibility that the adjective *Ephesia* might not be derived from the name of the city of Ephesos. In fact, the *Etymologicum Magnum* seems to consider it as a descriptive adjective (*Et. M.* 402.28): ἢ ἀπὸ ἐφεσίων τινῶν οὐσῶν ἐπαοιδῶν δυσπαρακολουθήτων, ὡς προείρηται· ὅθεν καὶ ἐφέσια λέγονται ('Or it is because they are liberating incantations, hard to understand, as it has been said, for which reason they are called "liberating".'). Wünsch[9] explains ἐφέσια as a

---

[4] Picard (1922) 131, cf. 434.
[5] Cf. Le Boulluec *ad* Clem. Alex. *Strom.* V.8.45, p. 175.
[6] McCown (1923) 128.
[7] Acts xix 19.
[8] Xenoph. Ephes. I.5.6. Cf. also Arnold (1989) 14–19.
[9] Wünsch (1900) 84–5.

derivative from ἐφίημι, with the meaning of 'to loosen', and it has even been proposed[10] that the term could have come from the Babylonian *epêšu* 'to fascinate'.[11]

4.3. THE TEXT

We know the text of these *Ephesia Grammata* from Clement of Alexandria (*Strom.* V.8.45.2):

Ἀνδροκύδης[12] γοῦν ὁ Πυθαγορικὸς τὰ Ἐφέσια καλούμενα γράμματα ἐν πολλοῖς δὴ πολυθρύλητα ὄντα συμβόλων ἔχειν φησὶ τάξιν, σημαίνειν δὲ Ἄσκιον μὲν τὸ σκότος, μὴ γὰρ ἔχειν τοῦτο σκιάν· φῶς δὲ Κατάσκιον, ἐπεὶ καταυγάζει τὴν σκιάν· Λίξ τέ ἐστιν ἡ γῆ κατὰ ἀρχαίαν ἐπωνυμίαν καὶ Τετράξ[13] ὁ ἐνιαυτὸς διὰ τὰς ὥρας, Δαμναμενεὺς δὲ ὁ ἥλιος ὁ δαμάζων, τὰ Αἴσιά τε ἡ ἀληθὴς φωνή. σημαίνει δ' ἄρα τὸ σύμβολον ὡς κεκόσμηται τὰ θεῖα, οἷον σκότος πρὸς φῶς καὶ ἥλιος πρὸς ἐνιαυτὸν καὶ γῆ πρὸς παντοίαν φύσεως γένεσιν.

Androcydes the Pythagorean says the far-famed so-called Ephesian letters were of the class of symbols and that *Askion* meant darkness, for it has no shadow; and *Kataskion* meant light, since it casts with its rays the shadow; and that *Lix* is the earth, according to an ancient appellation; and that *Tetrax* is the year, in reference to the seasons; and that *Damnameneus* is the sun, which overpowers; and *ta Aisia* is the true voice. And then the symbol intimates that divine things have been arranged in harmonious order—darkness to light, the sun to the year, and the earth to nature's processes of production of every sort.

Hesychius offers a much shorter version of the same interpretation (s.v. Ἐφέσια γράμματα):

ἦν μὲν πάλαι ⟨s'⟩, ὕστερον δὲ προσέθεσάν τινες ἀπατεῶνες καὶ ἄλλα. φασὶ δὲ τῶν πρώτων τὰ ὀνόματα τάδε· ἄσκι, κατάσκι[14], λίξ, τετράξ, δαμναμενεύς, αἴσιον. Δηλοῖ δὲ τὸ μὲν ἄσκι σκότος, τὸ δὲ κατάσκι φῶς, τὸ δὲ λὶξ ⟨γῆ, τετράξ δὲ ἐν⟩ιαυτός[15], δαμναμενεὺς δὲ ἥλιος, αἴσιον δὲ ἀληθές. ταῦτα οὖν ἱερά ἐστι καὶ ἅγια.

---

[10] Cf. Ogden (1999) 47.
[11] Cf. McCown (1923) 130, who proposes the possibilities that the formula came from Babylonia or from Anatolia.
[12] Cf. note 2.
[13] Τετράξ Stählin ex Hesych.: Τετρὰς L.
[14] ἄσκι, κατάσκι cod. (*denuo infra*) : ἄσκιον, κατάσκιον Latte.
[15] Add. Latte et Clemente.

Ephesian letters; Formerly there were 6 (*sc.* words), but afterwards some deceivers added others. They say that these are the names of the first ones: *Aski, kataski, lix, tetrax, Damnameneus, Aisia*. And *Aski* means darkness, *Kataski* means light, *Lix* means earth and *Tetrax* the year, *Damnameneus* is the sun, and *Aision* is truthful. Therefore these things are holy and sacred.

Hesychius seems to admit the sacred character of the *grammata* (albeit through an allegoric interpretation), whereas he considers that it is typical of false hypocrites to use it with longer formulas. Androcydes, the author of a Περὶ Πυθαγορικῶν συμβόλων, was a Pythagorean who, even if his character and his times are doubted,[16] probably lived after the third century BC. His interpretation obviously comes from a personal point of view, not based on the origin of the formula.

The text also figures on a gemstone of the Southesk collection,[17] where the formula appears as ἀσκι κατασκι αιξ τετροξ δαμναμενευς αἴσια. In a magical papyrus, the invention of this sort of Abracadabra is attributed to Orpheus[18] (*P. Mag.* VII 450):[19]

ἐὰν δὲ κατορυκτικὸν ποιῆις ἢ ⟨εἰς⟩ ποταμὸν ἢ γῆν ἢ θάλασσαν ἢ ῥοῦν[20] ἢ θήκην ἢ εἰς φρέαρ, γράφε τὸν λόγον τὸν Ὀρφαϊκόν[21], 'ασκει καὶ τασκει'[22] λέγων, καὶ λαβὼν μίτον μέλανα βάλε ἅμματα τξε᾽ καὶ ἔξωθεν περίδησον, λέγων πάλιν τὸν αὐτὸν λόγον καὶ ὅτι· 'διατήρησον τὸν κάτοχον' ἢ κατάδεσμον, ἢ ὃ ἂν ποιῆις, καὶ οὕτως κατατίθεται.

But if you cause [the plate] to be buried or [sunk in] river or land or sea or stream or coffin or in a well write the Orphic formula saying '*askei kai taskei*' and, taking a black thread, make 365 knots and bind [the

---

[16] Burkert (1972) 167, 175 n. 73. Jordan *per litt.* manifests reasonable doubts about the testimonies of the Ἐφέσια γράμματα mentioned in §2 as referring to this formula.
[17] Cf. Carnegie (1908) 141–2; Bonner (1950) 5 n. 14; Preisendanz (1961) 520.
[18] On the attribution of works to Orpheus, cf. Bernabé (2002).
[19] Translation by Betz (1986) 130; cf. Calvo-Sánchez Romero (1987) 217f.
[20] ἢ ῥοῦν Crönert : ηγουν Π.
[21] Cf. Luck (1985) 171. The text was missing in the collections of Orphic texts; it is now edited in Bernabé (2005), under the number 829. From now on, I will refer to those fragments included in this edition as *OF*, followed by the number of each fragment.
[22] According to McCown (1923) 132 ασκει καὶ τασκει 'stands here for the whole formula', which seems to me correct. However, I believe his opinion that ασκει καὶ τασκει is not τὸν λόγον τὸν Ὀρφαϊκόν is a rather forced interpretation of the text. It is clear that the λόγον is ασκει καὶ τασκει, because below it is said λέγων πάλιν τὸν αὐτὸν λόγον (evidently ασκει καὶ τασκει). Cf. also Rocca (2009) 34.

thread] around the outside of the plate, saying the same formula again and 'keep him who is held' (or 'bound'), or whatever you do. And thus [the plate] is deposited.

We complete our list with one last reference from the *Testamentum Salomonis*, where a demon introduces himself (7.4): ἐγὼ καλοῦμαι Λὶξ Τέτραξ 'I am called *Lix Tetrax*.'

Roscher[23] tried to turn the formula into a hexametric sequence by changing the order of the words: Ἄϊσια, Δαμναμενεύς, Τέτραξ, Λὶξ, Ἄσκι, Κατάσκι. Such an ambition has been rightly criticized by McCown.[24] It is clear that in all the testimonies ασκι κατασκι goes at the beginning of the formula. Except for the (totally misguided) attempts at interpretation by Androcydes, the ancient sources quoted above consider the Ephesian letters to be perfectly incomprehensible and there is no credibility in Stickel's endeavour[25] to explain the sequence as if it comes from a Semitic language. As we shall see, the *Ephesia Grammata* evolve from a completely comprehensible Greek narrative text, originally composed in dactylic hexameters.

4. 4. A SERIES OF INCANTATIONS (ἐπωιδαί) WITH VERY SIMILAR WORDS

In the last few years, some very old versions of the *Ephesia Grammata* have started to appear, containing several metrical incantations[26] that are quite similar as a whole, but which include many variations in the details. What is more interesting is that they contain every single word of the Ἐφέσια γράμματα. In this section I do not intend to draw a *stemma* nor to present the edition of each text;[27] instead, I will just present the relevant parts for this paper, since they contain the elements that eventually give rise to the *Ephesia Grammata*. Each

---

[23] Roscher (1901) 88–9, with the acceptance of Preisendanz (1961) 516.
[24] McCown (1923) 129 n. 7 and 132 n. 23. Notice also the pretty unfounded divertimenti of Schultz (1909a–b) 219ff.
[25] Stickel (1860).
[26] On the ἐπωιδαί, cf. Pfister (1924); Furley (1993).
[27] Cf. Bernabé (2005), although it only contains the 'Getty Hexameters' partially and it does not include the fragments edited by Rocca (2009).

version will be marked with a letter that I will use later in order to refer to them in shorthand.

A. Lead tablet from Egypt (between the second and fourth centuries AD[28]), preserved in Cologne,[29] lines 64ff. (*OF* 830a.1–5):

ασκι κατὰ σκι̣⌊ερῶν⌋ ὀρέων μελαναυγέα χῶρον
⟨Φερσεφόνης⟩ ἐγ κήπο̣υ̣⌊ἄγει πρὸς ἀ⌋μο{υ}λγὸν ἀνάγκη̣ι̣
τὴν τετραβάμονα π̣⌊αῖς ἁγίην Δή⌋μητρος {s} ὀπ̣⌊η⌋δ̣όν,
αἶγ' ἀκ̣α̣μαντορόα{s}. ⌊νασμοῦ θ⌋αλεροῖο γ⌊ά⌋λ̣ακτος
θη̣σόμενον.

1 ασκι] ἔσκε? Jordan |κατὰ σκι̣⌊ερῶν⌋ Jordan |μελαναυγέα χῶρον Daniel-Maltomini : μελαναυγεῖ χώρωι Jordan : μελαναυγηαχωρον **lam.** || 2 ⌊Φερσεφόνης⌋supplevi : ⌊Περσεφόνης⌋ Jordan, qui cett. add. et suppl. |]μουλγοναναγκης **lam.** || 3 omnia suppl. Jordan :]μητροσσοπ[ ]δων **lam.** || 4 αἶγ' ἀκ̣α̣μαντορόα{s} Jordan, quod dub. recipiunt Daniel-Maltomini ('scriba nominativum voluisse videtur'): at plane ἀκαμαντορόα genet. cum νασμοῦ desideratur : ἐξαμακαντορηας **lam.** | cett. suppl. Jordan || 5 θη̣σόμενον ('sugere') Daniel-Maltomini dub. : θεσ⟨σ⟩όμενον Merk. ap. Jordan : θεσσόμενον **lam.**

aski (when?)[30] down the shady mountains in a dark-and-glittering land
a child leads out of Persephone's garden by necessity for milking[31]
that four-footed holy attendant of Demeter,
a she-goat, to suckle from the untiring stream of rich milk...

B. *P. Mag.* LXX 12 (*OF* 830b)[32]

ἄσκει κατὰ σκειερῶν ὀρέων (...)
τετέ[λ]εσμαι

---

[28] According to Jordan, it dates between third and fourth centuries AD and, according to Daniel–Maltomini, between the second and third centuries AD.
[29] First ed. Wortmann (1968a) 57ff.; and again by Jordan (1988); cf. also Fauth (1985–1986); *SEG* 38, 1988, n. 1837 (p. 524); Daniel–Maltomini (1990) n. 49, pp. 193ff. It has normally been placed in Oxyrhynchus, but Jordan *per litt.* warns me that only its Egyptian origin is certain.
[30] Cf. §7. It is extremely hard to translate all these ἐπωιδαί, because of the insecurity of the texts, but also because they were probably written in such a way that they could not be clearly understood. I follow Jordan's translation (Jordan 1988, 252–3) slightly changed.
[31] On the possible meanings of ἀμολγός, cf. Rocca (2009) 36–7, who considers that this is the evening twilight, when the cattle return home.
[32] Cf. Schmidt (1937); Betz (1980); (1986) 297–8; Jordan (1988) 257–8; Calvo-Sánchez Romero (1987) 385–6; Jordan (2001) 187. There is also a silver tablet from the first century BC/AD, preserved at the Perkins Library of Duke University, whose first three words HASCE CATA SCLERON reflect our Greek text.

The Ephesia Grammata: Genesis of a Magical Formula

καὶ εἰς μέγαρον κατέ[βην Δακτύλων.

1 ἄσκει (ἔσκε?) κατὰ σκειερῶν ὀρέων Jordan : ἀσκει κατασκει ερων ορεων Π ‖ 3 μέγαρον κατέ[βην Δακτύλων Preisendanz (μαγαρον... δακτυλον Π) | δακτυλον secl. Jordan (1988), cf. infra.

aski (when?) under the shadowy mountains . . . I have been initiated and into the Dactyls' chamber I descended.[33]

Betz has noted[34] that in this spell there seem to be liturgical reminiscences of a mystery cult related to the Idaean Dactyls. Jordan (1988), on the other hand, brackets δακτυλον because he considers that it is probably an intrusion of a marginal or interlineal note pointing out that the text is 'dactylic'. However, we should remember that Clement[35] ascribes the invention of the 'Ephesian Letters' to the Dactyls of Ida, that Damnameneus, one of the six *Ephesia Grammata*, is indeed the name of a Dactyl,[36] and that Plutarch[37] affirms that those who have learned by heart the names of the Dactyls use them as a protection against fear. Jordan's argument is thus not conclusive because the magic formula of the ἐπωιδαί normally distorts the meter (the same process that we observe with certain σύμβολα of the gold tablets).[38]

C. Lead tablet from Phalasarna,[39] fourth century BC, preserved at the National Museum of Athens, lines 6ff. (*OF* 830c).

ασκι κατασκι κατασκι αασιαν ενδασιαν ἐν ἀμολγῶι [αἴ]ξ
αἶγα βίαι ἐκ κήπο⟨υ⟩ ἐλαύνε⟨ι⟩ {τε}. τ[ῶι δ' ὄ]νομα Τετραγ[ος·]
σοὶ δ' ὄνομα Τρεξ. ⟨ ‾ ˘ ˘ ‾ ⟩ ἀνεμώλιος ἀκτή.
(. . .)
'Τραξ Τετραξ Τετραγος.' 6

---

[33] I follow Jordan's translation (Jordan 2001, 193) slightly changed.
[34] Betz (1986) 298; cf. (1980) 292 n. 27.
[35] Clem. Alex. *Strom.* I.15.73.1.
[36] Cf. §10.
[37] Plut. *quom. quis suos in virt. sent.* 15 p. 85B: οἱ μὲν γὰρ ἐκμεμαθηκότες τὰ τῶν Ἰδαίων ὀνόματα Δακτύλων χρῶνται πρὸς τοὺς φόβους αὐτοῖς ὡς ἀλεξικάκοις, ἀτρέμα καταλέγοντες ἕκαστον, 'True it is that those who have got by heart the names of the Idaean Dactyls use them as charms against terrors, repeating each name with calm assurance' (transl. by F. C. Babbitt).
[38] Cf. Bernabé-Jiménez (2008) 63.
[39] First ed. Ziebarth (1899); cf. Wünsch (1900); McCown (1923) 132ff.; Levi (1922) 394; *IC* II (19) 7; Eitrem (1922); Maas (1944); Jordan (1992); D'Alessio (1993); Furley (1993) 96ff.; Brixhe–Panayotou (1995); Kingsley (1995) 269ff.; Jordan (2000a) 99, cf. also *SEG* 42 (1992) n. 818 pp. 233–4; 43 (1993) n. 615, pp. 203.

Δαμναμενεῦ. [vac.] δάμασον δὲ κακῶς [ἀ]έκοντας ἀνάγκα[ις]

---

1 post κατασκι¹ add. ⟨ἄσκι⟩ Guarducci prob. Furley | κατασκι αασιαν ενδασιαν Jordan : κατασκια αασιαν ενδασιαν Brixhe–Panayotou : κατασκι αἴσια ⟨λιξ⟩· λασίαν Guarducci | [αἴ]ξ accepi monente Jordan, qui vero verbum secludit : λιξ leg. Ziebarth : prima litt. hodie deperdita : [λ]ιξ Brixhe–Panayotou : {[λι]ξ} Guarducci || 2 ἐλαύνε⟨ι⟩ {τε} scripsi (coll. G1) : ἐλαύνετε Jordan | τ[ῶι δ' ὄ]νομα Jordan : [τὸ] ο⟨ὔ⟩νομα Guarducci : an [τᾶι δ' ὄ]νομα? Rocca : τεύ[χω (?) ('avec le sens de "produire" [ici "prononcer"]? cf. hom. τεύχειν βοήν vel simile') ὄ]νομα Brixhe–Panayotou | Τετραγ[ος] Brixhe–Panayotou : τετραγ lam. : unde dub. Τέτραξ [ὑμέτερον] Guarducci || 3 ο⟨ὔ⟩νομα Guarducci | post Τρεξ lac. ind. Jordan | ἀνέμωι Διὸς Guarducci || 6 'or τε τραξ τε τράγος?' Jordan, cf. SEG 42 (1992) n. 818 p. 233 || 7 ἀνάγκα[ις] dub. Brixhe–Panayotou (fort. 'moyens de contrainte, violence, punitions') : ἀνάγκαι legit Ziebart, prob. Jordan : ι hodie non legibile

aski kataski kataski aasian endasian, at milking time the goat
leads the goat perforce from the garden. His[40] name, Tetragos.
Your name, Trex... a windy promontory.
Trax, Tetrax, Tetragos
Damnameneus, subdue them ill, perforce, constrained.

D. Lead tablet, probably from Selinus, fourth century BC (Getty Hexameters)[41]

D1 side A col. i 8–12
hόσσα κατὰ σκιαρῶν ὀρέων μελαναυγέϊ χώρωι
Φερσεφόνης ἐκ κήπου ἄγει πρὸς ἀμολγὸν ἀνάγκη[ι]
τὴν τετραβήμονα παῖς hαγίην Δήμητρος {h}ὀπηδόν,
αἶγ' ἀκαμαντορόα νασμοῦ θαλεροῖο γάλακτος
βριθομένη⟨ν⟩

---

1 hόσσα] ἔσκε Jordan : βᾶσα Faraone | 3 hαγίην vel hαγνὴν (fortasse potius) Jordan–Kotansky : 'l. ἀγνῆς' Janko : hαγιην lam. || 2 l. ἐκ | ἄγει vel ἄγοι Jordan : αγαι lam. || 3 hαγίην Jordan : hαγνῆς Janko : ιαγιην lam. | ἀνάγκη[ι] Jordan : ἀνάγκη lam. || 4–5 Jordan

Having come down (? reading βᾶσα) the shady mountains in a dark-and-glittering land
a child leads out of Persephone's garden by necessity for milking

---

[40] On the possible readings of the form preceding ὄνομα, cf. Rocca (2009) 39.
[41] First ed. Jordan–Kotansky (2011).

The Ephesia Grammata: Genesis of a Magical Formula 81

that four-footed holy attendant of Demeter,
a she-goat with an untiring stream of rich milk
laden.

D2 col. ii 13–21

ασκι κατασ]κι κατασκι αασσια {ασια} ενδασι[α πρὸς?

    ]δε |ἀμολγὸν αἶξ αἶγα βίαι ἐκ κή ⌊που ἐλαύνει⌋
v |τῶι δ' ὄνομα Τετραγος ηηδε[
a |τετροαναραγε τεтραγ[
c |(. . .)
a |Τραξ Τετραξ Τ⌋ετραγ⌊ος⌋
t

---

1 ενδασι[α scripsi : ενδασι[αν Jordan | πρὸς? dub. Jordan : ἐν ἀμολγῶι Janko || 2 ἀμολγόν⟨δ⟩' Janko | κή⌊που Jordan | ἐλαύνει⌋ e G1 G2 supplevi : ἔλαυνε Jordan-Kotansky : ἐλαύνετε⌋ Jordan || 3 ἄγετε τραγ[Jordan || 5 |⌊Τραξ Τετραξ Τ⌋ετραγ⌊ος⌋ suppl. Janko : min. c. 15]τραγ[Jordan

aski kataski kataski aassia endasia
    the goat leads the goat of necessity from the garden at milking time
    His name Tetragos. This
    tetroanarage Tetrag[os] . . .
    trax, tetrax, Tetragos.

E. Lead tablet from the fourth century BC, found in the place of Locri Epizephyrioi, the so-called Centrocamere,[42] lines 2–3 and 7–8 (*OF* 830e).

ασκι κ]ατασ[κι]υσκι ασιαν ενδασιαν ἐ[ν ἀμολγῶι.]
¯ ˘ ˘ ¯]ν ἐ⟨κ⟩ κάπο⟨υ⟩ ⟨ἐ⟩λα[ύνει τῶι δ'] ὄνυ[μα Τ]ετρακο⟨ς⟩
. . .
Τραχ Τετρ[αχ Τετραγος   7
Δαμναμεν]ε[υ,] δάμασον δὲ κακῶς ἀέ[κοντας ἀνάγκαι.]

---

2 ἐ[ν ἀμολγῶι Costabile, prob. Jordan : cetera Jordan || 3 ¯ ˘ ˘ ¯]ν ἐ⟨κ⟩ κάπο⟨υ⟩ ⟨ἐ⟩λα[ύνετε (malui ⟨ἐ⟩λα[ύνει τῶι δ'] rest. Jordan :]νειαπολλ[lam. :]ΝΕΙΑ πόδα[ς Costabile | ὄνυ[μα Τ]ετρακο⟨ς⟩ Jordan : τ]ετρακο iam Costabile || 7–8 suppl. Jordan || 7 an Τετραχος?

aski kataski uski asian endasian at milking time.
(He) leads (the goat?) from the garden. His name Tetrakos
. . .
Trach, Tetrach, Tetrag/chos
Damnameneus, subdue them ill, perforce, constrained.

---

[42] First ed. Costabile (1999) 29ff. Again, it is edited by Jordan (2000a) 100.

F. Lead tablet from Himera, fifth century BC,[43] recto 1–4 (*OF* 830f).

ασ̣κι κ[ατ]ασ{ι}κι vac. max. 5
υσκ[κ]ι ασα ε⟨ν⟩δα̣[c 2]O ἀμολ[γῶι vac.?]
ΟΣΔ[1–2]ΠΑ ἐ⟨κ⟩ κά[π]ο⟨υ⟩ ἐλαύ[νει.]
τοὶ δ'ὄνο⟨μ⟩α Τετρα[γος.]

---

omnia suppl. Jordan ‖ 3 ²]ΠΑ] fort. αἶ]γ̣α | ἐλαύ[νε.] scripsi mon. Jordan : ἐλαύ[νετε.] Jordan : ἐνλυ[tab.

aski kataski
uski asa enda at milking time
(the goat?) from the garden.

G. Lead tablet from Selinus, fifth century BC.[44]

G1 recto 2–4

]υσσκι κατὰ σκιρὸν ἐν δ'ἀμ[ο]λγο͂[ι
αἶγ]α βίαι ἐ⟨κ⟩ κάπου ἐλαύνει τᾶιδ' ὄνομα Τετ[ραγος

]δαμνυμενα δάμασον δὲ κακὸς ἀ⟨ἐ⟩κοντας[

---

omnia suppl. Rocca

uski under the shadowy, at milking time
(he) leads the goat perforce from the garden; his name Tetragos.

G2 verso 1–3

σ]κιρὸν ἐν δ' ἀμο[λγ]ο͂[ι
ἐ]λαύνει τ[ᾶ?]ιδ' ὄνομα Τετρ[αγος

δάμ]ασον [δ]ὲ κακὸς ἀ⟨ἐ⟩κοντα[ς

---

omnia suppl. Rocca

shadowy, at milking time . . . leads. . . . his name Tetragos.

H. Lead tablet from Selinus, fifth century BC.[45]

H1 recto 2–4

]υσσκι κατ[ὰ σκιρὸν
] βίαι ἐ⟨κ⟩ κάπου[

---

[43] Cf. the apograph of Manni Piraino (1976) 697–8, first ed. Jordan (2000b).
[44] First ed. Rocca (2009) 23–7.
[45] First ed. Rocca (2009) 28–9.

The Ephesia Grammata: Genesis of a Magical Formula   83

δ]αμνυμενα[

---

omnia suppl. Rocca

uski under the shadowy . . . perforce from the garden . . . *damnumena*

H2 verso 2-4

ασσκι[
αἴξ αἶγ[α
Τετρα[γος

---

omnia suppl. Rocca

aski . . . the goat (leads?) the goat . . . Tetragos.

4. 5. VARIANTS

I list the variants of the words in the formula as follows:
Variants of the words in the formula

Clem.	ἄσκιον	κατάσκιον	λίξ	τετράξ[46]	δαμναμενεύς	αἴσια
Hsch.	ἄσκι	κατάσκι	αἴξ	τετράξ	δαμναμενεύς	αἴσιον
gemma	ασκι	κατασκι	αιξ	τετροξ	δαμναμενευς	αισια
PMag	ασκει	καὶ τασκει	–	–	–	–
Test. Sal.	–	–	λίξ	τετράξ	–	–
L.Rom.	*hasce*	*cata scleron*				
A	ασκι	κατὰ σκι[ερῶν]	αἶγ'	τετραβάμονα		
B	ἄσκει	κατὰ σκ{ε}ιερῶν	–	–	–	–
C	ασκι	κατασκι (bis)	{αἴ]ξ αἶγα	Τετραξ[47]	Δαμναμενεῦ δάμασον	ααασιαν[48]
D1	*hóssa*	κατὰ σκιαρῶν	αἶγ'	τετραβήμονα	–	–
D2	ασ]κι	κατασκι (bis)	αἴξ αἶγα	Τετραγος[49]		αασια[50]
E	[ασκι]	κ]ατασ[κι[51]	—	Τ]ετρακο⟨ς⟩[52] Δαμναμεν]ε[ῦ] δάμασον	ασιαν[53]	

---

[46] Stählin : τετράς cod.
[47] Before Τετραγ[ος, then Τρεξ and finally the string Τραξ Τετραξ Τετραγος.
[48] Followed by ενδασιαν.
[49] After τετροαναραγε τέτραγ[and then the string ⌊τραξ τέτραξ τ⌋έτραγ⌊ος⌋.
[50] Followed by {ασια} ενδασια.
[51] Followed by]υσσκι.
[52] With the string Τραχ Τετρ[αχ Τετραγος.
[53] Followed by ενδασιαν.

F	ασκι	κ[ατ]ασ {ι}κι[54]	—[55]	Τετρα[γος	—	ασα[56]
G1	]υσσκι	κατὰ σκιρὸν	αἶγ]α	Τετ[ραγος	]δαμνυμενα δάμασον	
G2	–	σ]κιρὸν	–	Τετρ[αγος	δάμ]ασον	–
H1	]υσσκι	κατ[ὰ σκιρὸν	–		δ]αμνυμενα[	–
H2	ασσκι[	–		αἶξ αἶγ[α	Τετρα[γος	–

4. 6. A PROBLEM OF PRIORITY

The presence of some of the words of the *Ephesia Grammata* in these earlier metrical incantations raises the problem of priority. On the one hand we could think that, at first, there was originally the famous string of names and that they evolved into the long incantations by modifying and adding certain words. But the opposite is also possible—that the hexametrical incantations were more ancient and the Ephesian letters were nothing but a diminished and reduced version of these, as Kotansky believes[57]: 'their appearance [sc. Ἐφεσίων γραμμάτων] in verses inscribed on lead... suggests strongly that they must have once been meaningful hexameters in their original context.'

There are a number of reasons that lead me to prefer the second option.[58] First, it is easier to imagine a process where a meaningful formula degrades and loses its sense, as when the French phrase *un beau chateau* 'a beautiful castle' is transformed into the meaningless words *ambó ató* in a Spanish children's song. The process of degradation in these documents is totally clear. In this regard, suffice it to have a look at the *stemma* proposed by Jordan,[59] who points to certain mistakes in the late Classical variants and suggests that they derive from an even earlier model of a different alphabet. Besides, if we consider that the shortest prosaic versions of the *Ephesia Grammata* are documented only in a late period, we should conclude that the six-word string is the final outcome of the drastic shortening of

---

[54] Followed by]υσκι.
[55] Perhaps we should read αἶ]γα ἐ⟨κ⟩ κά[π]ο⟨υ⟩?
[56] Followed by ε⟨ν⟩δα[(perhaps we should read ε⟨ν⟩δα[σια?).
[57] Kotansky (1991) 126 n. 22.
[58] Already announced by McCown (1923) 132ff.
[59] Jordan (2002).

the original incantation. Concerning the presence of ἄσκι at the beginning of the hexametrical versions, Jordan[60] believes that by a kind of back formation the prosaic version of the *Ephesia Grammata* might have influenced the transmission of the original reading.[61]

Let us, finally, examine each of the words making up the short formula that Clement and Hesychius transmit.

4.7. Ἄσκι

Obviously, the main variant is ασκι, the term that makes up the first dactyl in combination with the first syllable of κατασκι (ασκει in **B** and in the *PMag.* VII 450 is a graphic variant). Jordan *ad loc.* hesitantly proposes ἔ̄σκε, perhaps a conjunction meaning 'when', by reading ἄγηι in the subjunctive. It is remarkable, however, that the Latin tablet has *hasce,* which seems to reflect ασκι. Whatever its origin, ασκι is already a *verbum magicum* that creates a rhyming jingle with the sequence κατασκι-, very similar to the type *abra-cadabra*. It is also possible that ασκι had this function from the very beginning. The variant *hóσσα* in **D1** offers no good meaning and it seems to be a *lectio facilior*. The correction βᾶσα by Faraone (*per litt.*) is likely.

In fact, it is so important to keep a rhyming sequence that every time one of the words is modified, the other has to be changed in the same way. B shows ἄσκει and, consequently, σκιερῶν is also written as σκειερῶν. Likewise Clement offers the terms ἄσκιον and κατάσκιον, in order to respect the phonic game.

In **G1** and **H1** υσσκι appears before κατα σκιρόν; this is a less desirable variant because it breaks up the jingle[62], a fact that may explain why this variant does not survive in the later versions. The same sequence has been added to ασσκι κατασκι in E and in F.

This word appears at the beginning of the hexametrical version and it still holds the first position in the short formula, becoming, in a certain way, its 'distinctive trait'.[63]

---

[60] Jordan (1988) 257.
[61] *Per litt.* he explains that, in any case, he believes that first there was a previous meaningful sentence.
[62] These are the same documents offering the odd variant δαμνυμενα instead of Δαμναμενεῦ. Cf. § 11.
[63] Cf. Rocca (2009) 34.

4. 8. Κατάσκι

It seems pretty clear that κατασκι comes from abbreviating the sequence κατὰ σκιερῶν. However, this abbreviation is not accidental; it has been provoked exactly where the four letters of ασκι are repeated. If ασκι originated, as I believe, as a rhyming *pendant* for κατὰ σκιερῶν, this tendency has persisted until the formula became a purely phonic game, with no semantic reference at all. Such a tendency must have started at a very early date. The first step is reflected in **G1, G2**, with the disappearance of ὀρέων and the conversion of σκιερῶν into σκιρ-[64]. On the other hand, **C** already presents ασκι κατασκι κατασκι, a repetition that aims to intensify the effect and expands the sequence with αασιαν ενδασιαν. **D2** extends ασκι κατασκι κατασκι with αασσια ασια ενδασι[α, although it maintains the meaningful sequence κατὰ σκιαρῶν in **D1**. The exemplar from Locri (**E**) also extends ασκι κατασκι, by introducing before ασιαν ενδασιαν yet another phonic sequence that we just know partially, that is,]υσσκι[65]. A very close variant (probably the same, although more degraded) is the one we find in **F** αςκι κ[ατ]ασ {ι}κι[66] vac. max. 5 / υσ[κ]ι ασα ε⟨ν⟩δα̣[c 2].

4. 9. Αἴξ/Λίξ

The variants Αἴξ/Λίξ suggest that one of these comes from the other as a result of a copyist's error between the two capital letters. The form λίξ appears in Clement as well as in the *Testamentum Salomonis* and it was read by Ziebarth in **C**, even though this part of the text is now lost. The text of Hesychius is actually a correction that Latte made from Clement's version, but I do not believe it is necessary at all.[67] The term λίξ is explained only in Clement ('earth') and in a gloss

---

[64] Rocca (2009) 36 suggests: 'se non è dovuto a un errore grafico va considerato come fenomeno ionico'. Without denying this possibility, I think that the wish to play phonetically with ασκι must have influenced the choice of this form.

[65] Cf. § 7.

[66] It is probably due to a *Lento* pronunciation of κατασκι.

[67] Rocca (2009) 35 prefers Λίξ, as he considers it a *lectio difficilior*. However, the presence of αἴξ in the ἐπῳδαί, together with the later appearance of λίξ, leads me to consider that λίξ is an error and that it gives rise to a more 'magical' word, since it is the most uncommon.

of Hesychius': λίξ· πλάγιος. καὶ λίθος πλατύς. On the contrary, αἴξ takes the name of the goat mentioned in **A, C, D1, D2, G1**, and **H2** and was probably read at the beginning of the lost part in line 3 of **E**; we could even read it in [$^{1-2}$]ΠΑ, in line 3 of **F**, as [αἶ]γα.

4. 10. Τετραξ

This word is the most unclear. It does not appear in **A** or in **D1** but, since they both show τετραβάμονα(-βή-), a form which does not coexist with Τετραγος, we could imagine that the ultimate origin of the form Τετραγος could be this ancient poetical compound. We could even think that, once again, the wish for phonetic games has modified it, perhaps by changing the genitive αἰγὸς τετραβάμονος into the genitive αἰγὸς τετραγος, a process that involves the reinterpretation of τετραγος as τε τράγος.[68] Then, as the result of a new rhyming scheme, the nominative αἴξ τετραβάμων becomes αἴξ τετραξ.[69]

The fact is that **C** offers Τετραγ[ος in line 2, Τρεξ in line 3 and the sequence Τραξ Τετραξ Τετραγος (also in **E**), an increasing phonic reiteration where, once again, there is a four-letter sequence Τραξ repeated after a two-letter sequence (very similar to the sequence 4+3+4 ασκι κατ ασκι[70]) and followed by what seems to be the genitive of Τετραξ.[71] In **D2, F, G1, G2**, and **H2** Τετραγος reappears, whereas in **E** we find the variant Τ]ετρακο⟨ς⟩ and later the sequence Τραχ Τετρ[αχ Τετραγος (thus Jordan, perhaps Τετραχος?). On Τραχ Τετρ[αχ Jordan[72] offers two different interpretations: Τραχ may be merely a different pronunciation of the vocable, itself no doubt intentionally mysterious, but if χ is here the 'spelling' of ξ, it may, like ε,ο for η,ω, reflect an alphabet that was used some time before the texts at

---

[68] Cf. Jordan (1992) 194.
[69] The gem presents a variant τετροξ.
[70] However, in the last one, the four-letter sequence starts with a vowel and requires a consonant before the second ΑΣΚΙ.
[71] It is not probable that τετραξ has to do with the bird τετράξ ὁ μείζων, probably 'hazel-grouse' or 'ryper' (Ath. 9.398f, Eust. 1205.27, *Poet.Lat.Min*. III p. 203 Baehrens), with the variant documented in dat. τέτρακι in Ar. *Av*. 488. Nor does it have anything to do with the small bird, like the σπερμ(ατ)ολόγος, Epich. 42.3, 85.2 K.-A., Alex.Mynd. ap. Ath.9.398c.
[72] Jordan (2000a) 101.

Phalasarna, Selinus, and Locri Epizephyrioi were inscribed in the fourth century and it may have implications for the date of the composition of the verses.

Since Τετραξ, Τετραγος is a nonsense word, it is considered by ancient authors to be a proper name. Whatever the origin of this mysterious form, which was already part of some very ancient magic sequences, we could understand that, in order to complete the short rhyming version of the formula, it could be attractive to add the sequence αἴξ, Τετράξ.

4. 11. Δαμναμενεύς

On the other hand, the case of Δαμναμενεύς is much more clear. This is the name of an Idaean Dactyl, well documented since the Archaic epic[73] and common in the magical papyri[74]. The relationship between our formula and the Idaean Dactyls is also reflected in B[75]. Δαμναμενεύς is a speaking name meaning 'the one who subdues'. The Greeks had already noticed the transparent etymology of the term, in such a way that Androcydes[76] interpreted Δαμναμενεύς as ὁ ἥλιος ὁ δαμάζων[77]. As Kotansky[78] points out, this is why in C7 and in E8 'the imperative ... δάμασον as well as the adverbial ἀνάγκαι ... provide twin etymological *aitia* of the god's name ... one who "subdues, tames, or conquers" by constraint.' At the beginning, the poetic version worked as a σχῆμα ἐτυμολογικόν with the imperative δάμασον, just as we see in C, E and, with the variant δαμνυμενα, in H1. In G2, however, we only have the imperative. Once the hexametrical incantation has been abbreviated and has added the rhyming schemes attractive for a magical use, it is logical that Δαμναμενεῦ alone remains in the shorter formula: on the one hand, it evokes a

---

[73] Hes. fr. 282 M.-W., *Phoron*. fr. 2.3 Bernabé and note *ad loc.*, cf. Nonn. D. XXXIII.326.

[74] P. Mag. II 163, III 80, 100, 443, 511, IV 2772, 2779, etc. Also in a gold phylacteria, edited by Faraone and Kotansky (1988) 258, line 26.

[75] The form δαμνυμενα documented in G1 and H1 seems to be the result of a simple transposition, like αμακαντορηα instead of ἀκαμαντορόα in A1.4.

[76] In Clem. Alex. *Strom.* V.8.45.2.

[77] Cf. also Faraone and Kotansky (1988) 285, comment on line 26.

[78] Kotansky (1995) 258 and n. 31.

The Ephesia Grammata: *Genesis of a Magical Formula* 89

self-generated subduing power, which forces the others to give in, and, on the other, it has within itself a phonic structure with the repetition of the sequence μν-μ-ν. But in the later versions, instead of the vocative, we find the nominative Δαμναμενεύς. The reason could be that at this point the *Ephesia Grammata* were no longer considered invocations of concrete beings, but rather as a magical formula per se, where the vocative has lost its significance.

4.12. Αἴσιον / -α

Clement and the gem present the form αἴσια, whereas Hesychius offers αἴσιον. Ancient epigraphical testimonies, however, present several forms beginning with α(α)σ-: αασιαν (C), αασια ασια (D2, in a clear dittography), ασιαν (E), ασα (F). It is not plausible to consider Brixhe-Panayotou's proposal of reading the first line in C ασκι κατασκι κατασκια ασιαν ενδασιαν, because in D2, where κατασκι is not repeated, we find αασσια ασια twice, with two initial α.

Let us consider the *sedes metricae*. In C, if we delete one of the two κατασκι as an evident dittography,[79] we will have the sequence ασκι κατασκι αασιαν ενδασιαν ἐν ἀμολγῶι. The beginning ασκι κατασκι gives us a sequence – ⏑⏑ | – ⏑ and the last part, ἐν ἀμολγῶι, fills the end of a hexameter ⏑⏑ | – – |, which leaves the sequence ⏑ | – ⏑⏑ | – ⏑⏑ | – for the enigmatic αασιαν ενδασιαν.

In D2 we find ασκι κατασ]κι κατασκι αασσια ασια ενδασι[α and perhaps πρὸς] ἀμολγόν. The end of the hexameter has been changed against the metrics; ἐν ἀμολγῶι seems to be more acceptable. In this case, what we find repeated is αασσια ασια instead of ενδασι[αν, filling the same sequence ⏑ | – ⏑⏑ | – ⏑⏑ | –.

In E again we find ασιαν ενδασιαν, preceded by]υσκι. And in F ασα ε⟨ν⟩δα[, after υσ[κ]ι.

My proposal is as follows: the sequence ⏑ | – ⏑⏑ | – ⏑⏑ | – can be filled with ἀασία, ἐνδασία, both in the nominative. We can explain the fact that they were initially nominative because of the presence of αἴξ in two of the samples (C and D2, in C it is *extra metrum*), a term that agrees grammatically with both of them. The first of these words,

---

[79] Jordan (2000b) 106 proposes it, hesitantly, for the presence of]υσ(σ)κι (perhaps κατ]υσκι?) in E and in F.

ἀασία, could be the feminine of an adjective ἀάισιος, formally related with the series of ἀάω, ἄτη, and so forth, and with a wide range of meanings extending from 'madness' to 'disaster'. ἀασία would mean 'what entails confusion' or 'disaster'. We can remember two compounds, documented by the lexicographers, ἀασιφόρος ('the one bringing damage')[80] and ἀασιφρονία ('damage to the mind' or 'folly').[81]

As for ἐνδασία, the term that would make up a rhyming pair with ἀασία, I think that it could derive (with the added suffix -ιος) from the adjective ἔνδασυς 'hairy'.[82] This sort of derivation would be parallel, for instance, with γλύκιος[83] from γλυκύς. Thus, according to my proposal we would have a correct and completely dactylic hexameter: ασκι κατασκι ἀασία ἐνδασία τ'[84] ἐν ἀμολγῶι. The adjective ἀασία with a strong and unusual meaning also entails a three-alpha sequence (excellent for a *vox magica*). It was selected to close the sequence and thus left the central part to the pair ending in -ξ. As time went by, the unusual form ἀασία, already decontextualized, would have been transformed into αἴσια, the neuter plural of αἴσιος, and its meaning reinterpreted as 'auspicious, favourable', very appropriate to the power that was traditionally ascribed to the *Ephesia Grammata*.

4.13. ANY LINK WITH THE ORPHIC SPHERE?

I believe it is important to highlight the fact that both the hexametrical and the prosaic versions of the *Ephesia Grammata* have clear connections with Orphic texts:

a) First, in *P. Mag.* VII 450 the sentence γράφε τὸν λόγον τὸν Ὀρφαϊκόν· 'ασκει καὶ τασκει' λέγων implies that the formula, so well known that only the first part need be quoted, is explicitly ascribed to Orpheus.

---

[80] ἀασιφόρος· βλάβην φέρων, Hsch. Et.Gud., cf. EM I.49. If it comes from the hexametric poetry it should be measured as ἀᾱσιφόρος.

[81] ἀασιφρονία· φρενοβλάβεια Apollon. Lex., Phot. a 14 Theodoridis.

[82] They are both documented, referring to plants, in Dsc. II.142 (ἔνδασυ), IV.41.1 (ἔνδασυν).

[83] Arist. EE 1238a 28.

[84] τ' to preserve the hiatus, but we could also think that the syllable stays long before the bucolic diaeresis.

b) In P. Derveni col. VI 2ff. we read:

ἐπ[ωιδὴ δ]ὲ μάγων δύν[α]ται δαίμονας ἐμ[ποδὼν
γε[γενημένο]υς μεθιστάναι.

This incantation of the *magoi* that can dislodge *daimones* has important contact points with the above-quoted text of Plutarch:[85] ὥσπερ γὰρ οἱ μάγοι τοὺς δαιμονιζομένους κελεύουσι τὰ Ἐφέσια γράμματα πρὸς αὑτοὺς καταλέγειν καὶ ὀνομάζειν ('For just as sorcerers advise those possessed by demons to recite and name over to themselves the Ephesian letters' [transl. by E. L. Minar Jr.]). The *magoi* are mentioned in both texts. This possession by *daimones* suffered by the δαιμονιζομένους in Plutarch is indeed a manifestation of the δαίμονας ἐμ[ποδὼν γε[γενημένο]υς from the *Derveni Papyrus*. And in their origins the *Ephesia Grammata* are, as we have seen, a sort of ἐπωιδή.

c) The two geographical areas where we find the old metrical incantations (Crete and South Italy) are also the places where the Orphic gold tablets have been found.

d) There is also a narrow community of images between the ἐπωιδαί and the gold tablets. Thus, **A** and **D1** mention a she-goat, 'that four-footed holy attendant of Demeter', which is carried out of the garden of Persephone to nurse (θησόμενον) in **A** or just full of (βριθομένην) milk in **D1**. From their contexts we imagine that also **E** and **F** must have talked about it. In **C** it is introduced in the non-metric nominative αἴξ. It seems that the formula has been reinterpreted in such a way that now the παῖς in **A** is also a goat. We find as well αἴξ αἶγα in **D2** and **H2**.

In my opinion there must be a certain link between the she-goat that must be carried out from Persephone's garden and some of the texts in the Orphic gold tablets.

Thurii, IV a. C. (*OF* 487) 4–6:
θεὸς ἐγένου ἐξ ἀνθρώπου· ἔριφος ἐς γάλα ἔπετες.
χαῖρ⟨ε⟩ χαῖρε· δεξιὰν ὁδοιπόρ⟨ει⟩ 5
λειμῶνας θ' {ε} ἱεροὺς καὶ ἄλσεα Φερσεφονείας.

You have been born a god from the man that you were. A kid, you fell into the milk.
Hail, hail; take the path to the right
towards the sacred meadows and groves of Persephone.

---

[85] Plut. *Quaest. conv.* VII.5.4, p. 706D, cf. § 2.

Thurii, IV a. C. (OF 488) 7-9:
δεσ{σ}ποίνας δ'{ε} ὑπὸ κόλπον ἔδυν χθονίας βασιλείας·
'ὄλβιε καὶ μακαριστέ, θεὸς δ' ἔσηι ἀντὶ βροτοῖο'.
ἔριφος ἐς γάλ' ἔπετον.

And I plunged down into the lap of my lady, the subterranean queen (sc. Persephone):
'Happy and fortunate, you will be a god, from the mortal you were'.
A kid, I fell into the milk.

Pelinna, IV a. C. (OF 485), 2-5:
εἰπεῖν Φερσεφόναι σ' ὅτι Β⟨άκ⟩χιος αὐτὸς ἔλυσε.
τα{ι}υρος εἰς γάλα ἔθορες.
αἶξα[86] (αἶψα L) εἰς γ⟨ά⟩λα ἔθορες.
κριὸς εἰς γάλα ἔπεσ⟨ες⟩.

Tell Persephone that Bacchus himself has liberated you.
A bull, you leapt into the milk.
A goat, you leapt into the milk.
A ram, you fell into the milk.

This is no time to go further into the meaning of the formula.[87] Quoting a passage from Lucian (*Pseud.* 16: ἀπειλῶν ἐξελαύνει τὸν δαίμονα) Kotansky[88] asserts that in using this expression the tablets 'probably have in mind protection and purification of the owner's actual estate: the she-goat will be then a kind of goat-demon like those of Near Eastern heritage'. I think, however, that there is nothing similar between this scapegoat and the 'she-goat, companion of Persephone and full of rich milk'. Again, the reference to the 'garden of Persephone' is another link with the tablets' imagery.

On the other hand, Ἀνάγκη appears personified next to Χρόνος 'Time' in the very beginning of the Orphic Theogony.[89] Finally, some

---

[86] αἶξα (instead of αἶψα) is a convincing reading proposed by Méndez Dosuna (2009).
[87] Cf. Bernabé-Jiménez (2008) 76-83.
[88] Kotansky (1995) 256; cf. Rocca (2009) 38.
[89] In the so-called *Theogony of Hieronymus and Hellanicus,* cf. Damasc. *De princ.* 123 bis (III 161.8 Westerink = OF 77) συνεῖναι δὲ αὐτῶι τὴν Ἀνάγκην, φύσιν οὖσαν τὴν αὐτὴν καὶ Ἀδράστειαν, ἀσώματον διωργυιωμένην ἐν παντὶ τῶι κόσμωι, τῶν περάτων αὐτοῦ ἐφαπτομένην. 'And with him (with Time) was Necessity, being of the same nature and incorporeal Adrastea, having her arms stretched out in the entire cosmos, reaching its limits', and also in the *Rhapsodies:* Procl. *in Plat. Remp.* II 207.27 Kroll ἀλλὰ κἀκεῖνος (sc. Ὀρφεύς) ἄλλην Ἀνάγκην παρήγαγεν πρὸ τῶν Μοιρῶν, 'στυγερῶπα τε Ἀνάγκην' (OF 110) λέγων προελθεῖν ἀπ' ἐκείνων (sc. a primis dis) 'but Orpheus also

parts of the texts that I have not collected here show a very similar vocabulary to the Orphic one, such as Νύξ and perhaps Αἰών, as the fundamental elements in **A**, or ὄλβιος in **C**[90].

e) In **B**, he who uses the formula claims that he has been initiated (τετέ[λ]εσμαι) and thereby makes a clear link between the magical vocabulary and the Mystery one. There are also several testimonies connecting Orpheus with the Idaean Dactyls[91].

f) The relationship between the formula and Ephesos is not, however, completely convincing, since it is more probable that it has arisen from a false etymology, from the adjective ἐφέσια 'liberating', which in a certain way is a sort of antidote for a magical binding spell (κατάδεσμος). I believe that it is more acceptable to consider this origin than to resort to the well-worn argument of a loanword from a non-Greek language.

4.14. CONCLUSION

At the end of our route we observe that even if there are still some obscurities surrounding the origin and the interpretation of the terms that make up the Ἐφέσια γράμματα, it seems that all of them were part of one or several ἐπωιδαί and that they were originally all meaningful words. Nevertheless, we notice that, already in the ancient documents, there is a deliberate preference for phonic play over semantic meaning. As a result, the original and comprehensible Greek terms become opaque and are gradually turned into meaningless *voces magicae*. The second tendency is to abridge the original hexametrical incantation of many verses so that it becomes a much shorter and prosaic formula.

---

made appear another Ananke before the Moirai, the "hateful Ananke" by claiming that it came from those (the first gods)'. Cf. as well Orph. *Arg.* 12f., where Ananke is mentioned in a sort of summary of the Orphic theogonies (*OF* 99).

[90] Cf. as well **C** 4 κατ' ἀμαξιτόν and Parmen. B 1.21 D.-K. ἰθὺς ἔχον κοῦραι κατ' ἀμαξιτὸν ἅρμα καὶ ἵππους 'the maidens drove the chariot and mares straight down the highroad'.

[91] Cf. D. S. V.64.4 (= Ephor. *FGrHist* 70 F 104), IV.43.1 (Dionys. Scyt. fr. 18 Rusten), IV.48.6 (Dionys. Scyt. fr. 30 Rusten), V.49.6. cf. Bernabé (2000) 47f. and *OF* 519–23.

The end of this process is what we call the Ἐφέσια γράμματα (it would probably be more acceptable to use lower-case letters, ἐφέσια γράμματα 'liberating letters'), a formula consisting of only six words. In order to create the short formula, the more remarkable words were taken from the verse incantations, especially those with an attractive phonetic sequence. Some of them were preserved with no alterations; others were altered by misinterpretation, a sort of popular etymology. None of them was comprehensible, a fact that explains why they were gradually reinterpreted in very different ways. Androcydes already knows the most abbreviated version of the formula in the Hellenistic period.

From a conjectural point of view, the process of making up the short formula could be as follows: the earliest sequence to be altered was ασκι κατασκι. In fact, the first word (ἔσκε?) was transformed at such an early date that there are no traces of a meaningful term replaced by the magic word ασκι, which probably emerged as a magical *pendant* for κατασκι. As for the second word, we find κατὰ σκιερῶν, preserved in **A** and **B**, and κατὰ σκιαρῶν in **D1** (in the three cases it always goes before ὀρέων). In **G1** and **G2** the form is σκιρὸν whereas ὀρέων has disappeared. Although **A** can be dated between the second century and fourth century AD, it seems that this document preserves the original sequence better than some of the earliest South Italian witnesses. The coincidence with the magical papyrus LXX (**B**) confirms the antiquity of the sequence.

In **C**, **D2**, **E**, and **F** the sequence appears as ασκι κατασκι, losing all connections with κατὰ σκιερῶν as a result of cutting the second word just where the four letters of ασκι are repeated. Both words were at the very beginning of the original ἐπωιδή and they are still at the beginning of the abbreviated formula almost like a sort of 'title' (as we saw in the shorthand reference in *P.Mag.* VII 450ff.).

In **A, C, D1, D2, E, G1**, and probably **F**, a she-goat appears as the protagonist of the first part of the ἐπωιδή in the environment of Demeter and her daughter. Through the power of magic, the goat was led out from the garden of Persephone (a clearly eschatological milieu) and in **A** and **D1** she seems to be a source of abundant milk. It is natural, then, that the very next word in the sequence of the *Ephesia Grammata* was precisely the animal that carries this enormous symbolic meaning, the goat, αἴξ. Perhaps *AIΞ* was read as *ΛIΞ* in a moment when the formula was no longer conceived as a whole of meaningful words.

In order to echo the term αἴξ, the sorcerers played with the phonic attractiveness of the mysterious word Τετραξ, a possible alternative for the ancient τετραβάμων, by making a homeoteleuton with αἴξ. Whereas the first tablets played a morphological game between αἴξ, αἶγα (nominative, then accusative), the later ones followed suit with Τετραξ, Τετραγος/κος (nominative, then genitive), with the variants Τραξ (Τραχ probably arises from a mistaken reading when changing from one alphabet to the other) and Τρεξ. In Τετραγος there was a play with the homophone τε τράγος. Whatever its origin, Τετραξ was a magical name, very important to know, and it maintained its connections with αἴξ, the term which is still its phonic pair in the formula.

Δαμναμενεύς was one of the Idaean Dactyls, whose name evoked the magical ability of constraining or obliging. In C and E he is still invoked through the etymological game Δαμναμενεῦ δάμασον so that, according to his name, he can exercise his capacity for coercion. In G1 and G2 we find the variant δαμνυμενα in similar contexts. Since invoking the one who embodied coercion (Damnameneus) was an important part of the incantation, his name is the next to be selected from the poetic version, albeit replacing the vocative with the nominative, because in the abbreviated version there is no longer any need to invoke him, just to enunciate his powerful name. The place it takes in the formula is the same as in the ἐπωιδαί, just after Τετραξ.

Ἀασία, on the other hand, an initial epithet of αἴξ meaning 'bearer of ἄτη' and a ἅπαξ λεγόμενον, was probably selected for the abbreviated formula because of its originally magical and eschatological character and then reinterpreted as αἴσια (neuter plural of αἴσιος, 'auspicious, opportune'), an undoubtedly more appropriate meaning for the power that was ascribed to the Ἐφέσια γράμματα. On the other hand, it could also have been transformed first in the ἐπωιδαί and then selected for the formula for the reason I have just referred to. Taking into account its position in C, D2, E, and probably F, the word ἀασία should have appeared after ασκι κατασκι, but it has been moved to the end of the formula, maybe with the intention of preserving the two pairs of rhyming words: ασκι κατασκι and αἴξ τετραξ. There must have been several attempts to continue this process, and even if they did not prevail, they have left some traces in our texts, such as the prolongation (and even replacement) of ασκι by υσσκι, the pair ἀασία ἐνδασία, or the use of different variants of the same word, like αἴξ αἶγα, even the sequences where every word has one syllable more than the preceding, like Τραξ Τετραξ Τετραγος.

5

The *Ephesia Grammata: Logos Orphaïkos* or Apolline *Alexima Pharmaka*?

Radcliffe G. Edmonds III

The tablet from Selinus at the Getty Villa provides an opportunity to reconsider the nature of the formula, which appears in a number of epigraphic sources and literary testimonia, known as the *Ephesia Grammata* and to analyse the reception of the formula over a range of places and times. Scholars have often focused on the question of the origins of the formula, trying to determine whether a mystery cult might have produced the hexameters and, if so, which cult. The label of the formula in one late example as a *logos Orphaïkos* has tempted some to look to Orphism, while the presence of Hecate has inclined others towards a chthonic cult.

However, the examples of the text that have survived to the present day, whether or not they came originally from a mystery cult, do not appear in a mystery cult setting. The hexameter verses of the *Ephesia Grammata* are used in the epigraphic texts as warding magics, as *alexikaka, alexipharmaka*, or, as the Getty tablet has it, *alexima pharmaka*.[1] The earliest versions seem to deploy the formula against harmful creatures or magical attacks, whereas, in the later versions and in most of the testimonia, the hexameter verses that begin with *aske kata skieron oreon* or the collection of six words, *aski, kataski, aix, tetrax, damnameneus,* and *aision,* have become a more general

---

[1] Getty text ἀλέξιμα φάρμακα l. 6, 23, 47, cf. Photius s.v. *Ephesia Grammata*: 'also *Ephesia alexipharmaka*; some names and phrases having an innate remedy for suffering.'

protective spell, good especially against daimonic attack.[2] Some later examples, such as the *defixio* in Cologne and the recipe in the Greek magical papyri that refers to the formula as a *logos Orphaïkos*, use the *Ephesia Grammata* to protect another spell against interference that might undo its effect. Over time, the connection with Paean and warding magic is lost, and the formula is connected with prestigious figures of magic, such as the Idaean Dactyls and Orpheus. The uses of the formula within the context of the later texts, however, show that the protective function of this warding magic still persists in all the versions.

The Getty tablet provides explicit information about the origin and function of the mysterious hexameter verses that become in the later tradition the *Ephesia Grammata*. While it is not clear who the narrating voice of the tablet itself might be, the *Ephesia Grammata* verses are labelled the immortal verses of Paean Apollo himself:

$$Παιήων\ σὺ\ δὲ\ πάντοσ'\ ἀλέξιμα\ φάρμακα\ πέμπεις$$
$$καὶ\ τάδ'\ ἐφώνησας\ ἔπε'\ ἀθάνατα\ θνητοῖσιν·\qquad(6\text{–}7)$$

Paean, for in every direction you send averting charms,
And you spoke these immortal verses to mortal men.

The deictic τάδε leaves no doubt that the verses that follow are thought to be Paean's own words, rather than simply further description of the narrative situation. The originating voice is just as clear in these lines:

$$Παιήων'] \ σὺ\ γὰρ\ αὐτὸς\ ἀλεξιμὰ\ φάρμα[κα\ πέμπεις]$$
$$[c.\ 6\text{–}7]γου\ κατάκουε\ φ[ρ]ασὶν\ γλυκὺν\ ὕ[μνον]\qquad(23\text{–}4)$$

Paean, for you yourself [do send] averting charms!
Give ear in your mind to sweet h[ymnic song]

$$[Πα]ι[ή]ων·\ ὁ\ γὰρ\ αὐτὸς\ ἀλεξιμὰ\ φάρμακα\ πέ[μπεις]$$
$$[οὐ]κ\ ἂν\ δ⟨η⟩λήσαιτ'\ οὐδεὶς\ \{ουδαι\}\ πολυφάρ[μακ\text{-}\text{-}\text{-}]\qquad(49\text{–}50)$$

[Pa]e[a]n, for in every direction you [send] averting charms,
Nor would anyone harm (us?) with much-cur[ing]...

In both introductions, moreover, the nature of the verses is specified: they are *alexima pharmaka*, warding magics. The verses themselves

---

[2] Hesychius s.v. *Ephesia Grammata* (ε 7401) 'Ephesia Grammata: Formerly there were 6, but afterwards some deceivers added others. They say that these are the names of the first ones: askion, kataskion, lix, tetrax, damnameneus, aision. It is clear that askion is darkness, kataskion is light, lix is earth, tetrax is the year, damnameneus is the sun, and aision is truth. Therefore these things are holy and sacred.'

must be classified as *pharmaka*, but not the kind of *pharmaka* that are baneful poisons; rather, they serve as protection against harm.

What kind of harm is difficult to see from the tablet fragments, but references on the second fragment provide some clues. Lines 26–8 set up a situation of impending crisis: whenever some thing (the supplement *kêr* is tempting) comes to threaten men or flocks or even the ships and other things produced by mortals' craft, then these verses will protect them. Lines 4–5 extend the protective power more generally: 'As many things as the broad Earth nourishes shall not harm him nor as many things as much-groaning Amphitrite rears in the sea.' Nothing that lives on land or sea can harm the one who has activated the power of Paean's verses.

The same protective function appears in later examples of the *Ephesia Grammata* verses. Bernabé shows the similarities between the texts that appear in a number of places from Egypt to Sicily, ranging in date from the fourth century BC to the fourth century AD.[3] While the examples from Himera, Selinus, and Locri (cp. Bernabé texts E, F, G, and H) have no framing language that provides context, the fourth century BC lead tablet from Phalasarna invokes protective deities. 'I call on Zeus Averter of evil (*Alexikakos*) and on Heracles Sacker of cities and on the Healer and on Victory and on Apollo.'[4] This invocation of the protective deities is followed by a variant of the verses, and the tablet's end again brings in the idea of protection from harm. 'He shall not destroy me with ointment or application or with drink or with spell', where the subject is probably the 'whoever' (*hos ke*) mentioned a few lines earlier, who is attempting to harm and perhaps even cast a spell upon (if that is what may be construed from *kollobalousi*) the speaker. While McCown thinks that this ending *alexipharmakon* is an error that the writer 'allows to creep in by mistake as he unintelligently copies from his book of recipes', it fits perfectly with the beginning and frames the *Ephesia Grammata* verses in the middle as the efficacious verses that provide the warding magics.[5]

---

[3] Bernabé in this volume excerpts only the parts of the text that include the *Ephesia Grammata* formula. For the entirety of the texts, see Jordan (2000a) 100, for text E from Locri Epizephyrioi; Rocca (2009) for texts F, G, and H from Himera and Selinus.

[4] Phalasarna Tablet: National Museum, Athens, Inv. X.9355. Text from Jordan (1992). Bernabé in this volume excerpts the formula in his text C (= *OF* 830c), but he omits the framing language and the remainder of the spell. For the full text and translation see the Appendix to this volume.

[5] McCown (1923) 134, n. 25.

PGM LXX, a papyrus formulary from the third or fourth century AD, contains a series of protective spells, among which appears the *Ephesia Grammata* formula, although only the first line, '*askei kataskei erôn oreôn*', is cited.[6] The charm is to be recited at the approach of some unnamed entity, whom Betz suggests is an underworld daimon bent on inflicting chastisement, since the charm is directed *pros phobon kolasios*, against fear of chastisement. The aim of the protective spells is to avert this entity, whatever it is—*kai paraitêsêi,* and you will avert it. Here again, the *Ephesia Grammata* formula is used to ward off some threat of harm.

In the third or fourth century AD *defixio* from Oxyrhynchus now in Cologne, the *Ephesia Grammata* verses appear at the end of a lengthy erotic spell.[7] The beginning of the spell (lines 1–56) invokes the powers of the dead and the underworld deities to inflict eros upon the target woman, and the various erotic prohibitions and compulsions are elaborated in characteristically graphic detail. The spirit of the dead is then adjured repeatedly by the threat of Hecate, who is herself requested to activate the spell (*epitelousai moi ton katadesmon touton,* lines 61–2). The aim of the spell ('Drive, bind Matrona...') is repeated once more, then the spell is finished off by a recitation of the *aski kataski* verses (lines 64–8), capped with an injunction to 'preserve this spell unbroken for eternity' (*phulaxon aluton ton katadesmon eis aiôna,* lines 73–4). The verses, although they too invoke Hecate, are specifically aimed at preserving the spell from outside influence that might dissolve it, any countercharm that Matrona or another might make. This prophylactic action is not quite the same as the warding function in the Phalasarna and Getty tablets, but it is still the single protective element in an otherwise entirely offensive spell.

The testimonia regarding the *Ephesia Grammata* words seem to reinforce the essentially defensive nature of the *Ephesia Grammata* verses. Many of these testimonia are collected by Bernabé in his contribution to this volume, but he is examining the origin rather than the function of the magical words. It is worth noting, however, that whatever the process of evolution that links the hexameter verses beginning with *aske kata skieron oreon* to the collection of words *aski,*

---

[6] Text in Preisendanz/Henrichs (1973–4), with a translation in Betz (1986). Bernabé in this volume excerpts parts of lines 10–12 as his text B (= *OF* 830b).

[7] The full text (*SEG* 38:1837) appears, with translation, in Jordan (1988), but Bernabé in this volume excerpts lines 64–8 as his text A (= *OF* 830a).

kataski, aix, tetrax, damnameneus, and *aision,* the same idea that the magical words serve to ward off harm persists.[8] The second century AD lexicographer Pausanias described them as 'encompassing in themselves the natural sense of warding off evil', and they are attested early as a protective amulet. The fourth century BC comic poet Anaxilas mocks a dandy who wears the *Ephesia Grammata* stitched on leather, while the late lexicographers relate the story of a boxer who was invincible until his knucklebone amulet with the *Ephesia Grammata* was removed.[9] The boxer's amulet was perhaps like an inscribed gem in the Southesk collection that bears all six names.[10] Menander describes the *Ephesia Grammata* used as *alexipharmaka* to protect either those getting married (*gamousin*) or, if we accept the emendation of McCown, those who are afflicted by demons (*daimosin*).[11] The received text would make these preventative magic at a crucial transition time, but the emendation fits with other attestations of the *Ephesia Grammata* in which they are used to protect against daimonic attack. In explaining how the philosopher should protect himself against the corrupting influence of bad music, Plutarch advises,

> For just as sorcerers advise those afflicted by demons to recite and name over to themselves the *Ephesia Grammata,* so we, in the midst of such warblings and caperings, 'Stirred by frenzies and whoops to the tumult of tossing heads,' if we bethink ourselves of those hallowed and venerable writings and set up for comparison songs and poems and tales of true nobility, shall not be altogether dazed by these performances... [12]

Plutarch mentions the same parallel between this use of the *Ephesia Grammata* as warding magic and the recollection of stories of ancient virtue in another context, where he compares the reciting of the names of the Idaean Dactyls to the recollection of the deeds of virtuous men.

> True it is that those who have got by heart the names of the Idaean Dactyls use them as charms against terrors, repeating each name with

---

[8] I agree with Bernabé and others who see the hexameter incantation as the primary form, later transformed into a series of *voces magicae,* just as the meaningful phrase 'hoc est corpus' was transformed into the chiming, unintelligible 'hocus pocus'.
[9] Cp. Eustathius on *Odyssey* XIX.247 (2.201–2); Anaxilas, *The Harp-Maker* (II 268 K) = Athenaeus, *Deipnosophistae* XII.14.12–18 548C.
[10] Carnegie (1908) 141–2; Plate XIII N5.
[11] Menander *Paidia* fr. 313 Kock, from Photius s.v. *alexipharmaka,* cp. McCown (1923) 131 n. 17.
[12] Plutarch, *Quaestiones convivales* 706e.

calm assurance; but it is also true that the thought and recollection of good men almost instantly comes to mind and gives support to those who are making progress towards virtue, and in every onset of the emotions and in all difficulties keeps them upright and saves them from falling.[13]

Marcus Aurelius makes a similar statement, 'In the *Ephesia Grammata* there was this message, to remember some one of the ancients who practised virtue.'[14] By the time of Marcus Aurelius, it is the philosophical substitute, the recollection of virtuous men that is recommended in place of the magic of the *Ephesia Grammata*, but the association between the *Ephesia Grammata*, the names of the Dactyls, and the protection from fear and harm remains. So efficacious are the *Ephesia Grammata*, the late testimonia tell us, that rather than just praying to Apollo, as in Herodotus, Croesus recited these words on the pyre to save himself. These magical words, derived perhaps from Paean's immortal verses, create the miracle that wards off harm from the Lydian king. Ultimately, they become symbols to be interpreted allegorically.[15]

The ascription to Orpheus comes only through the reference in the papyrus formulary, dating to the third or fourth century AD, which instructs the magician to use the 'Orphic spell' (*logos Orphaïkos*) to ensure that the binding spell in the recipe remains unbroken.

> Write the Orphic formula, saying, 'Askei kai taskei' and, taking a black thread, make 365 knots, and bind [the thread] around the outside of the plate, saying the same formula again and, 'Maintain the restraining' (or 'the binding'), or whatever you do. And thus it is deposited. For Selene, when she goes through the underworld, breaks whatever spell she finds. But when this rite has been performed, the spell remains unbroken so long as you say over the formula daily at this spot.[16]

---

[13] Plutarch, *Quomodo quis* 85b.
[14] Marcus Aurelius, *Meditations* XI, 26.
[15] Clement of Alexandria, *Stromata* 5.8.45.2–3. 'Androcydes the Pythagorean, indeed, says that the so-called Ephesian letters, which were well known among many, were of the order of symbols. And he said that Askion is darkness, for this has no shadow; and Kataskion is light, since it casts a shadow with its rays; and Lix is the earth, according to the ancient name; and Tetrax is the year, according to the seasons; and Damnameneus is the sun, the tamer; and Aisia is the true word. And truly the symbol signifies that the divine things have been set in order: darkness to light, the sun to the year, the earth to every kind of genesis of nature.'
[16] *PGM* VII 451–458.

As in the Cologne *defixio*, the *Ephesia Grammata* serves to prevent the spell from being broken. Once again, the formula has a defensive power, but, instead of being ascribed to Apollo Paean or even to the Idaean Dactyls, it is labelled as Orphic. Nothing in the framing of the formula in any of the other examples or testimonies indicates an Orphic context—why should it be labelled Orphic here?

The question leads to the oft-trampled quagmire of defining Orphism, and I don't want to stray too far here. For my part, I would agree with West, that 'A poem becomes Orphic simply by being ascribed to Orpheus... There was no doctrinal criterion for ascription to Orpheus, and no copyright restriction. It was a device for conferring antiquity and authority upon a text that stood in need of them.'[17] However, Alberto Bernabé and his pupil Raquel Martín Hernández have recently argued for a close link between the *Ephesia Grammata* and Orphism, so I think it is worth addressing their arguments.[18] Beyond the basic similarity of being mysterious ritual inscriptions on thin sheets of metal, the lead tablets with the *Ephesia Grammata* formula and the so-called Orphic gold tablets show a number of similarities that strike these scholars as significant. Both sets of texts involve Persephone, a goat, and milk, and both sets have been found in the regions of southern Italy and Crete.

Martín moreover draws parallels between the imagery of the *Ephesia Grammata* verses and the descriptions of Crete (in, for example, Diodorus Siculus), arguing for a connection with the cult of the Idaean Dactyls of Crete.[19] Orpheus is numbered among the founders of the cult of the Dactyls, and Clement makes them the inventors of the *Ephesia Grammata*.[20] Not only are the *Ephesia Grammata* identified with the names of the Dactyls in Plutarch, but the name Damnameneus is among the names of the Dactyls on several of the varied lists. Moreover, the reference in *PGM* LXX to 'when under the shadowy mountains' is followed by a reference to the chamber of the Dactyls. Betz has argued that an initiatory rite for the Idaean Dactyls lies behind this reference,[21] while Jordan suggests that the

---

[17] West (1983) 3.
[18] Cf. Martín (2010) 142–63; Bernabé (2003) and in this volume, §13.
[19] Martín (2010) 156–63.
[20] Cf. Clement *Stromata* I.6, the scholiast to Apollonius Rhodius at I.1129, and Strabo, *Geography*, 10.3.22 for lists of the names of the Dactyls that include Damnameneus.
[21] Betz (1980) 287–95. A passage from Porphyry's *Life of Pythagoras*, 17, provides a striking parallel to the descent into the chamber of the Dactyls in *PGM* LXX. 'When

unmetrical reference to the dactyls is merely a marginal note referring to dactylic verses that has crept into the text.[22] Finally, Bernabé and Martín cite the Derveni author's reference to the *epaoidai* that the *magoi* use against impeding daimons as an Orphic parallel to the use of the *Ephesia Grammata* for those afflicted with daimons.[23]

None of these arguments will bear much weight. Firstly, in the Derveni papyrus, whatever the context of the rituals described there, it is the *magoi* who perform spells against the daimons, not Orpheus, just as in Plutarch, the *Ephesia Grammata* of the *magoi* are contrasted with the remedies of the philosopher. Secondly, the roles of Persephone, the goat, and the milk are all significantly different in the gold tablets than in the *Ephesia Grammata* verses. Persephone appears in the tablets, not as the possessor of a garden that is the scene of the action, but as the enthroned Queen of the Underworld. The goat, whether the *eriphos* kid of the Thurii tablets or even the hypothetical *aix* of the Pelinna tablet, is rushing or falling into the milk, not producing milk endlessly. A resemblance between symbols does not indicate a shared meaning—a goat, milk, and even Persephone signify different things in different contexts.[24]

A goat with a ceaseless supply of milk is most reminiscent of the myths of the suckling of the infant Zeus on Mount Ida.[25] However, the connection of Orpheus with the Idaean Dactyls is not so strong as to make anything Dactylic Orphic as well. Orpheus is the ritual

---

he landed in Crete, he betook himself to the mystics of Morges, one of the Idaean Dactyls, by whom he was purified with the thunder-stone, at daybreak lying prone beside the sea and at night beside a river, his head wrapped in the fleece of a black ram. Moreover, he went down into the Idaean Cave, as it is called, wearing black wool, passed thrice nine days there in accordance with custom, and offered a funeral sacrifice to Zeus.' (text and translation from Cook, 1914, vol.I: 646)

[22] Jordan (1992) 258. *Dactulôn*, 'a cretic, cannot stand in a hexameter... probably an intrusion from a marginal or interlinear note meant to signal the reader that the lines are in verse and are to be intoned as such.'

[23] P.Derv. col. vi. '... prayers and sacrifices appease the souls, and the enchanting song of the *magoi* is able to remove the *daimones* when they impede. Impeding *daimones* are revenging souls. This is why the *magoi* perform the sacrifice, as if they were paying a penalty.'

[24] Cf. A2 = OF 489B; D1.4 = OF 485, where several scholars have suggested that the lamella's clear text of AIPSA be emended to AIGA. For the importance of reading the familiar mythic elements in the gold tablets within the context of the tablets themselves, see Edmonds (2004) ch. 2 *passim*.

[25] Cf. the version in Diodorus of Sicily, V. 70.2–3. See Johnston in this volume for other associations with milk.

founder supreme, and his name becomes attached to a wide variety of rites, from Demeter in Sparta, to Hecate at Aigina, to the Eleusinian Mysteries at Athens. Orpheus' name could add the lustre of antiquity or special sacrality to a rite, putting it among the class of the oldest and best rites founded by Orpheus himself. The Dactyls are connected with a variety of other figures (including Heracles, who appears in the Phalasarna tablet), and there is nothing in any of the testimonia or the examples of the texts to suggest that the connection with Orpheus was activated, that the potential link within the tradition was actualized.

However, just as the Orphic label could be used to enhance the prestige of a festival, so too, it was used to add glamour to enchantments such as the formula in *PGM* VII. Pausanias tells us that Orpheus is known to be terrific at enchantments (*mageusai deinon*), and the chorus in Euripides' *Cyclops* boast that they know a charm by Orpheus that can harm the monster.[26] The Orphic label for this charm to protect the spell is thus most likely another of the 'advertisements' so common in the magical papyri, adding importance to a recipe by associating it with a famous name. The association with the names of the Idaean Dactyls comes not through Orpheus, but through a process of evolution in which the sounds of the hexameter verses are distorted and altered, transforming a series of magically powerful dactylic hexameters into a list of the names of the inventors of dactylic hexameter.

It is perhaps worth noting that another set of verses is found with the *Ephesia Grammata* verses in the two latest examples, the *defixio* in Cologne and *PGM* LXX. The iambic trimeters that list the *symbola* of Hecate, including the bronze, gold, and iron sandals, are used in both places to invoke the goddess to give power to the spell. The role of Hecate Einodia in the *Ephesia Grammata* hexameters may well have suggested that she was the power to be invoked for the repulsion of hostile forces, and so the trimeters, which were well known enough to be allegorically explained by Porphyry, were added to strengthen the magician's claim upon the power of Hecate.[27]

---

[26] Pausanias VI.20.18. Euripides *Cyclops* 645–8. 'But I know an entirely excellent incantation of Orpheus, so that on its own accord the burning brand moves towards his skull and sets afire the one-eyed child of earth.'

[27] Porphyry, *Peri Agalmatôn* 8.58–65. 'The moon again is Hecate, (the symbol) of the configurations about her and of the power of the configurations—wherefore her power is threefold: that of the new moon as she bears the white-robed and

The *Ephesia Grammata*, then, show no evidence of connection early on with a mystery cult, whether attributed to Orpheus, devoted to the Idaean Dactyls, or even connected with Demeter and Kore.[28] Rather, the successive uses of the formula suggest that the earliest connection of the formula is to Apollo Paean, who prescribed the verses as *alexima pharmaka*.[29] Only later, as the formula is used more broadly, does it become attached to the Idaean Dactyls and ascribed to the magician and greatest founder of mysteries, Orpheus.[30] The immortal verses that Paean chants to mortals in the fourth century BC end up in the fourth century AD as 'the Orphic spell', a supplementary charm to prevent a binding spell from being broken. The examples of testimonies to the *Ephesia Grammata*, both the hexameter verses and the set of words, show the transformation from explicitly labelled *alexima pharmaka* to the meaningless hocus-pocus words that nevertheless retain the sense of warding magic. This process illuminates the way the ritual power of the verses was received and transformed over centuries of the tradition.

golden-sandalled [. . . .] and the torches alight. The kalathos, which she bears aloft, is the symbol of the production of crops, which she nurtures in the increase of her light. The bronze-sandalled goddess is, again (the symbol) of the full moon.' For a recent examination of the testimonies to these verses, see Martín (2010) 163–77.

[28] Jordan and Kotansky (2011) 54 suggest that the *Ephesia Grammata* were 'the traditional legomena of a rite of initiation into the worship of Demeter and Kore.' Cf. Jordan (1992) 245: 'The parallel verses, which we plan to present in detail elsewhere, go back, some of them, to at least the 5th century BC and seem to come from a chthonic cult.'

[29] See Rutherford in this volume for the suggestion that the text might best be classified as a 'paean' or an 'incantation paean' because of this connection with Paean. Johnston in this volume, on the other hand, focuses on the narrative in the verses as a historiola with a magical function.

[30] See Faraone in this volume for the connections between these hexameters and other hexametrical charms for healing and protection.

6

Magical Verses on a Lead Tablet: Composite Amulet or Anthology?

Christopher A. Faraone

6.1. INTRODUCTION

All the scholars, myself included, who discussed the Getty Hexameters at the seminar in November 2010 were in agreement, voiced or tacit, that the lead tablet upon which the verses are inscribed was used as an amulet, and not without good reasons: they begin with a reference to hiding the text 'in a house of stone', and they twice quote versions of the famous *Ephesia Grammata*, an incantation said, for example, to have protected Croesus from the flames of his funeral pyre or an unnamed boxer from defeat at the Olympic games.[1] The tablet was also found evenly folded six times, a feature that is common in the case of amulets.[2] Long after the 2010 seminar I was struck, however, by a curious afterthought: perhaps the lead tablet was actually an anthology of sorts that preserved a series of originally separate incantations. There are, in fact, some peculiarities about the Getty tablet that do not fit the model of a composite amulet. It is laid out, for instance, in two side-by-side columns, a very rare occurrence on amulets, and there are indications of the kind of scribal habits that one finds in handbooks: marks to the left of the first column, for example, seem to indicate a section break, as do the

---

[1] For the literary references to the *Ephesia Grammata*, see Bernabé, Ch. 4, section 2.
[2] Jordan and Kotansky (2011) 54. The Phalasarna tablet is also folded six times horizontally; see the drawing in Jordan (1992).

indentation and vertical margin line at the bottom of the second.[3] The text itself, moreover, is long and variegated, while the other early lead amulets from Locri, Himera, and Selinus only have, as far as we can tell, one short text: the *Ephesia Grammata*.

Most puzzling, perhaps, are the repeated verses addressed to Paean, which—as Rutherford discusses in Chapter 8—suggest the type of refrains (*epithegmata*) that one often finds in those special hymns (paeans) that were addressed to Apollo or Asclepius and were designed as appeals for safety and health. This type of hymn would, of course, be perfectly appropriate for an amulet, especially one designed to ward off destruction from a house or an entire city. There is, however, one serious problem with this approach: in none of these repeating lines is the god Paean actually asked to help or heal. A second option discussed briefly by Rutherford is that these verses are designed to be refrains in a sung incantation, such as we find in the binding spell (*hymnos desmios*) sung and danced by the Furies in Aeschylus' *Eumenides*, or the love spell performed by Simaetha in Theocritus' second *Idyll*. This is, at first glance, a more promising starting point, because in both of these literary examples, the refrain seems to reiterate the purpose of the spell and, in the case of the binding hymn, even gives us a title for it: 'Over our victim this is our song.... the chant of the Furies, that binds the mind, sung with no lyre, a song to shrivel up men' (ἐπὶ δὲ τῷ τεθυμένῳ τόδε μέλος ... ὕμνος ἐξ Ἐρινύων, δέσμιος φρενῶν, ἀφόρμικτος, αὐονὰ βροτοῖς).[4] By repeating this refrain, then, the Furies remind us what their song does (it binds and withers), and that they are its authors. Simaetha's refrain also seems to reiterate the purpose of the love spell in the form of a command: 'O *iunx*, you yourself drag to my house that man of mine!' (ἶυγξ, ἕλκε τὺ τῆνον ἐμὸν ποτὶ δῶμα τὸν ἄνδρα). Here the word *iunx* can refer both to the special bird used as an effigy in a love spell and to the incantation itself.[5] So one might argue, then, that the repeated

---

[3] Two short parallel horizontal lines appear to separate lines 7 and 8 of the first column and thus seem to mark the beginning of the first quotation of the *Ephesia Grammata*. At the bottom left of the second column, the scribe began to write the second version of the *Ephesia Grammata*, but then apparently decided that it should be indented (perhaps following his exemplar?); he apparently drew a vertical guideline to remind himself where the indented margin was.

[4] Text and translation by Sommerstein (2008) *ad loc.* with some changes. For discussion, see Faraone (1985).

[5] Faraone (1999).

verses in the Getty Hexameters are closer to this kind of refrain, especially if we recall that, like the *iunx*, the word Paean/*paean* can designate both an agent, a god who can be invoked, as well as a hexametrical text that can be performed. The comparison with Simaetha's refrain, however, points up the important problem that was mentioned earlier: Paean/*paean*, unlike Iunx/*iunx*, is never actually asked to do anything in the Getty Hexameters.

There is, however, an even more striking difficulty with this second hypothesis: the alleged refrain seems to introduce different kinds of hexametrical texts—an oracular text of the type 'Apollo commands' (discussed in Chapter 3), as well as two different versions of the *Ephesia Grammata*, an earlier hexametrical version and a later, more corrupted version in a different dialect.[6] Now it is true that in Simaetha's spell, each refrain introduces a new type of ritual (most aimed at burning or melting) in a composite and very long performance, so perhaps the author of the Getty Hexameters aimed at a similar effect.[7] We certainly find inscribed on the gold and silver amulets of the Roman period composite amuletic texts of similar length and differing content.[8] But the inclusion of two versions of the same incantation suggests another possibility: that the text on this lead tablet was not, in fact, designed to be an amulet, but rather an anthology, in which the repeated verses about Paean operate as markers which divide one incantation from the next. In an anthology, of course, it is entirely plausible that we might find two versions of the same spell, a phenomenon that we see, for example, in a much later magical papyrus called the 'Book of Moses' (*PGM* XIII) that records two versions (the second much enlarged) of the same recipe,[9] or a second/third century AD copper amulet from Acre (near Syracuse) that seems to have been copied from a handbook and contains three *phylaktêria* of Moses (*GMA* 32), each introduced by rubrics:

---

[6] See Janko, Ch. 2 in this volume.

[7] Gow (1950) 40–1 describes the different sympathetically magical actions as follows (according to his ordering of the verses): barley burnt (18–21); laurel burnt (23–6); husks burnt (33–6); wax melted and rhombus turned (28–31); triple libation (43–6); fringe of coat burnt (53–6); and *throna* kneaded (58–62).

[8] See e.g. *GMA* 52, a long silver amulet from Beirut, which combines one after the other six different kinds of protective texts, e.g. exorcism, direct prayer ('protect!'), invocation formula (*epikaloumai*), second exorcism, flee-formulas (addressed to diseases), and Christian acclamations.

[9] Smith (1984).

(i) 'a phylactery which Moses used to protect himself....' (the name *Sabaôth* on a gold tablet); (ii) 'a phylactery of Moses, when he went up Mount Sinai' (a prayer to Jahweh followed by the text of Deut. 32.1–3); and (iii) 'a phylactery of Moses, when he went up Mount Sinai' (beginning of the same prayer to Jahweh followed by claims for the efficacy of the amulet). And with regard to the lead medium, one should also mention a Selinuntine *lex sacra* inscribed on lead that dates to the same period: a lead handbook.[10]

In what follows, then, I will argue that the text on the Getty tablet may have been composed as an anthology (perhaps originally memorized by oral performers) that preserves a number of different hexametrical spells (with two different versions of one of them). I will suggest, however, that the person who inscribed the Getty Hexameters onto this lead tablet—and who presumably added the four lines boasting of its efficacy as a written text 'in a house of stone'—may have misunderstood this anthology to be a single composite incantation. My argument will proceed along two tracks: I begin with comparative evidence for the existence of two other early anthologies of hexametrical incantations, one of which seems to have been transmitted as a single spell, and I close with a discussion of the form and function of rubrics—both metrical and prose—used in the Archaic and Classical periods to separate, identify, and (I suggest) help memorize individual hexametrical charms within an anthology.

6.2. ANTHOLOGIES

A fragment of a papyrus of the Augustan age, the so-called 'Philinna Papyrus',[11] was designed as an anthology of hexametrical charms (lines 6–20):[12]

[7–8]ας Σύρας ⟨Γ⟩αδαρηνῆς [ἐπαοιδή] πρὸς πᾶν κατάκαωμα

[⟨σεμνοτάτης δὲ⟩ θεᾶς παῖς μ]υστοδόκος κατεκα[ύθη,

---

[10] Jameson, Jordan, and Kotansky (1993).

[11] *PGM* XX. I give the text as it appears on p. 265 of the second volume of *PGM*. Maas (1942) 33–8 reconstructed the text by joining P. Berol. 7504 and P. Amherst II, col. ii(A) with the help of a fragmentary fourth-century AD version of a very similar text, *SM* 88. For a discussion of its anthology format, see Faraone (2001b).

[12] For this text and translation, see Faraone (1995a).

Magical Verses on a Lead Tablet 111

ἀκρ]οτάτῳ δ' ἐν ὄρει κατεκαύθη· ⟨πῦρ δ' ἐλάφυξεν⟩
ἑπτὰ λύκων κρήνας, ἐπτ' ἄρκτων, ἑπτὰ λεόντων·
ἑπτὰ δὲ παρθενικαὶ κυανώπιδες ἤρυσαν ὕδωρ
κάλπισι κυανέαις καὶ ἐκόμισαν ἀκάματον πῦρ.

φιλίννης Θε[σσ]αλῆς ἐπαοιδή π[ρὸς] κεφαλῆς π[ό]νονν

φεῦγ' ὀδύν[η] κεφαλῆς φεύγει δὲ [λέων] ὑπὸ πέτ[ρα]ν·
φεύγουσιν δὲ [λύ]κοι, φεύγ[ουσι] δὲ μώνυχες [ἵπ]ποι
[ἱέμενοι] πληγαῖς ὑπ' [ἐμῆς τελέας ἐπαοιδῆς]

The [incantation] of [ ]a, the Syrian woman from Gadara for every inflammation:

[The son of the ⟨most august⟩ goddess,] the initiate was scorched. On the highest mountain he was scorched. ⟨The fire gulped down⟩ seven springs of wolves, seven of bears, seven of lions, but seven maidens with dark-blue eyes drew water with jugs of lapis lazuli and quieted the untiring fire.

The incantation of Philinna from Thessaly for headache:

Flee headache! [Lion] flees under a rock! Wolves flee and single-hoofed horses flee propelled by the blows of my perfect charm!

Lines 1–5 (which precede the text quoted here) preserve the end of a third hexametrical incantation, which is fragmentary and has lost its rubric: all we can tell is that it ends with the common coda 'bring to perfection this efficacious incantation' (discussed in Chapter 3 in this volume). Given the nature of this papyrus (an anthology) and the corruption of the metre of the individual charms, scholars have rightly argued that the hexameters themselves had been previously performed and/or copied a number of times and therefore probably had an even earlier, independent existence in the oral tradition. Indeed, the rather beautiful couplet ('but seven maidens. . . .') at the end of the spell of the 'Syrian woman from Gadara' has been admired for its poetic artistry and connected with a lost Hellenistic liturgy, or an even earlier Near Eastern tradition of healing incantations.[13] Of

---

[13] Although Maas (1942) thought the final two hexameters had an 'archaic ring' to them, scholars usually suspect that these verses are a Hellenistic composition, perhaps influenced by Isiac liturgy; see esp. Koenen (1962) 167–74. More recently, however, Faraone (1995a) points out that the mythological setting of the burning *mystodokos* goes back to very old Mesopotamian models and argues that we should leave open the possibility that Maas was correct about the archaic date of the last two verses.

special interest, however, is the pattern of presentation: a prose rubric expressed in a somewhat formulaic manner (author's name in the genitive + ἐπαοιδή + the purpose of the spell introduced by the preposition πρός), followed by the hexametrical incantation itself. We should also note the consistency of form and purpose: all three charms are hexametrical and the two that have their rubrics are curative, rather than protective.

There is, however, a better and earlier parallel for exploring the possibility that the Getty Hexameters were originally an anthology of discrete charms: the lead tablet from Phalasarna, which dates to the late Classical or early Hellenistic period and contains a number of short and disjointed hexametrical charms and prayers inscribed one after the other. I have, for clarity's sake, divided the translation below into thematic sections, but these sections are *not* in any way marked on the lead tablet, for example, by ruled lines or indentation:[14]

> Section 1: I command you (κελεύω) to flee from these houses of ours.... (lines A–B)
>
> Section 2: I call on (καλέω) Zeus, the averter of ills, Heracles, the sacker of cities, Iatros, Nike, Apollon. (lines C–D)
>
> Section 3: Epaphos, Epaphos, Epaphos, flee, flee at once (φεῦ[γ'] ἅμα, φεῦγε, λύκαινα), she-wolf! And you, dog, flee at once (φεῦγε, κύων, ἅμα σ[ύ]), and PROKROPROSATE, ... associate. Let them run maddened, each to his own house. (lines F–H)
>
> Section 4: Version of the *Ephesia Grammata* (lines I–Q)
>
> Section 5: Whosoever hurts me and those who KOLLOBALOUSI evils—hawk's feather, PELEIOPETON, white-horned(?) AMISANTON of a she-goat, claw of a lion, tongue of a bearded lion-serpent(?)—shall not harm me with ointment or application or with drink or with spell, spoiler of all things. (lines R–V)

It is, in fact, the patchwork design of this tablet that makes it so difficult to translate these verses as a continuous text or to restore the corrupted portions, which are several.

The text begins with a two-verse 'command' formula to some illnesses or demons to flee (Section 1)—such Apolline commands are known from inscribed rings and other amulets of the Roman and late-antique periods, but the genre probably goes back to a tradition

---

[14] See the Appendix to this volume for the full Greek text and discussion.

Magical Verses on a Lead Tablet

of hexametrical Apolline oracles (as was mentioned earlier) that recommend ritual and choral performances in times of crisis.[15] This initial section is followed by a cletic invocation ('I call on...') to Zeus, Heracles, Iatros, Nike, and Apollo (Section 2). (The very obscure line E seems to be half gibberish, but may be connected with the preceding prayer.) The text changes, then, from prayer to charm in the three-line 'flee-formula' in Section 3, which is similar in content and verbal expression to the headache charm from the Philinna Papyrus, which is also only three verses long.[16] After another single line of incoherent verse (I), we find the longest charm on the amulet (Section 4): a corrupted version of the *Ephesia Grammata*. The tablet closes with Section 5, where the first and final two verses (lines Q and S–T) resemble the boast of the disguised Demeter in the *Homeric Hymn to Demeter*, where she claims that she is expert in protective magic.[17] The long intervening line (R) is unmetrical and seems to be a list of *materia magica*, perhaps used as amulets. It would appear, then, that most of these disarticulated sections of the Phalasarna tablet could be used independently as short, free-standing charms for protection or healing, but have been collected together in this text either as a kind of composite charm or as an anthology of charms used for reference. The Phalasarna amulet shows no signs, however, of the kinds of rubrics or performance information that we saw in the Philinna papyrus, and it seems less unified in its purpose, mixing together protective incantations such as the *Ephesia Grammata* and curative ones such as the flee-formulas.[18]

---

[15] For full discussion see Faraone (2009a) and in Ch. 3 of this volume. Note that here, as in the oracular texts quoted there, the verb of command appears at the end of the line.

[16] These 'flee-formulas' seem to have originated as hexametrical chants performed during scapegoat rituals, for which see Faraone (2004b). They are attested frequently in the Roman period, at which time a pursuer is often added to hasten the departure of the disease or demon. There is, for example, a magical gemstone which depicts Perseus holding the Medusa's head and carries the brief non-metrical inscription: φύ[γε] ποδάγρα, [Π]ερσεύς σε διώκει ('Flee, gout, for Perseus pursues you'), and another on which Heracles strangles the Nemean lion: ἀναχώρει χολή, τὸ θεῖόν σε διώκει ('Withdraw, bile, for the divinity pursues you!'). Other examples of this genre include a stomach-ache charm to be engraved on an iron ring: φεῦγε φεῦγ', ἰοῦ χολή, ὁ κορυδαλός σε ζητεῖ ('Flee, flee, o bile of poison, the crested lark pursues you!'); and an oral charm for curing a sty: φεῦγε φεῦγε, κρείων σε διώκει ('Flee, flee, a stronger one (i.e. a god) pursues you!'). See Heim (1982) nos. 57–60.

[17] Maas (1944) 36–7 and Faraone in Ch. 3 of this volume.

[18] For a similar disjointed collection of hexametrical incantations, these being maledictory rather than amuletic, in Homeric *Epigram* 13.7–23, see Faraone (2001c).

114   The Getty Hexameters

Table 6.1 Phalasarna and Getty compared

Source	Command	*Ephesia Grammata*	'shall not harm'
Phalasarna	A–B (*keleuô*)	I–Q	U–V (last two lines)
Getty	25 (*an[ôga*)	8–20 and 33–42	50 (last line)

The composite text of the Phalasarna tablet suggests, then, that a series of originally disconnected incantations, mostly of short length, were at some point collected together, without any rubrics or formal divisions. Indeed, if we remove from the Getty Hexameters all of the verses dealing with Paean, they, too, would appear to be a similar patchwork quilt, with two sections quoting different versions of the *Ephesia Grammata*, a third using an oracular command formula, and the last quoting a short boast about future freedom from harm. In fact, if we ignore (see Table 6.1) the first quotation of the *Ephesia Grammata* (8–20), the individual charms on the Getty Hexameters (24–31, 33–42, and 50) seem to follow the same sequence as those on the Phalasarna tablet.

6.3. RUBRICS

What role, then, do the Paeanic verses play in the Getty Hexameters? Could they serve, like the rubrics on the Philinna Papyrus, as some kind of divider or rubric between the individual charms? We have, in fact, already seen a number of examples of such rubrics, some prosaic and at least one in the same meter as the incantation itself: when the Furies sing 'This is the binding-song of the Furies', they are making both a statement about ownership or copyright for their spell, and a statement about its purpose, much like the two surviving rubrics on the Philinna papyrus, which retain this same two-fold objective: 'the charm of [missing female name] the Syrian from Gadara for every inflammation' and 'the charm of Philinna of Thessaly for every inflammation'. One important distinction, however, between the rubric embedded in the binding song and the two on the papyrus is the self-referential use of the deictic marker 'this' by the Furies.

We find similar rubrics, in fact, in two other texts. The first is one of the oldest Greek inscriptions, the so-called Nestor's Cup Inscription (*SEG* 14 [1957] no. 604):

Νέστορός εἰμι εὔπτοτον ποτέριον.
ὃς δ' ἂν τόδε πίεσι ποτερί[ου] αὐτίκα κεῖνον
ἵμερος αἱρέσει καλλιστε[φά]νου Ἀφροδίτης.

I am the cup of Nestor, good for drinking.
Whosoever drinks from this cup, desire for beautifully crowned Aphrodite (i.e. sex) will seize him instantly.

The last two lines are hexametrical and comprise a *bona fide* erotic charm designed to force passion suddenly upon the person who drinks from the cup.[19] Here the word *potêrion* at the end of the first line probably refers not only to the cup upon which the text is inscribed, but also—like the word *iunx* in Simaetha's incantation—to the text itself written on the cup.[20] Thus this first line contains two of the three common features of a rubric: *deixis* (first-person 'I am the cup' = third-person 'This is the cup') and statement of authorship or ownership ('of Nestor'). This rubric is, moreover, followed immediately by a boast in the form of a future more vivid condition ('Whosoever drinks from this cup, desire... will seize him instantly') similar to those discussed in Ch. 3 ('shall not harm'). The first line of the Nestor's Cup Inscription, then, although unmetrical, serves nonetheless as a rubric for the physical object on which it is inscribed (the cup) and as a mnemonic device for recalling the incantation nicknamed 'the cup of Nestor'.[21]

Another early text begins or ends with a similar rubric, and this one—like the verses that name Paean in the Getty Hexameters—was composed as part of a hexametrical poem: the fragmentary verses (quoted and discussed briefly in Chapter 3 of this volume) that appear at the start or finish of the two earliest and longest Orphic gold tablets:[22]

Μνημοσύνης τόδε θρῖον(?)· ἐπεὶ ἂν μέλλῃσι θανεῖσθαι
[ἐν πίνακι χρυσέῳ] τόδε γρα[ψάτω ἠδὲ φορείτω].

This is the leaf(?) of Memory. Whenever he (i.e., the initiate) is about to die, let him write this [on a golden tablet and carry it].

---

[19] See Faraone (1996) for full discussion.
[20] Faraone (1996) collects examples of *potêria* spells from the later magical handbooks.
[21] Faraone (1996).
[22] These lines are lacunose on both tablets, so I give the composite text and translation of Janko (1984) 91–2, with the supplements to the second line by West (1975) *ad loc.* For a detailed discussion of various other proposals for the third word in the first line ('leaf'), see Faraone (2009b) and Ch. 3 n. 20 in this volume.

Here, as in the case of the rubric on the cup from Pithecussae, the deictic pronoun suggests that the rubric can refer both to the gold tablet on which the text is inscribed ('a leaf') and to the text itself.[23]

I have purposely framed this discussion as a choice between refrain and rubric, and to get at the differences between the two, I provide a summary of the refrains and rubrics examined above in Table 6.2. A consistent feature of the two refrains, of course, is that they repeat the same text precisely each time. The Getty references to Paean come close to this kind of consistent repetition, but there are, in fact, some significant variations:

Παιήων, σὺ δὲ πάντοσ' ἀλέξιμα φάρμακα πέμπεις
καὶ τάδ' ἐφώνησας ἔπε' ἀθάνατα θνητοῖσιν.   (6–7)

'Paean, for you send averting charms in every direction,
and you spoke these immortal verses to mortal men.'

Followed by the *Ephesia Grammata* (8–20).

[Παιήων,] σὺ γὰρ αὐτὸς ἀλεξιμὰ φάρμα[κα πέμπεις]   (23)

'[Paean,] for you yourself [send] averting charms'

Followed by an Apolline command-oracle (24–31).

[Παιήων, σὺ δ]ὲ πάντοσ' ἀκεσσφόρος ἐσσὶ καὶ ἐσθ[λός]   (32)

'[Paean, for you] in every direction are cure-bringing and excell[ent].'

Followed by the *Ephesia Grammata* (33–42).

[Πα]ι[ή]ων ὁ γὰρ αὐτὸς ἀλεξιμὰ φάρμακα πέ[μπει].   (49)

'[Pa]e[a]n, for he himself s[ends] averting charms

Followed by the 'neither x nor y shall harm' formula (50).

Judging by the criteria that head the columns on Table 6.2, we note first that each of these sentences identifies Paean as the source or author of the incantatory verses (*pharmaka*) that follow, which he is said to 'send' (in two cases 'in every direction'). They also tell us the general purpose of these *pharmaka*: in three of four cases they are 'protective' (*alexima*), and in the remaining case Paean himself (or

---

[23] Faraone (2009b) surveys the use of real leaves as media for amuletic incantations, including Socrates' claim in the *Charmides* to have learned a Thracian headache cure and a pair of Orphic gold tablets from Thessaly cut in the shape of ivy leaves.

Magical Verses on a Lead Tablet 117

Table 6.2 Refrains and rubrics summary

	Source	Purpose	*Deixis?*	Metrical?	Condition?
RUBRICS					
Nestor's 'Cup'	Nestor	no	'this is'	no	'whoever'
Orphic 'Leaf'	Memory	no	'I am'	yes	'whenever'
Philinna	Philinna	headaches	no	no	no
Papyrus	Syrian woman	inflammation	no	no	no
REFRAINS					
Aeschylus	Furies	binding	'this song'	yes	no
Simaetha	no	brings man	no	yes	no

the song paean itself) is said to be a 'bringer of cures' (*akesphoros*). This could potentially be an important difference, of course, because amulets tend to fall into two general categories, those that protect a person before sickness arrives and those that cure a person after he or she is already sick. The text that follows, however, is the second version of the *Ephesia Grammata*, which was earlier introduced as a protective charm, but now appears as a curative one.

The repetitive verses about Paean, then, seem to share two of the three common features of the rubrics discussed above: a declaration of ownership and a statement of purpose. Only once, however, do we see any sign of deictic language, and it appears in the verse appended to the first statement about Paean:

> Παιήων, σὺ δὲ πάντοσ' ἀλέξιμα φάρμακα πέμπεις
> καὶ τάδ' ἐφώνησας ἔπε' ἀθάνατα θνητοῖσιν. (6–7)
>
> 'Paean, for you send averting charms in every direction,
> and you spoke these immortal verses to mortal men.'

Here the deictic τάδε refers to and introduces the hexametrical verses that follow, much like the repeated refrain of the Furies' binding song ('*this* song') or the rubric of the gold tablet ('*This* is the leaf of Memory....'). This is, in fact, the only place where the Getty tablet actually claims that Paean composed the verses inscribed on the Getty tablet and that he did so for the benefit of mortals. The second repetition of the verse about Paean is followed by a long command (presumably by Apollo) that begins: 'I command you to utter [this hymn]....' Here, of course, the deictic phrase 'this hymn' has been restored and (even if it were not restored) it does not appear to be part of the rubric/refrain itself. This command does, however, take the form of a condition

('... utter [this hymn], whenever [doom] approaches...') similar to the instructions that follow the rubric on the gold tablet ('This is the leaf of Memory. Whenever he is about to die, write it...') and the Pithecussan cup ('This is the cup of Nestor. Whosoever drinks....')

6.4. CONCLUSION

We have seen, then, that the patchwork quilt of different types of incantations inscribed on the Getty tablet, as well as the appearance of the *Ephesia Grammata* in two different forms, suggests that these hexameters may have served at some point as an anthology of sorts. One important variation in the repeating verse ('cure-bearing' instead of 'protective') shows, moreover, that although most of the Getty spells were used for protection, at least one (the second version of the *Ephesia Grammata*) was thought to be curative. The command-spell likewise seems to derive from a different tradition of oracular hexameters. All these features suggest, then, that the Getty Hexameters may have been designed, at least originally, as an anthology of different amuletic charms; but I suspect that this format and purpose may have been ignored or misunderstood by the person who took the trouble to inscribe these verses on the lead tablet that has come down to us. He seems, first of all, to have prefaced all these different charms with a conditional boast about the protective power of all the verses, if they are inscribed on tin and hidden in a house of stone. Nothing, he wrote, will harm the person who does this, and the text seems to end with a similar boast about future protection from harm.

The person who framed the Getty tablet between these two boasts about protection, then, probably thought that all of these verses were protective, and probably meant for them all to serve as a kind of composite amulet, despite their different origins and rhetorical forms. I suggest, moreover, that a similar evolution may have happened in the case of the Phalasarna tablet, which (as we saw earlier) has nearly the same range and sequence of different texts as the Getty Hexameters, but with no repeating verses to separate one charm from the other. This makes sense, of course, of the late-Classical or early Hellenistic date of these texts, a time when Greeks began to inscribe magical incantations that had previously been performed orally: the *defixiones* found in late Classical Athens and Selinus, for example, seem to reflect the same purpose (to bind human speech and thought) and the same performative context (before an important legal trial) as the orally performed binding song of the Furies;[24] the Orphic gold tablets also seem to record late Classical texts that had previously been memorized and reperformed orally. I suggest that the Getty and Phalasarna tablets do the same. In each case the novel inscription of these formerly oral incantations leads to a new appreciation of their power as inscribed texts: *defixiones*, especially in Selinus, explore different ways to distort the written names of their victims, either by scrambling the letters or twisting the text in an inward spiral,[25] while the Getty Hexameters and the two oldest Orphic leaves make novel assertions about the power of these written verses, when placed in a house or inscribed at the moment when death threatens. It is, I suggest, in precisely this climate of experimentation and innovation that the oral anthology of incantations, both protective and curative, that lie behind the Getty Hexameters, begins to be appreciated erroneously but also creatively as a single and continuous composite amulet.

[24] Faraone (1985).
[25] Jordan (1993).

7

Myth and the Getty Hexameters[1]

Sarah Iles Johnston

7.1. INTRODUCTION

One of the most puzzling aspects of the Getty Hexameters is the story that the narrator claims was first told by a god called the Healer ('Paean', col. i, Side A):[2]

6	Paean, for in every direction you send averting charms,
7	and you spoke these immortal verses to mortal men:
8	"As down the shady mountains in a dark-and-glittering land
9	a child leads out of Persephone's garden by necessity for milking
10	that four-footed holy attendant of Demeter,
11	a she-goat with an untiring stream of rich milk
12	laden; and she follows, trusting in the bright goddesses
13–15	with their lamps. And she leads Hecate of the Roadside the foreign divinity as she cries out in a frightening, foreign voice: 'I by my own command through the night...
16	...having sallied forth, I recount divinely [uttered?]... ...to mortals and of the goddess of the splendid [gifts]'"
18–20	[letters]

The story raises many questions. What will the goat's milk be used for, and what is the significance of the goat having been pastured in

---

[1] Versions of this paper were delivered at Université de Liège and Washington University. I thank the audiences there, as well as the participants of the seminar held at the Getty Museum in November 2010, for their suggestions. I am also grateful to Fritz Graf and David Frankfurter for their help as I developed the published version of the paper.

[2] Translation by Christopher Faraone and Dirk Obbink.

Persephone's garden? Why is the goat called Demeter's attendant? Who is the child that leads the goat? Why does Hecate suddenly appear—what will *she* announce? And finally, what has any of this to do with the stated purpose of the spell, overall—to protect the owner from 'as many things as broad Earth nourishes and much-groaning Amphitrite rears in the sea' (lines 4–5)?[3]

The last question is the easiest to answer, at least superficially. These characters and their actions comprise a *historiola*—that is, a 'little story' embedded in a magical spell that is analogous in some way to the situation that the spell is supposed to address.[4] Typically, at least some of the characters in a *historiola* are gods or heroes—typically, a *historiola* is the type of story that we are accustomed to call a *myth*. These gods and heroes have names that are familiar to their audiences; their names already evoke histories, actions, and personal characteristics that are potentially relevant for the analogy that the *historiola* sets up.[5] The gods and heroes, moreover, inhabit a realm that is rife with powers greater than those available in the quotidian realm. Thus, the analogy that the *historiola* offers has great potency, compact though it may be.

The *historiola* embedded in the Getty Hexameters is the earliest Greek-language example of the phenomenon that we possess, dating, as we see it on the tablet, to the late fifth or early fourth century BC, but indebted to an older predecessor, as Janko suggests in his contribution to this volume.[6] *Historiolae* that share lines and phrases with it—that, indeed, seem to be derived either from the *historiola* narrated in the Getty Hexameters or from a source common to all of

---

[3] And more particularly (as Side A, col. ii goes on to specify), against war, ships that bring doom to mortals, and anything that might harm flocks and herds.

[4] The word *historiola* was adopted by scholars of ancient magic from scholars of folklore, who, in turn, seem to have invented it, at least in the sense that we now use it (there is no ancient precedent): Maas (1942) 37 with n. 22; Heim (1892/93) 495 with notes. A large number of European *historiolae* from a range of periods can be found in the essays contained in Roper (2009) and Roper (2004); overall, the material offered there provides wonderful *comparanda* for ancient *historiolae*, as I will occasionally note below.

[5] See my article 'Demeter, Myth, and the Polyvalence of Festivals,' forthcoming in *History of Religions*.

[6] The tablet from Himera that shares three lines with Side A, col. ii (Bernabé F) is dated to the early fifth century, and two other tablets from Selinus itself (Bernabé G and H) that share phrases with the Getty text are dated to the fifth century as well. Janko (this volume) posits that the Getty tablet copies an earlier archetype and suggests that at least some of the material may be as early as the late sixth century.

them—appear in eight other texts, stretching from the fifth century BC to the third or fourth century AD, and geographically from Crete, to Rome, to Egypt.[7] However, until we reach the Philinna Papyrus of the first century BC, we find no other text in the Greek language that narrates a different *historiola*—and it has been persuasively argued that the Philinna *historiola*, although recounted in Greek, owes its content to Egyptian (and also, perhaps, Near Eastern) models.[8] *Historiolae* found in the Greek magical papyri of later antiquity owe a great deal to Egyptian models as well, and are almost always populated by gods from the Egyptian pantheon.[9]

Explanations for this situation can only be conjectural. Did the concept of using *historiolae* (which is found in many other Mediterranean and European cultures) simply fail to catch on in Greece? That answer is unsatisfactory insofar as it fails to account for the fact that variations of the *historiola* narrated in the Getty Hexameters *were* used over a large chronological and geographic range. Have the vagaries of time robbed us of evidence that the technique was, in fact, more widely used in Greece? This answer is also unsatisfactory, for the same reason: we would be left to explain why so many texts that use variations of a single story just happened to survive. Were the spells in which *historiolae* were embedded usually transmitted orally? Again, if so, why are variations of the Getty *historiola* recorded in writing over and over and the conjectured others not recorded at all?

Later in this paper I shall try to give, if not final answers to these questions, then at least some context that may allow us to move towards answers. For the moment, at any rate, we can note that the narrator of the Getty text tells us that the letters of the 'sacred verses' that comprise the *historiola* are to be inscribed on tin and hidden in a 'house of stone' in order to avert all sorts of evils—both those of the Earth and those of the sea. The situation for which the *historiola* is

---

[7] I will usually refer to these texts in this essay by the letters Bernabé assigns to them in his contribution to this volume.

[8] Philinna Papyrus = P. Berol. 7504 plus P. Amherst 2 col. II (A) plus P. Oxy. Ined. (= Pack [1967] no. 1872). Interpretation: Ritner (1998) (who argues for a purely Egyptian background); Faraone (1995) (who argues for a mixture of Egyptian and Mesopotamian elements); Koenen (1962); Maas (1942). Fuller bibliography at Ritner (1998) 127 n. 3. I am persuaded by Ritner's arguments that this particular spell draws on Egyptian elements, although I more generally support, methodologically, Faraone's openness to looking for diverse cultural influences behind any given spell.

[9] An exception is *PGM* VI.1–47, a late antique divinatory spell that tells of how Apollo first tasted the divinatory plant laurel.

supposed to serve as an analogy, then, is a very broad one. Six of the eight other texts that include lines or phrases found in the Getty *historiola* leave their purpose unstated (implying that their power is broadly applicable);[10] the remaining two are spells to win love and to ward off fear of punishment.[11] In other words, the story narrated by the Getty *historiola* and related variants had no single, specific purpose or even cluster of purposes; we must start from the assumption that this narrative relayed by the *historiola* was understood to be very widely effective indeed. The fact that the *historiola* is often accompanied by a version of the *Ephesia Grammata* (in our hexameters, lines 33, 36, and 41, and see further Bernabé and Edmonds in this volume)—or perhaps even evolved into the *Ephesia Grammata*, as Bernabé persuasively argues[12]—points in this direction as well, for the *Ephesia Grammata* were widely applicable as protective devices against a huge variety of ills or even, more positively, as a means of ensuring good luck. The presence of Paean, Zeus, and probably Apollo and Heracles in the Getty Hexameters points in this direction, too, for all four were widely invoked against a variety of threats.[13]

7.2. WHAT ARE *HISTORIOLAE*?

I have described *historiolae* as myths embedded in magical spells, which are analogous to the situations that the spells are supposed to address. Such analogies help to establish the myths as *paradigms* to which the situations confronted by the practitioner and his client are then expected to adhere.[14] What happens within the mythic realm in which a *historiola* is set is also supposed to happen within the

---

[10] Bernabé C, E, F, G, H as well as an unpublished Latin text that seems to translate lines of our hexameters, which Bernabé discusses on page 90 n. 32 *supra*.

[11] Bernabé A (directed towards obtaining sexual favors) and B (directed against fear of punishment).

[12] And cf. Jordan (2000) 97.

[13] For Zeus, Apollo and Heracles, see lines 46–8.

[14] I adopt the term 'paradigm' from Frankfurter (1995). Frankfurter, however, pairs it with 'precedents,' which I avoid because I want to emphasize the potential for *historiolae* to narrate actions that occur *for the first time* as the narration takes place.

quotidian realm in which the practitioner and his client dwell. If a client is ill with fever, then the practitioner might invoke a paradigm of 'successful cure' by telling how Isis cures Horus of fever, analogically equating his client with Horus. If a woman is having trouble delivering her baby, then the practitioner might invoke a paradigm of 'successful birth' by telling how Christ sends the archangel Michael to help a doe give birth, analogically equating his patient with the doe. If a baby has a headache, then the practitioner might invoke the paradigm of 'banished headache' by telling how Christ pushes the Evil Eye off a rock to stop it from persecuting another baby, analogically equating his young patient with the baby in the story.[15]

It is important to note that setting the action of a *historiola* within the mythic *realm* does not necessarily mean setting it within something that scholars often call mythic *time*—that is, within the distant past. Although some *historiolae* do use the past tense to narrate their myths, implying that their paradigmatic action occurred at an earlier time, others use the present tense, which can be understood in either of two ways. 1) The present tense may imply that narrating something that already took place causes it to happen *again, right now*, thus bringing its paradigmatic power into the quotidian realm in a particularly vivid manner. 2) The present tense may also imply that what is narrated is happening *now for the first time*, at the very moment that the practitioner is narrating it.[16] The words of the practitioner may be understood as a performative utterance, which *causes* the story to unfold in the mythic realm at the same time as the quotidian events it simultaneously affects. This situation is generally analogous to the way that some other magical speech acts operate. 'I bind so-and-so,' for example, is a performative utterance that causes the binding to happen at the moment the words are spoken or inscribed on a *defixio*. If we extend this logic to *historiolae*, then describing what a god does to solve a problem can be understood to cause the god to act simultaneously in that way, and by extension bring the same power to bear within the quotidian realm.

Of course, it is possible that a *historiola* of this second kind may become popular and be adopted by others, in which case the

---

[15] Horus: see below, section 5. Christ and the doe: *ACM* #49 = Berlin 8313. Christ, Mary, and the Evil Eye: a Transylvanian *historiola* still in use, as recorded by Éva Pócs (2009) 29.
[16] Cf. Podemann Sørensen (1984) 10.

continued use of the present tense comes to be understood as causing the events of the story to happen again (thus moving it into the first kind). But I emphasize that the second possibility exists because recognizing this will help us to move away from the long-held assumption that *historiolae* simply 'repeat' or 'recast' pre-existing myths. Rather, those who narrated *historiolae*, whether they were professional ritual specialists or ordinary people called on to address sudden emergencies with whatever means they had at their disposal, felt free to create new myths that would best serve as analogies for their situations. This gave the narrators of the *historiolae* considerable power, for they could create myths that precisely fit the circumstances for which they wanted the *historiolae* to serve as paradigms. It also meant that *historiolae* were quite free to evolve, shifting details from occasion to occasion as necessary. The *historiolae* that contributors to Jonathan Roper's two volumes on European charms have collected—much richer collections than we are able to obtain from ancient cultures—show considerable flexibility in their details as they move across temporal, linguistic, and cultural lines, as well as a notable freedom to introduce 'apocryphal' stories about Christian saints and even, indeed, about Christ himself.[17] Because of this characteristic, we may best understand a *historiola* and its relationship to the quotidian problem it is meant to resolve not by looking for a single myth or even group of myths that the *historiola* 'renarrates,' but rather by seeking the cultural significances of the characters, objects, and themes that populate the *historiola*, and of the patterns of action in which they are involved.

In this chapter, I approach the issues I have just outlined in three stages. In section 4, I will identify the core theme of the Getty *historiola*. In section 5, I will propose that this theme echoes some Egyptian myths that are in turn anchored in broader Egyptian traditions and lore. I will also propose that some of the specific details of the Getty *historiola* look back to Egyptian models. In section 6, I will explore the resonances of that theme within the *Greek* world by contextualizing the theme within the set of traditions and lore shared by the culture for which this particular *historiola* was created. I will also look at the ways in which the Egyptian models were modified to suit Greek traditions and the Greek understanding of how myths work.

---

[17] Cf. the analysis of Faraone (1995), which traces a *historiola* to several different Near Eastern traditions. Many of the essays in Roper (2004) and Roper (2009) demonstrate this point as well.

7.3. HOW DO *HISTORIOLAE* WORK?

First it is useful to survey the different methods by which *historiolae* establish paradigmatic analogies between the stories they convey and the quotidian situations they are meant to address. As Jørgen Podemann Sørensen first observed, there are at least five ways to do this, each of which involves embedding the *historiola* within the larger ritual text in a particular way:[18]

1. The practitioner may identify himself with one of the characters in the *historiola*, usually a god. For example, in *PDM* xiv.594–620, the speaker takes on the role of Anubis. As David Frankfurter has noted,[19] this type of *historiola* thereby *collapses* the boundary between the mythic and quotidian realms. Because the practitioner often speaks in the voice of the character with whom he identifies, this also tends to be the most vivid and dramatic of the five types of *historiolae*. It has a sense of immediacy that other types do not.

2. The *historiola* may narrate the story of how a solution for the present situation was once found—a solution that will once again be implemented by the present practitioner. For example, at *PGM* IV.94–153, Isis complains to Thoth about Osiris committing adultery and Thoth tells her how to remedy this—a remedy that will be used again by the present practitioner.

3. Similarly, the *historiola* may describe an object or material that is used in the ritual addressing the present situation, and explain how it came to be recognized as powerful. For example, *PGM* VI.1–47, a divinatory spell that uses laurel, tells how Apollo first discovered the divinatory properties of the plant.

4. The *historiola* may draw an overt comparison between the present situation and the situation that was resolved in the mythic realm. For example, a Coptic spell from Egypt refers to the fact that God enabled Sarah to conceive late in life and asks that he grant the same benefit to another woman who is trying to conceive.[20]

5. The *historiola* may incorporate a reference to the client whom the practitioner is attempting to help—perhaps even mentioning his or her name. As with number 1, this works to erase the boundary

---

[18] Podemann Sørensen (1984), as developed by Frankfurter (1995).
[19] Frankfurter (1995) 469–70.
[20] *ACM* No.83 = Pierpont Morgan Library M662B 22.

between mythic and quotidian realms—although not as effectively as number 1 does, given that number 1 often incorporates first-person speech in the voice of a god. An example is found in *PGM* IV.94–153, described above; the speech in which Thoth advises Isis requires the practitioner speaking it to insert his client's name in place of Isis' name at several points.

The *historiola* in the Getty Hexameters falls into the first of Podemann Sørensen's five types, for its narrator repeats the words of the Healer in the first-person voice. Interestingly, the Healer, who also speaks in the first-person voice, is said to have told his story in the *past* ('having spoken,' line 7), a framing device that lends authority to what follows, but the Healer's narration is set in the *present* ('brings out,' line 9; 'follows,' line 12). As I noted in section 2 above, use of the present tense may be taken to imply that the action is occurring in the mythic realm as the words of the *historiola* are spoken (or written). This not only allows the practitioner to tailor precisely the actions he wishes the gods to perform, but (like the use of the first-person voice) works to collapse the distance between the mythic and quotidian realms, thus enhancing the *historiola*'s paradigmatic, analogical force.

Such a combination of first-person narrations in the past and the present is unusual and suggests two things. 1) The *historiola* as we see it in the Getty Hexameters probably reflects different stages of development. That is, the authoritative attribution of the narration to the Healer, set in the past tense, probably was added after the narration itself had been in existence for some time; it looks as if the Getty Hexameters preserve an existing *historiola* that has been embedded in what can be understood as a secondary framing *historiola*. 2) This combination—authority anchored in the past and the advantages of present-tense narration—may be one reason that our *historiola* was used repeatedly over a broad span of time and place—it was perceived to be highly successful.

But there is one further difference between the type-1 *historiola* as Podemann Sørensen and Frankfurter have described it, and the type-1 *historiola* that we see in the Getty Hexameters. Most typically, a type-1 *historiola* is meant to be *recited aloud*.[21] The practitioner who

---

[21] There are exceptions. For example, *ACM* #48 = Schmidt 1, a Coptic healing spell on papyrus in which Horus and Isis carry on a conversation, was meant to be worn as an amulet; the Horus-*cippi*, too, rely on a written or depicted *historiola*. But the vast majority of examples clearly are meant to be spoken, and at times spoken over

uses the *historiola* to build analogical force literally identifies himself with the god by speaking in his voice, bringing divine authority directly to bear on the present situation in which he is operating. In the Getty Hexameters, in contrast, the narrator tells us that the physical letters (*grammata*, line 3) of the 'sacred verses' (*hierôn epeôn*,[22] line 2) are to be inscribed (*kekolammena*, line 3) on tin and hidden in a 'house of stone' (*laos en oikôi*, line 3). That is, they comprise a phylactery, the 'voice' of which is eternalized in written form so as to be forever effective. In line 7, the phrase 'immortal verses' (*epe' athanata*), which describes the *historiola* that immediately follows, underscores this quality. The present tense used by the Healer in his narration, then, not only erases the distance between mythic and quotidian realms, but also reflects the fact that the words of the Healer will continue to work as long as their physical representations (the *grammata*) survive. The closest analogues to the Getty Hexameters in this respect are Egyptian *historiolae* recorded on various materials for use as amulets or recorded on *cippi* over which a person could pour liquids that he or she would then drink (thus absorbing the power of the words). These examples, however, most often tend to use *historiolae* of types 2 and 4.

7.4. WHAT IS THE *HISTORIOLA* IN THE GETTY HEXAMETERS?

Where does the *historiola* of the Getty Hexameters begin and end, properly speaking? The beginning is relatively easy to spot: the Healer's narration begins in line 8, where the first-person speech

---

materials that will be empowered by the pronouncement: e.g., Borghouts ## 14, 15, 18, 20, 21, 22, 26, 27, 28, 29, 30. For a different approach to the issue of spoken vs. written *historiolae*, see Faraone (this volume).

[22] I find no other uses of the phrase *hieron epos* in ancient texts. '*Hieros Logos*,' a relatively common phrase in contrast, typically refers to a rationale, an explanation or an *aition* for a ritual, rather than to utterances that are 'sacred' in and of themselves (Graf and Johnston [2007] Chapter 6). This important difference between the two phrases suggests an acute awareness on the part of the tablet's creator of the fact that he was recording what was originally a performative utterance. As with the *defixiones*, which appear in the Greek world at approximately the same time as the Getty tablet and which similarly fix oral commands in written form, the Getty Hexameters may bring us near to the origin of the use of writing for such purposes.

begins. The end presents us with a challenge, for there are two possibilities. The Healer's narration might have ended after Hecate completed her own speech, somewhere in the fragmentary lines that conclude Side A. That is, we could understand the Healer himself to be narrating Hecate's speech, either as a continuation of the action involving the goat, or as a second *historiola* within a *historiola*. But it is also possible that the Healer's narration ended *before* Hecate began her speech, after the mention of the lamps in line 13. We could understand the second half of line 13 and line 14 ('... And Hecate of the Roadside, the goddess, guides the god as she cries out in a frightening, foreign voice:....') as words that the narrator of the Getty Hexameters (as opposed to the Healer) spoke in his own voice in amounts to an introduction to a second *historiola*.

The latter scenario seems more likely, especially if we identify 'the god' whom Hecate is said to guide (*theôi*, line 14) with the Healer, for it would be odd for the Healer to refer to himself in the third person within a *historiola* that he himself relates. (The Healer is the likeliest referent for *theôi*: other than Hecate herself, he is the only god who has appeared in the text—the garden is said to belong to Persephone and the goat to Demeter, but neither goddess has actually acted within the story.)[23] I will proceed on the assumption that this second scenario is the correct one—that we have two *historiolae* in the Getty Hexameters. One is intact, running from line 8 to line 13, and one is fragmentary, running from line 13 to somewhere in either the final, lost lines of Col. i, Side A, or the first two lines of Col. ii, Side A. Because so much of this second *historiola* is missing, I will not comment on it further in this chapter, save to make three remarks. 1) Hecate is said to convey ritually important information in several other texts and is often portrayed elsewhere as a guide of both immortals and mortals.[24] Thus, whatever it was that she recounted and did in the now-lost lines of the Getty Hexameters, she plays roles that were typical for her within Greek tradition. 2) Two of the other later texts that narrate a variation of the first *historiola* include fragmentary remains of this second *historiola* as well; even if formally distinct from one another, the two *historiolae*

---

[23] Janko (this volume) takes *theôi* to refer to the child instead.
[24] *HHDem.* 24–8, 52–9, and 438–40; Call. fr. 466 Pf., *ARV*² 1012.1, Pi. *Pa.* 2.49; schol. Theocr. 2.12; Orphic fr. 317 Bernabé with Johnston (2011); see also Johnston (1990) 21–48.

apparently were understood to work in tandem.[25] 3) Hecate's pronouncement that she has come 'by [her] own command' (*autokeleustos,* line 15; cf. line 2 of col. iii Frr. 4+3+2+1 back in the *editio princeps*) finds echoes in later texts where gods declare that they have performed tasks either willingly or against their will.[26] Thus, here in the Getty Hexameters we have an apparent allusion to what would become a long-lived *topos*: the issue of whether gods could—and should—be coerced by 'magical' actions or not.

The first *historiola* in the Getty Hexameters comprises the following elements:

1. A child comes down from a mountain.
2. The child brings out from Persephone's garden a goat to be milked; the goat is Demeter's 'attendant'.
3. The goat provides abundant milk.
4. [The goat] follows [the child], trusting in lamps; these lamps are referred to as goddesses.

The central action of the story is the milking of the goat—a point that is confirmed by side A, col. ii of the tablet, which, after invoking the Healer to provide charms of aversion against a variety of evils, includes the phrases 'a goat for milking', and 'the goat from the garden by force'. It is also confirmed by five other texts that use *historiolae* similar to ours:

1. The Oxyrhynchus tablet (Bernabé A) includes the phrase 'when under the shadowy mountains in the dark-gleaming land the child leads of necessity from the garden of Persephone at milking time the holy four-footed servant of Demeter and when the goat with her ceaseless flow of rich milk...'.
2. The Phalasarna Tablet (Bernabé C) includes the phrases 'at milking time', 'goat', 'drive from the garden by force the goat'.

---

[25] The Oxyrhynchus tablet (= Bernabé A) and the unpublished silver tablet in Latin. Also, *PGM* LXX.11–15 calls itself a 'Charm of Hecate-Ereschigal against Punishment'.

[26] See, e.g., a series of oracles collected by Porphyry (all included under fr. 347 in Smith's edition), as recorded by Eusebius and considered by some scholars to be from the *Chaldean Oracles: Ch. Or.* fr. dub. 219 = Eus. *PE* V.8.3–4; *Ch. Or.* fr. dub. 220 = Eus. *PE* V.8.7; *Ch. Or.* fr. dub. 221 = Eus. *PE* V.8.6; *Ch. Or.* fr. dub. 222 = Eus. *PE* V.8.5; *Ch. Or.* fr. dub. 223 = Eus. *PE* V.8.6; cf. Eus. *PE* V.6.2–7.2. Also, numerous passages from the *PGM* talk about either persuading a god to cooperate (e.g., *PGM* I.42–195) or compelling him or her to do so (e.g., *PGM* IV.52–85).

3. One of the two fifth-century lead tablets from Selinus (Bernabé G) mentions leading the goat from the garden at milking time by force.
4. The other text from Selinus (Bernabé H) mentions force, a garden, and a goat.
5. The unpublished silver tablet (not in Bernabé's list) includes Latin translations of lines 8–15 of the Getty Hexameters—the story of the child leading the goat out of Persephone's garden to be milked and the early portion of Hecate's appearance.

Depending on how we reconstruct two other texts (the fourth century BC lead tablet from Locri Epizephyrioi = Bernabé E and the fifth century BC lead tablet from Himera = Bernabé F), we may have two further instances.

7.5. MILK IN EGYPT

To understand the way in which the *historiola* that we see in the Getty Hexameters and these other related *historiolae* served as paradigms, providing models for success that were analogical to the situations that the spells were intended to address, we need to understand what the concept 'provision of abundant [goat] milk' meant to an ancient audience. What does milk have to do with the arousal of sexual desire, the aversion of fear, or wholesale protection from harm? We seem to be far away from the tidy analogies provided by some of the *historiolae* I mentioned in sections 2 and 3, where a feverish child is identified with feverish Horus, a labouring woman is identified with a labouring doe, or a barren woman with the barren Sarah. We are also far away from any other Greek myth that might help us: outside the Getty Hexameters and the related texts, there is no myth about Demeter or Persephone that makes them the owners of goats or the providers of milk.[27] How shall we proceed?

---

[27] There is a line in Ovid's story of Demeter's arrival in Eleusis (*Fasti* IV.445) that may remind us of the Getty text: *filia parva duas redigebat monte capellas* (describing the daughter of Celeus who comes to greet the disguised goddess). It is very unlikely that Ovid is echoing some earlier myth, related to the Getty text but now unknown to us, in which this girl and her goats played a more important role. Rather, Ovid's description reflects the fact that children were (and still are, in rural areas) given

We will start by looking at some Egyptian myths that are likely to have inspired the Getty *historiola*, and the traditions from which those myths were drawn. Then, in the next section, we will contextualize the *historiola* within Greek culture. In general, Egypt offers itself as a likely source of inspiration for our *historiola* for two reasons. First, *historiolae* were a distinctive element of Egyptian religious practices throughout three millennia; although we find them in other ancient Near Eastern cultures as well, cumulatively, we have more *historiolae* from Egypt than from all the other cultures combined.[28] Second, Selinus' location made it a place that repeatedly encountered a variety of foreign influences, but particularly Phoenicians, who were actively present in the city from at least the early fifth century. The Phoenicians are virtually certain to have encountered Egyptian *historiolae* during their continuous interaction with the Egyptians throughout their long history; a fragment from an (undated) Horus-*cippus,* including a *historiola*, has been found in Byblos.[29] The Phoenicians also incorporated members of the Egyptian pantheon, notably Isis, Hathor, and Osiris, into their religious system.[30] Thus, it is likely that the Phoenicians carried Egyptian myths and ritual techniques into Selinus. Of course, it is also possible that a local Selinuntine ritual specialist travelled to Egypt himself and brought the technique home, or that travelling Egyptians brought it to Selinus. Given the city's coastal location, interactions between it and a number of other cultures must have been fairly frequent.

Isis, Horus, and milk

As early as the Ebers papyrus (*c.*1500 BC) a number of healing spells call upon the practitioner to apply milk to cure a patient. Often, it is specified that the milk should be from 'a woman who has borne a male child'. As Robert Ritner has discussed, this phrase alludes to stories in which Isis cures her wounded or feverish son Horus with

---

responsibility for herding small animals such as goats, as well as the fact that goats are by nature mountain-grazers. (See below, p. 181, for examples.)

[28] Cf. Ritner (1998) 1028 n. 4, who describes the *historiola* as 'characteristic of Egyptian magical spells from the Pyramid Texts onwards'.

[29] Montet (1928) 249–32 no. 948; cf. Faraone (1995) 309 with n. 34.

[30] Below, n. 51, and cf. Faraone (1995) 308–9 more generally on the interaction amongst Near Eastern cultures and the resultant transmission of *historiolae.*

her milk or other fluids that stand in for her milk, such as her spittle; the milk applied by the practitioner in the spells is assimilated to that of the goddess.[31] In other words, the phrase 'milk from a woman who has borne a male child' is in essence a compact *historiola*. The range of applications for such milk is quite wide: fever, burns, eye ailments, nose problems, muscle aches, and swellings.[32]

Greco–Egyptian magical papyri of later antiquity also reflect this tradition of the goddess' powerful milk. A Demotic magical text advocates using the milk of 'a woman who has borne a son' to create an eye unguent that will enable the user to see the gods—in other words, to have eyes such as Horus himself had.[33] Sometimes a spell narrates Isis' application of her milk to a burning (feverish) Horus more fully, as in Papyrus British Museum 10059 [37] (*c.*1325 BC)[34] from which I give an excerpt here:

> ... Isis came out of the spinning house [at the hour] when she loosened her thread. 'Come, my sister Nephthys! See, my deafness has overtaken me. My thread has entangled me! Show me my way that I may do what I know (to do), that I may extinguish for him with my milk, with the salutary liquids from between my breasts. It will be applied to your [Horus'] body so that your vessels become sound. I will make the fire recede that has attacked you!

Other spells reflect the tradition less directly by advocating the use of cow's milk for a number of purposes (both Isis and Hathor, who was Horus' mother in the earliest tradition and whom we will meet in the next myth, were associated with the cow and sometimes depicted with a cow's head). For example, a falcon (the animal with which Horus was frequently associated) that is drowned in cow's milk becomes a divine messenger; when the practitioner drinks the milk in which the falcon was drowned, 'something divine' enters his heart, as well. Poured as a libation, the milk of a cow deifies a newly made

---

[31] Ritner (1993) 83 and 103; Ritner (1997) 135; Dawson (1932). Dawson sketches the extraordinarily long life of the concept 'milk of a woman who has borne a male child'. On other fluids, see particularly Faraone (1995).

[32] Ebers papyrus: for burns: 69, 5; 69, 7; for the eyes: 59, 8; 60, 14; 62, 10; 62, 17; for the nose: 90, 19; 90, 21; for the muscles: 80, 15; for swellings: 74, 13. London Medical papyrus: for burns 6, 7; 14, 13; 15, 1. Hearst papyrus: for the muscles: 8, 12.

[33] *PDM* xiv.1078–89.

[34] Trans. Borghouts #30.

statuette. Mixed with other substances, it consecrates a ring.[35] Clearly, belief in the power of Isis' milk—or milk assimilated to that of Isis—was ritually played out in numerous ways.

The tradition survived into Christian Egypt as well. A lengthy Coptic text containing spells against various ailments, for example, tells a mother with inadequate milk to:

> ... serve your child,
> Give milk to Horus your son,
> Through the power of the Lord God.
> Cow, cow of Amun, mother of the cattle,
> They have drawn near you.
> In the morning you must go forth to feed (them).
> They have drawn near you.
> In the evening you must come in to let them drink.

This *historiola* works by analogizing the hungry child to Horus and the mother with inadequate milk to Horus' divine mother (alias the 'cow of Amun', who is either Isis or Hathor here), and then commanding the divine mother to be present and provide nourishment.[36] Interestingly, the hungry child in question is grammatically female[37] but nonetheless is assimilated to Horus, which underscores how widely the tradition behind this *historiola* could be applied. Interestingly, too, the spell continues, first with a list of seven things that hamper milk production, including 'the real weed that does not provide a staff for a herder, does not provide a goad for the cowherd', that is, a weed that fails to cooperate in animal husbandry that supports milk production; and then with what looks like a second related *historiola*. The speaker addresses 'my cowherd, my shepherd, my herder', who seems to be in distress (his garments are torn and he is running); then gives a list of '7 white (?) sheep, 7 black sheep, 7 young heifers, 7 great cows'; and finally makes a petition: 'let every cow and every domestic animal receive her offspring ... express the thoughts of your heart(s) that every domestic animal may receive her offspring'. In short, the spell not only draws on the tradition of Isis'

---

[35] Falcon: *PGM* I.1–42, specifically 5; statuette: IV.3125–71, specifically 3149; ring: XII.201–69, specifically 215. Breast-shaped libation vessels alluding to the milk of Isis/Hathor were used in non-magical rituals in Egypt; for the evidence, Griffiths (1975) 208–12.
[36] *ACM* #43 = Michigan 136.6.   [37] Frankfurter (2009) 233.

caring for Horus with her milk, as alluded to in the first *historiola* 'serve your child, give milk to Horus your son, etc.', but also draws on one or more traditions in which a threat to milk production among animals was confronted and averted—which speaks again to the fluidity with which *historiolae* might combine traditions to create new myths or ritual programmes.

Hathor, Horus, milk, and a gazelle

'The Conflict of Horus and Seth,' narrated in Papyrus Chester Beatty I (*c.*1160 BC),[38] is another myth about the injured Horus. Horus and Seth are fighting in the river, in the guise of hippopotami. Isis, coming to the aid of her son, spears Seth but then allows him to escape, out of sisterly pity. In anger, Horus beheads his mother and climbs atop a mountain in the desert (Isis' head is subsequently replaced by Thoth with that of a cow). At Re's instructions, the other gods pursue Horus, but he flees to an oasis. Finding Horus, Seth chases him back on to the mountain and tears out both of his eyes, but then lies to Re about the matter, saying that Horus was nowhere to be found. Eventually, Hathor discovers Horus on the mountain and bewails the loss of his eyes. She seizes a gazelle and milks it, then applies the milk to Horus' eye-sockets thus restoring his sight—and in the course of doing so, also restores the '*wedjat*,' or (right) 'eye of Horus', which when reproduced in the quotidian world guaranteed protection, wealth, and good health by warding off all evil. Amulets depicting this eye were so popular, in fact, that '*wedjat*' could be used to mean 'amulet' more generally.[39] In other words, Hathor's ministrations of gazelle milk restored to the world a powerful agent against threats of all kinds—very much along the lines of the promise that our *historiola* makes to protect against 'as many things as the broad Earth nourishes ... or much-groaning Amphitrite rears in the sea.'

The fact that Hathor uses *gazelle* milk is significant. Throughout Egyptian history, gazelles were strongly associated both with the

---

[38] See also discussion of Papyrus Beatty I and other sources in Griffiths (1970) 349–50 (*ad* Plut. *De Is.* 20), where a very similar myth is recounted—Isis loses only her crown, however, not her head, and receives a cow-headed helmet from Hermes in compensation. See also Strandberg (2009) 181–2, 191.

[39] Pinch (1994) 109; Hart (2005) 73.

provision of milk and more generally with healing and regeneration.[40] They were frequently depicted feeding their young in both two-dimensional and three-dimensional art, and, particularly in the Old Kingdom, they were shown mating, giving birth, and (especially) suckling their young even amidst scenes of the hunt, as if to remind the viewer that life triumphs in the face of death.[41] Faience bowls, characteristic of Hathor cult, often show images of suckling gazelles, which is perhaps, suggests Åsa Strandberg, an allusion to the story of Hathor curing Horus.[42] A number of scarabs show a gazelle with a hieroglyph meaning 'young' above her head, as if to refer to regeneration; two scarabs show a suckling gazelle.[43] A scarab now in the Metropolitan Museum shows a gazelle and the eye of Horus, seemingly a reference to the story of Hathor restoring Horus' eyes.[44] On Horus-*cippi*, a gazelle protome occasionally appears on the young god's brow as if to intensify his beneficial powers.[45] Throughout Egyptian history, the death and resurrection of Osiris was said to have occurred at a place named 'Gehesty', which means 'the Place of the Two Gazelles'. It is not clear to what actual place (if any) this name refers, but in several ancient texts it is described as a mountain in the desert, which brings us back again to the story of Hathor's healing of Horus with gazelle milk.[46]

In sum, there were Egyptian myths about Isis/Hathor using either her own milk or the paradigmatically regenerative milk of the gazelle to heal Horus, and more broadly there was a strong Egyptian tradition according to which divine milk—or human or animal milk that had been assimilated to divine milk—could perform a number of curative, restorative, or protective functions.[47] In the final section of

---

[40] Strandberg (2009). Interestingly, the antelope, another member of the *bovidae* family that bears some resemblance to the gazelle, emblematized evil in Egyptian lore: Frankfurter (2004).

[41] Strandberg (2009) *passim*; see especially 57–100 for suckling gazelles in hunt scenes and particularly her summation remarks on pp. 71, 83, 92, 98–100. Gazelles (and only gazelles) were sometimes shown nursing their young in scenes where they are led to sacrifice as well: pp. 106, 112, 115–16, 128.

[42] Strandberg (2009) 189.

[43] Strandberg (2009) 158–9.

[44] Strandberg (2009) 190 and fig. 82.

[45] Strandberg (2009) 135–40, 190–3.

[46] Strandberg (2009) 162–70.

[47] Another Egyptian myth, found in Papyrus Jumilhac (late Ptolemaic or early Roman period), expressed the singular powers of milk as well: the milk of a cow-goddess, variously identified as Hathor or Hesat, is used to regenerate the body of the

this essay, I will take up the question of how such myths and traditions might have contributed to the creation of our *historiola*—that is, how we might imagine such a process of cultural transformation to have taken place. For the moment, however, I would note the likelihood that some or all of these did in fact contribute to the *historiola*'s creation is strengthened by two further points. First, the milk-providing animals in the myth of Hathor and in our *historiola* are similar. In appearance, habitat, and behaviour, the gazelle is much like the goat. Both are members of the *bovidae* family; the ancient goat, which had longer horns than the modern goats with which we are familiar, bore a particularly strong resemblance to the gazelle. And although the Greeks knew of the African gazelle by at least the late fifth century (referring to it under the more generic term for deer, *dorkas*, or *xorcas*),[48] the gazelle was not native to Europe; one can imagine that, as the person who put our *historiola* into its current form incorporated elements from Egyptian models, he would have put a closely similar local animal into the gazelle's role. Goats were, moreover, along with sheep, the animal most commonly milked by the Greeks—already in *Odyssey* IX we see Polyphemus milking his goats, and as I will discuss further on, a number of myths tell of abandoned children being suckled by goats. If one were 'translating' the Egyptian myth of Hathor and the gazelle into a story that would ring true for Sicilian Greeks, trading a gazelle for a goat would be one obvious way to do so.

Second, by the early fifth century at latest, Isis was identified by the Greeks with Demeter,[49] who is the mistress of the goat in our *historiola* and to whom a major sanctuary in Selinus was dedicated—a sanctuary that we know was the site of other private rituals likely to have been performed by the sort of ritual practitioner who probably created the Getty tablet.[50] It is worth remembering, too,

---

god Anty who had been flayed as punishment for decapitating that same goddess (Pinch, 2002, 103; Hart, 2005, 23–4). The fact that Anty is a falcon-god makes it likely that this myth and the one told about Horus in Papyrus Beatty I influenced one another.

[48] Hdt. IV.192, VII.69.

[49] Indeed, Walter Burkert has proposed that the Eleusinian episode in the Homeric *Hymn to Demeter* (early sixth century?) was based on an earlier Egyptian story of Isis' sojourn in Byblos, rather than the other way around, as scholars usually assume (Burkert, 1987, 20–1). Cf. Faraone (1995) 315.

[50] Our oldest *defixiones*, dating from the first half of the fifth century, were found in Selinus, some of these under the floor of the temple of Demeter Malophorus: Gager (1992) 117, 138–42 with further bibliography in notes.

apropos the strong Phoenician presence in Selinus, that Byblos had a cult of Isis dating back to at least the seventh century BC, and that Hathor is referred to as the 'Lady of Byblos' in Middle Kingdom documents.[51] All three of these goddesses—Greek Demeter and Egyptian/Phoenician Isis and Hathor—may have contributed traits and traditions to the goddess worshipped in Selinus. It may even be the case that Selinus was the Greek point of entry for the foreign technique of using *historiolae* in part because one of their major local divinities lent herself so easily to assimilation with a goddess who already had a strong presence in existing Egyptian *historiolae*.

7.6. MILK IN GREECE

Yet our *historiola* vigorously presents itself as Greek: it is in the Greek language, it uses hexameters, and is populated by gods who carry Greek names. To fully understand how it worked, we must contextualize it within Greek culture. Several Greek traditions concerning milk will help us. After examining them, I will propose that the Getty *historiola* does not rely on establishing a precise analogical relationship between the mythic realm and the quotidian realm, as do Egyptian *historiolae* such as we saw in sections 2 and 3 of this chapter, but rather operates on a basis that made sense within the Greek way of looking at myths.

In order to do this, I will not restrict myself to traditions that specify *goats'* milk. As noted earlier, goats were, along with sheep, the animals most commonly used to provide milk in ancient Greece. 'Goats' milk' was, therefore, an unmarked category in Greece, and although I have argued that the goat in our *historiola* looks back to the gazelle in the story of Hathor, I assume that in the *historiola* itself the more salient point is the provision of milk per se, rather than the specific source of the milk. With a few exceptions, the same can be said about milk in the other Greek traditions about to be examined.

---

[51] Griffith (1970) 54, 319–22. Griffith concludes that the cult of Osiris in Byblos can be traced back to the New Kingdom; the cult to Hathor is attested by the Hyksos period and figurines of Isis appear in Phoenicia by at least the seventh or early sixth century BC. The *locus classicus* for Isis in Byblos is Plutarch's myth of Isis' travels to Byblos while searching for Osiris: *De Is.* 15–16. Hart (2005) 65 states that Hathor was called the 'Lady of Byblos' in Middle Kingdom documents.

The Gold Tablets

Lines found in four of the Gold Tablets, which promised post-mortem bliss to initiates into the mysteries of Dionysus, describe an animal falling into or jumping into milk:

1) You have become a god instead of a mortal. A kid [young goat], you fell into milk (Tablet 3 G&J = Bernabé OF 487, line 4)
2) A kid, I fell into milk (Tablet 5 G&J = Bernabé OF 488, line 10)
3) Bull, you jumped into milk
   Quickly, you jumped into milk
   Ram, you fell into milk (Tablet 26a G&J = Bernabé OF 485, lines 3–5)
4) Bull, you jumped into milk
   Ram, you fell into milk (Tablet 26b G&J = Bernabé OF 486, lines 3–4)

Like most recent scholars, I have followed Günther Zuntz's lead in understanding these phrases as proverbial expressions of happy plenitude.[52] Particularly persuasive support for this interpretation lies in similar proverbs that Zuntz cites from the ancient paroemiographers, each of which expresses blissful abundance: 'a donkey in bran', 'a cow in the crops' (or 'manger' or 'heap of corn'), 'like water for a frog', 'like suet for a weasel'. If it be objected, as Zuntz notes, that 'falling into milk' would seem to involve 'an excessive and indeed a pernicious supply of the "desired good"', it may be urged that such exaggeration, again, is characteristic of proverbs'. As ancient *comparanda* for such proverbial excess he cites 'sweetness choked by honey', 'hiding oneself in honey', and 'an ant-hill of good things'. Our own language similarly gives us 'swimming in money' and 'rolling in dough'.

When Zuntz was writing, only Tablets 3 and 5 were available. The subsequently discovered Tablets 26a and 26b, with their variant expression of 'jumping into milk' (that is, of *voluntarily* immersing oneself in milk), support his suggestion that 'falling into milk' is to be understood as a desirable experience of plenitude. But what of the animals that replace the kid in these variations? It is harder to understand why an adult animal—a bull or a ram—would take pleasure in an abundance of milk. It is impossible to offer an answer to this quandary, at least on the basis of our present evidence, but

---

[52] Zuntz (1971) 323–7. Cf. Graf and Johnston (2007) 128–9.

I will venture some remarks that bring us closer to one.[53] First, it is unlikely that the terms 'kid', 'bull', and 'ram' refer to Dionysus himself, and thereby attest to the initiate's identification with the god through identification with the animal.[54] Not only do we lack any mythic or cultic connection at all between Dionysus and rams, but this hypothesis entails a problem of gender: the two tablets mentioning a bull and a ram were found in the grave of a woman: would female initiates have identified themselves with the god by means of terms for (adult) male animals? I suspect that the first editors of tablets 26a and 26b were right in suggesting that the statements about the bull and ram voluntarily jumping into milk developed as 'hyperbolic' (and perhaps also locally restricted) variants of the statement about the kid falling into milk.[55] Second, and to the same general point, with the exception of one Imperial-period inscription from Thessaly that mentions a *galaktophoros*, we have no evidence that milk was connected with any Dionysiac ritual.[56] In short, it is unlikely that the phrases refer, in any literal sense, to something that the tablets' owner experienced while participating in the Dionysiac mysteries. Rather, all of these phrases, including 'a kid falling into milk', are meant metaphorically.

Some scholars who agree that the phrases are metaphorical have suggested that 'falling' or 'jumping' into milk, particularly as an adult (either an adult animal or, by extension, an adult human), is meant to signal rebirth, either in the underworld or in the world above. Alberto Bernabé and Ana Isabel Jiménez San Cristobel support this idea by pointing to images of goddesses suckling both children and adults,

---

[53] For a thorough review of the various scholarly proposals concerning these phrases, Bernabé and Jiménez San Cristóbal (2001/2008) 76–83; cf. Graf and Johnston (2007) 128–9.

[54] As argued for example by Dieterich (1891) 37 = (1911) 91; Turchi (1923) 48; Albinus (2000) 147.

[55] Tsantsanoglou and Parassoglou (1987). Cf. Guarducci (1990) 17, who suggests that milk came to be broadly identified with happiness and thereby could appropriately be applied to other animals; here she approaches my own conclusions.

[56] *Galaktophoros*: IG IX², 65 (*BCH* 37 [1913] 97 n. 7), Robert (1934) II 793 ff. = *OF* 664 Bernabé. It is not clear whether this is a procession connected with mysteries or with public rituals. We do hear, from Sallustius (*De diis* 4), about the initiate's being fed milk 'like a newborn' during the mysteries of Attis, and we know from Apuleius that breast-shaped vessels, used to pour milk, were carried in Isiac processions (Apul. *Met.* XI.10; cf. the Egyptian breast-shaped vessels mentioned in n. 35 above) but it is difficult, to say the least, to extrapolate from these pieces of evidence back to the earlier, Bacchic Gold Tablets.

which are found in graves throughout the western Mediterranean beginning in the fourth century BC; Britt Marie Fridh-Haneson has argued that these images allude to the expectation that the deceased will be adopted by a goddess after death and given the 'milk of immortality'.[57] Perhaps this is correct for some or all of Fridh-Haneson's cases, but even so, jumping or falling into milk is different from suckling milk; there is no reason to assume that images of animals jumping or falling into milk were meant to signify rebirth, even if images of the dead suckling milk did so. Both images (falling/jumping into milk and suckling milk) are likelier to have drawn, independently, on a much wider cultural conceptualization of milk as a very desirable substance.[58]

Paradise

In my next set of *comparanda*, an abundance of milk, often paired with an abundance of honey, is characteristic of ancient Greek and Roman portrayals of paradise.[59] Rivers of milk and honey (and sometimes wine) are frequent features of the transient state of paradise that occurs during Dionysiac ecstasy as well.[60] (Particularly given this fact, it may be that the Gold Tablets' mention of milk not only draws on a proverbial expression, as Zuntz suggested, but also nods to the idea that milk is something that an initiate into the Bacchic mysteries expects to find after death.) The connection between milk-drinking and geographically distant races such as the Hippomolgoi

---

[57] Bernabé and Jiménez San Cristóbal (2001/2008) 79 and 306–10; Fridh-Haneson (1987).

[58] Perhaps the first editors of Tablets 26a and 26b were right in guessing that the images of a bull and a ram jumping into milk were later, hyperbolic variations of what they suggested was the original phrase ('A kid, I fell into milk'): Tsantsanoglou and Parassoglou (1987) 13. Overall on the relationship between these tablets and the goat in the Getty Hexameters, see both Bernabe and Edmonds in this volume; I agree with the latter that there is no firm reason to accept that the hexameters (in either the form we have them on the Getty tablet or elsewhere) had any significant 'Orphic' connection.

[59] Paradise: e.g., Ov. *Met.* I. 111; Verg. *G.* 1.132; Lucian *True History* 2.3, 2.13, 2.26; *Sat.* 7; cf. Pi. *N.* 3.78 and the Biblical 'Land of Milk and Honey.' See also Graf (1980); Bonner (1910); Usener (1902).

[60] Eur. *Bacch.* 142 and 704–11; Pl. *Ion* 534a; Aesch. Socrat. fr. 11; Hor. *Odes* II.19.10; Sen. *Oed.* 494; Philostr. *VA* VI.10; Nonnus XLV.306; cf. Philostr. *Imag.* I.14. Dionysus causes milk and nectar to flow from the looms of the Minyads at Ant. Lib. 10.

may point towards milk as a paradisiacal fluid as well: those who are marginal are often understood to be excessive in both positive and negative ways.[61]

Animal nurses

Milk is properly the food of babies, and there are numerous myths about divine or heroic children who, in the absence of their mothers, are miraculously suckled by animals. Zeus is suckled by the goat Amalthea,[62] Phylakides and Philandros (sons of Apollo) by the Cretan nymph Akakallis, Asclepius and Aegisthus[63] are suckled by goats as well.[64] Cyrus the Great,[65] Aeolus, and Boeotus are suckled by cows,[66] Telephus is suckled by a doe,[67] Hippothoos by a mare,[68] Pelias and Neleus by a mare and a dog,[69] Antilochus by a dog,[70] Paris and Atalanta by bears,[71] and Cybele by panthers.[72] On the Roman side, Romulus and Remus were suckled by a wolf, and Camilla by a mare.[73]

It may be tempting to dismiss these stories as fanciful variations on a biological necessity—a child will starve without nourishment—but this will not do. Myths are quite capable of ignoring what is unimportant to their larger tasks, even if what they ignore looms large in everyday life; we need to ask why so many myths tell of children being suckled by animals. One reason is that the suckling of a child by an

---

[61] Hippomolgoi: *Iliad* XIII.5. See also Hes. *Cat.* 150.15 and 151, Hdt. I.216, Lucian, *True History* 1.24; cf. Graf (1980).

[62] In some myths the goat is called Amalthea, in others, 'Amalthea' is the name of the nymph who owned the goat. Call. *H.* 1.45–8, Hyg. *Fab.* 139 and 182; Ov. *F.* V.115; Str. VIII.7.5, p. 387; Eratosth. *Catastr.* 13; schol. Aratus 161; Apollod. *Bibl.* I.5; D.S. V.70.2.

[63] Aegisthus: Hyg. *Fab.* 87 and 252; Ael. *VH* XII.42. Asclepius: Paus. II.26.3–5.

[64] Phylakides and Philandros: Paus. X.16.5.

[65] Cyrus: Hdt. I.122; Ael. *VH* XII.42.

[66] Aeolus and Boeotus: see the fragments of Euripides' *Melanippe the Wise* and *Telephus*, with remarks by Nauck; Hyg. *Fab.* 252.

[67] Telephus: Apollod. *Bibl.* II.7.4, Soph. fr. 89, Ael. *VH* XII.42, Hyg. *Fab.* 252.

[68] Hippothoos: Hyg. *Fab.* 187, cf. 252; Ael. *VH* XII.42.

[69] Peleus and Neleus: Schol. *Il.* X.334; Eust. ad *Od.* XI.253, p. 1681; Ael. *VH* XII.42.

[70] Antilochus: Hyg. *Fab* 252.

[71] Atalanta: Ael. *VH* XIII.1. Paris: Ael. *VH* XII.42.

[72] Cybele: D.S. III.52.1.

[73] Romulus and Remus: Livy I.4, Plu. *Rom.* 4, Hyg. *Fab.* 252. Camilla: Verg. *A.* XI.570–2, Hyg. *Fab.* 252.

animal usually takes place after the child has been abandoned to die or hidden away to protect it from enemies: the child's survival against all odds, thanks to the animal, proves that Fate has big things in store for him or her. Yet there is more to it than that. The stories of Jason and Ion, for example, in which a threatened child is whisked away to safety without any mention of how he is to be nourished, indicate that the *topos* 'suckling milk from an animal' exists independently of the *topos* 'survival against all odds', even if the first often contributes to the second. The frequency with which myths insist on narrating the miraculous provision of milk to an otherwise abandoned child, then, suggests a fascination with milk that accords it a special status. This fascination is also reflected in numerous medical texts that prescribe milk (human or animal) as a cure for a variety of ailments—as do Egyptian medical texts. The Hippocratic corpus recommends it for menstrual problems.[74] Dioscorides recommends it as an eye ointment,[75] as does Pliny, who adds that it also cures ear problems, lung ailments, fevers, and bowel diseases, and that it also serves as an antidote to certain poisonous substances.[76]

7.7. MILK IN THE GETTY *HISTORIOLA*

Milk, in short, was understood by the Greeks to be powerful stuff: an elixir that nourished, cured, and perfected everything it touched; a liquid whose abundance, like that of honey, marked the advent of paradise; a fluid that metaphorically connoted a safe and happy state. The provision of 'an untiring stream of rich milk' that lies at the heart of the Getty *historiola* (and the later *historiolae* with which it shares phrases) resonates with this broad cultural signification of milk; by ritually recounting the story of a goat that is led forth to provide abundant milk, those who narrated these *historiolae* brought to bear upon a variety of situations (fear of punishment, sexual desire, the need for protection against a range of evils) the metaphorical benefits

---

[74] Hippocr. *De morbis mulierum* I.120.
[75] Diosc. *De Materia Medica* V.99.
[76] *HN* XXVIII.21 (77). The milk of a woman who has already weaned her baby is especially effective, he says, and the milk of a woman who has borne a boy—or even better, twin boys—is the most powerful of all (except for skin problems, where the milk of a woman who has borne a girl is preferred).

of that milk. The mention in the Getty Hexameters and some other texts of leading the goat forth 'by compulsion' or 'by force' underscores how crucial the milk is to the solution of the problems; as in so many other 'magical' contexts, what the divine world will not provide freely must be obtained by whatever means necessary.

But we need to pause on the use of the words 'metaphorically' and 'metaphorical' in the previous paragraph. The Getty *historiola* is far less precise in its analogies than other *historiolae*. Typically in *historiolae*, as we saw in section 3 earlier, the similarities between the figures or objects in the mythic realm on whom the paradigm is built, and the figures and objects in the quotidian realm who are supposed to align themselves with the paradigm, are straightforward and close—sometimes the two are identical, or nearly so. A labouring woman is analogically connected to a labouring doe (and each will be helped by the Archangel Michael); the laurel that a practitioner intends to use in a divinatory ceremony is analogically connected to the laurel that Apollo first used; the scorpion sting suffered by a practitioner's client is analogically connected to the scorpion sting suffered by Anubis (and each will be helped by an unguent invented by Isis).[77] We can schematize this sort of analogical relationship as A : B :: a : b (e.g., Anubis' scorpion sting : cured by Isis' unguent :: client's scorpion sting : cured by practitioner's unguent, made to Isis' specifications).

We can approach the analogizing in which the Getty *historiola* engages by reasoning that, just as milk was viewed as a panacea, so too would a *historiola* that drew its paradigmatic power from milk be viewed as a panacea, and therefore be just as broadly applicable. But there are two further issues to be considered if we want to take this route. First, unlike the medical writers' suggestions that milk be applied to sore eyes or a spell's instructions to use milk to consecrate a ring, there is no obvious way in which milk, or any liquid standing in for milk, can be 'applied' to ward off evil, to attract a woman, or to accomplish any of the other things towards which our *historiola* was directed over the centuries. Second, the text of the Getty Hexameters is quite clear that it is not *milk itself* that does the trick, but inscription of *the story about abundant milk* that will ward off all evils. In other words, the analogy that underpins the Getty *historiola* operates not in the mode of A : B :: a : b, but more like what George Lakoff and Mark

---

[77] Example taken from *PDM* xiv.594–620.

Johnson have dubbed a 'conceptual metaphor', that is, a metaphor in which a concrete image ('milk') is used to represent an abstract concept ('unlimited help, protection, or benefit').[78] In the case of the Getty Hexameters, the abstract concept is then kept permanently available by inscribing on tin the concrete image that stands in for it. The use of conceptual metaphors is quite common in everyday speech (both modern and ancient) and has ritual parallels not unlike those I propose for the Getty Hexameters (the amuletic use of Eucharistic wafers in early modern Europe is an example: Christ's sacrifice is given concrete expression as a foodstuff representing his body, and then is worn to keep the benefits of that sacrifice always at hand), but conceptual metaphors are unparalleled in ancient *historiolae*. In this sense, the *historiola* we see in the Getty Hexameters marks a significant departure from the norm.

But it does align well with the norms of Greek myth-telling as we know it in the fifth century. Let us consider, for example, myth as it was narrated in epinician poetry—a genre that we know was familiar in Greek Sicily, as well as in mainland Greece. When a Pindar or a Bacchylides set out to laud victors in the games, he usually did so by narrating one or more myths, but the myths he chose typically had neither a direct nor a straightforwardly analogical connection to either the victor at hand or the athletic events in which the victor had triumphed.[79] Rather, through a complex network of allusions, imagery, and verbal echoes, themes expressed by the chosen myth *metaphorically* invite rumination on the nature of the present victor's accomplishments, on athletic victory more generally and the glory that follows in its wake, and on the effects such glory will have upon the victor, his family, and his city. Skilfully done, the narration of myth thus plays a crucial role in bringing about the tangibly significant benefits that proper celebration of athletic victory could garner (and admonishing against its concomitant risks), but it does so without drawing explicit, one-to-one equations between the mythic

---

[78] Lakoff and Johnson (1980). They use the terms 'source domain' to describe the realm from which the concrete image is taken and 'target domain' to describe the realm of the abstract.

[79] There are a few exceptions. *Olympian* 3 includes the myth of Heracles founding the Olympic Games and planting olive trees along the race-course, for example, and *Olympian* 1 narrates Pelops' chariot race, which some traditions associated with the foundation of the Olympic Games. Even in these cases, however, no direct relationship is drawn between the myth and the victor.

realm in which the narration is situated and the quotidian realm within which the present victory occurred. *Isthmian 4*, for example, hints that we are to compare the young victor, Melissos, to Heracles (Pindar goes so far as to point out that both were small in build, lines 49–53), but the ode leaves it up to us to conclude in exactly what way we should read Heracles' story into that of Melissos. In a similar vein, tragedy, especially Euripidean tragedy, narrates myths that provoke thought about contemporary issues without ever drawing explicit analogies between them. We might be right in guessing that Euripides means us to ruminate on the Peloponnesian War when we read or listen to his *Suppliant Women*, but Euripides himself does not make that point. The closest Greek mythic narration ever comes to a mode of operation like that we see in *historiolae* is to be found in the *pars epica* of certain Greek prayers, where a god is reminded of what he did in the past in order that he might be persuaded to do something similar in the present, but the result is not guaranteed; the words of the prayer themselves are not efficacious, and so we are still far from the performative utterances that comprise most *historiolae*, especially those of Podemann Sørensen's first type, the type to which the Getty *historiola* belongs.[80] Aitiological narration, to take up another common function of myth in Greece, shares a function with type 2 *historiolae* insofar as *aitia* explain why certain rituals are performed, but the goals again are different: the recitation or inscription of an *aition* was not, in itself, imagined to effect, or even help to effect, the desired results of the ritual.

In sum, the conceptualization of myths that underlay most *historiolae* was quite different from any that was at home in Greece; this is one of the likeliest reasons why we lack *historiolae* that can properly be called 'Greek', as noted in section 1 of this chapter: the technique never caught on more widely because its underlying assumptions about what myth could do were too foreign. One would not think of causing Demeter to provide miraculous milk (her own or that of an animal) by shifting her name into a *historiola* where that of Isis or Hathor had previously stood; nor would one think that narrating a story of Demeter's provision of miraculous milk would cause milk to become miraculous in the quotidian world. The Getty Hexameters probably represent an experiment, conducted at a time

---

[80] On the efficacious nature of words in *historiolae*, see further Podemann Sørensen (1984) 7 and Frankfurter (1995) *passim*.

when other 'magical' techniques, such as those underlying the *defixiones*, were entering Greece from the East, and conducted in a place where we know that other such techniques entered early on, but conducted with attempts to align the technique more closely with the Greek understanding of how myths about divinities (and the divinities themselves) worked.[81] In section 5 of this chapter, I sketched some possible ways in which the technique may have reached Selinus; in this section I hope to have emphasized that from wherever and however the technique of creating *historiolae* entered Selinus, it was not one that sat easily alongside established Greek views.

7.8. DEMETER, PERSEPHONE, AND THE CHILD

I have already discussed the significance of Demeter in the Getty *historiola* as a goddess with whom Isis and Hathor were equated, but two other *dramatis personae* need to be considered: the child (or servant[82]) who descends from the mountain in order to lead the goat from the garden to the place where she will be milked, and Persephone, from whose garden the goat is led.

The first thing that may strike us about this constellation is that it comprises a notably indirect way to involve the two goddesses in the central act of the *historiola*, the provision of milk. Neither goddess actually acts within the story; any work to be done is done by the child. This stands in contrast not only to the stories of Isis and Horus, and Hathor and Horus reviewed in section 5 of this chapter, but also to most *historiolae* from other cultures, where the gods or heroes are directly involved in the paradigmatic action:[83]

'Come to me, Mother Isis, Sister Nephthys! Look you, I am suffering inside my body...'[84]

---

[81] See note 50 above.

[82] Already in Aeschylus (*Ch.* 653) *pais* can mean 'servant'. Here, I proceed on the assumption that *pais* means 'child'. Cf. n. 27 above.

[83] There are a few exceptions. Notably, in the spell mentioned earlier in which a labouring doe asks Christ for help when he encounters her on a mountain, Christ tells her that she cannot tolerate his glory and that he will send the Archangel Michael to her aid instead: *ACM* #49 = Berlin 8313.

[84] Borghouts #34 = Papyrus British Museum 10059 [46] 14, 8–14.

'Isis sat speaking to the oil, ABARTAT, and lamenting to the true oil, saying "You are praised..."' [etc., from the spell to cure scorpion stings, mentioned above].

'Three men met us in the desert [and said to the Lord] Jesus, "What treatment is possible for the sick?" and he says to them "[I have] given olive oil and have poured out myrrh [for those] who believe in the [name of the] father and the Holy [spirit and the son].'[85]

'The Virgin Mary walked in the grass
Where she heard the snake hiss.
"I shall tie you
And force you
With my five fingers
In the name of the Holy Father".'[86]

Behind the absence of divine action in our *historiola* lies, in part, the sensibilities that I described in the preceding section: the Greeks did not imagine that one could make the gods do things by narrating stories about their doing things. But behind the absence may lie the Greek expectation that, in particular, the gods do not engage in the humbler sorts of labour. They fight alongside their favourites in war, or occasionally disguise themselves as human servants for their own purposes,[87] but with the exception of Hephaestus, Greek gods perform menial duties strictly under duress—Apollo owned cattle, but it was only as a punishment for killing the Cyclopes that he was compelled to herd cattle himself.[88] And indeed, when Demeter herself assumes a servile position as nursemaid to the Eleusinian prince Demophoon, she does not, in fact, actually suckle the child from her breast, but instead uses other divine means to nourish him.[89]

---

[85] *ACM* #4 = Oxyrhynchus 1384.

[86] Herjulsdotter (2009) 55—from a Swedish charm against snakebite.

[87] Thus Demeter disguised herself as an old woman while living amongst humans and took a job as nurse maid (*HHDem.* 101, Ov. *F.* IV.517–18, Apollod. *Bibl.* I.4.5, and many other places—the story is the *aition* of the Thesmophoria). Hera disguised herself as Semele's old nurse Beroë to deceive her (Ov. *Met.* III.256–315, Apollod. *Bibl.* III.4.3, Hyg. *Fab.* 167, 179; cf. D.S. III.64.3–4. The story is perhaps already in Aeschylus: fr. 168 R; schol. ad Ar. *Ran.* 1344.).

[88] Hes. Fr. 54 M–W; Acus. 2F19; Pherec. 3F35, 3F131; E. *Alc.* 1–9; Apollod. *Bibl.* III.10.4.

[89] Note, for example, *HHDem.* lines 235–7 '... he grew like a *daimôn*, not eating grain, not sucking from the breast, but Demeter used to anoint him with ambrosia, as if he had been born of the goddess...' and see the excellent article of Pirenne-Delforge (2010), which notes that Greek goddesses, in fact, do not breast feed their children but rather choose either to hand them over to others, such as the nymphs, to be suckled, to

Unlike Isis, Demeter could not be expected to provide miraculous milk herself. And unlike Hathor, under no circumstances could Demeter or Persephone be expected to grab a goat, much less sit down and milk her. Children, in contrast, in ancient Greece and in many other Mediterranean and European cultures, commonly serve as goatherds: the young Ganymede was herding flocks when Zeus abducted him from Mount Ida, and the young Branchus was herding flocks on a mountain when Apollo fell in love with him; Daphnis and Chloe met while they were children, herding the goats and sheep of their foster parents; and then there is Aesop's famous 'boy who cried wolf' while herding.[90]

Was this child a particular child? I have been translating *pais*, following Faraone, as 'a child', but it might also be translated as 'the child'—perhaps the audience of our *historiola* was meant to think of a *specific* child known from local myth, cult, or both, somewhat along the same lines as the 'child from the hearth' in the Eleusinian mysteries, or the child Demophoon, who appears in a number of myths about Demeter. (I do not mean to suggest that the Selinuntine child is to be *equated* with either the Eleusinian child or Demophoon; rather, I offer them as figures analogous with some child whom the local populace could have recognized as having a connection to Demeter in either myth or cult.)

The other important character in our *historiola* is Persephone. I have found no other occurrence of the phrase *Phersephonês kêpou* (or *Persephonês kêpou*) in any text, nor have I found uses of *kêpos*, period, more generally within texts such as the magical papyri that are likely *comparanda* for the *historiola*. The closest apparent parallels for our phrase come from stories (some set in Sicily) in which Persephone picks flowers in a meadow (*leimôn*) from which she is abducted, and from a late fourth-century Gold Tablet from Pherae that represents the post-mortem place of the blessed as a meadow belonging to Persephone.[91] But *kêpos* suggests a cultivated and perhaps enclosed

---

nourish them on ambrosia, as Demeter did for Demophoon, or both.' Hera's suckling of Heracles is the notable exception, which Pirenne-Delforge addresses in depth; it appears relatively late in Greek sources and may be Etruscan in origin.

[90] Ganymede: Lucian *Dial. Deor.* 10; Branchus: Conon *Narr.* 33; Aesop 210 Perry. Outside antiquity one need go no further than Johanna Spyri's *Heidi* for an example.

[91] Persephone snatched while in a meadow: *HHDem.* 7, Ov. *M.* V.391–2, Ov. *F.* IV.420–42, Paus. IX.31.9, Orph. fr. 387 Bernabé, Orph. *Argo.* 1192–6. Diodorus Siculus (V.4.2–3) mentions that Persephone received as recompense for her rape

area, in contrast with *leimôn*, which evokes the idea of an open, relatively uncontrolled, space; these apparent parallels are probably false leads. We are left once again in the realm of conjecture. 'Persephone's garden' may have been an actual spot, perhaps within the Selinuntine sanctuary of Demeter, or it may have been a place of the imagination, drawn from a local myth of Persephone that situated her abduction within a more domesticated space than did similar myths (cf. some Sicilian myths say that Persephone was abducted while weaving, i.e., while occupied within a controlled domestic space).

In spite of this uncertainty, the phrase *Phersephonês kêpou* does provoke two further observations. First, the creator of our *historiola* recognized the importance of including Persephone in his story; his models, Isis and Hathor, worked on their own, but in the Greek world and especially in Sicily, to think of Demeter was to think of Persephone as well. This was another adjustment that the creator made to the traditions on which he modelled his *historiola* in order that it might better align with Greek expectations.

Second, the introduction of Persephone into the narrative by means of her *garden* (whether that garden be an actual place or an imaginary one), together with mention of the mountain from which the child descends—that is, the introduction of geographic details within our *historiola*—aligns squarely with the fact that *historiolae* from many cultures frequently locate the actions of their narratives within places that evoke those of the quotidian world. Thus, for example:

'Isis comes down from the mountain at midday, in summer, the dusty maiden; her eyes are full of tears and her heart is full of sighs...' [etc.; from a love spell in the magical papyri].[92]

'...Horus [the son of] Isis went up upon a mountain in order to rest... [etc.; from a *historiola* in a Coptic spell against stomach-ache].[93]

'The Virgin Mary walked in the grass
Where she heard the snake hiss....'
[etc.; from the Swedish charm against snakebite cited above].

certain meadows (*leimônas*) around Enna in Sicily. In Nysa in Caria there was a place called the Meadow (*leimôn*) near an entrance to the Underworld (Str. XIV.1.45). Underworld meadow: Tablet 27 G&J; cf. the Underworld meadows mentioned at *Od.* XI.539, 573 and XXIV.13; Pi. fr. 129; Ar. *Ra.* 373 and 449; Plu. fr. 178.

[92] *PGM* IV.94–153.
[93] *ACM* #49 = Berlin 8313.

'Our Lord Jesus Christ and the Virgin Saint were walking in the fields.
The Saint Virgin Mary found a white stone.
She sat on it and started weeping...'
[etc., from a cure for eye ailments, collected in France in the 1880s][94]

'Saint Lazarus and Our Lord were going for a walk in our town...' [etc., from a manuscript belonging to a French bone-setter, dating to about 1900].[95]

Such *emplacement* of narrative action subtly reiterates a principle that underlies all *historiolae*: what happens in the mythic realm can happen within our quotidian realm as well. Indeed, the term 'mythic realm', useful though it may be for discussing the way in which *historiolae* provide paradigms that will be taken up within another, 'quotidian realm', has the unfortunate side-effect of suggesting that the actions of *historiolae* occur in places that are completely separate from our own.[96] This is contradicted not only by the insistently familiar settings of *historiolae* themselves (mountains, streets, grassy areas and fields, and even 'our town'), but also by the ontological underpinnings of the cultures that produced the *historiolae* quoted in this chapter: gods and heroes may be understood to make their homes in a place that is geographically distant (higher or lower than where humans make their homes; beyond the western ocean, etc.), but that place is not understood to be cut off from our places; sacrificial smoke can rise from our altars to their nostrils, for example, prayers uttered by our mouths reach their ears, and when they choose to visit us for whatever reason, they find it quite easy to do so.[97] The locative details of many *historiolae,* including the one narrated by the Getty

---

[94] Davies 2004 (104).   [95] Davies 2004 (98).

[96] I find it impossible to suggest a really satisfying alternative to the word 'realm', however; most of the words we might be tempted to substitute, such as 'sphere,' evoke place at least as strongly as does 'realm'. 'Mythic *mode*', perhaps?

[97] It is interesting that our *historiola* specifically chooses a mountain as one of its locations; Egyptian and Coptic *historiolae* frequently set their action on mountains. In addition to those instances already mentioned in this chapter, see for example, *PGM* XX.4–12 with the parallels discussed in Faraone (1995); *PDM* xiv.1219–27. Notably, gazelles are closely associated in Egyptian thought with desert mountains as well: Strandberg (2009) *passim*, esp. 24, 47, 190–1, and see the table of contents for many discussions of the 'desert hunt' of the gazelle. Is it possible that the Getty *historiola* evokes Egyptian precedents in its reference to the mountain? But see also Frankfurter (2009) 231 and 233, who suggests that mountains in *historiolae*, like marshes and deserts, represent 'intermediary places,' and help to '[amplify distress] through depictions of distance.'

Hexameters, firmly remind the audience that the effects described by the narration apply to *their* circumstances, as well as to those of the gods and heroes that populate the story.

7.9. CONCLUSION

It is time to pull together the different threads of my argument. I have suggested that the *historiola* we see in the Getty Hexameters constitutes a myth that draws on the 'rich and complex mélange of traditions'[98] available from cultures throughout the Mediterranean—particularly those of Egypt and Greece, perhaps with Phoenician contributions. It imports to the Greek world myths that had long been at home in Egypt, but it shows a sensitivity to cultural expectations, adapting what it imports to Greek experiences with the natural world (thus, goats instead of gazelles provide miraculous milk, for example) and to Greek assumptions about the gods (thus, the gods of the Getty *historiola* do not themselves provide milk or milk animals).

Even before entering Greece, however, the myths on which our *historiola* draws undoubtedly had themselves been subjected to adaptation—or rather, like most traditional materials, they were in an ongoing state of revision to suit the changing situations in which they were invoked. In section 2, I emphasized the importance of *not* understanding a culture's corpus of myths as a limited number of pure forms from which 'versions' more-or-less true to those forms are derived, but rather understanding the versions *to be* the myths. In section 5, I looked at a number of Egyptian texts that preserve a tradition according to which milk associated with certain goddesses is miraculous. Some of these texts were myths that narrated stories about Horus and his mothers, Isis and Hathor; some were *historiolae*—shorter myths intended to have a practical effect upon the quotidian world—that shared characters or plots with the longer myths. Some of the texts were what we would call medical prescriptions or magical spells, although they shared with the myths and *historiolae* features that look back to the same tradition, such as the stipulation that the milk of a woman who has borne a son is especially efficacious. In all of these

---

[98] Faraone (1995) 325.

cases, there is a notable fluidity of detail circling around the central theme of miraculous milk: sometimes it comes directly from a goddess's breasts, and sometimes from the udder of a gazelle via the hands of a goddess. Sometimes it restores damaged eyes, sometimes it cures a fever, and sometimes it consecrates a statuette. When this Egyptian tradition of miraculous milk entered the Greek world, all of these articulations already coexisted: although I am proposing that the myth of Hathor using gazelle milk to restore the *wedjat* particularly lies behind the specific form that our *historiola* took, it is important to realize that the more general *tradition* of miraculous milk expressed by that myth found an easy foothold in Selinus because the Greeks themselves had a tradition in which milk signified a paradisiacal state of plenitude (as reviewed in section 6 of this chapter), as well as a local goddess who could comfortably be drafted into a leading role in a 'milk myth'. The 'new' myth of Demeter, Persephone, the child, and the goat that we find in the Getty *historiola* was hardly new in this sense: it was at heart yet another articulation of a theme at home in both cultures, borrowing and adjusting details from one so as to thrive in the other.

What *was* new—what does represent a significant departure from what had gone before—is the logic by which the Getty *historiola* operates. Like Greek myth in general, it utilizes metaphor: milk already had a strong association with blessedness and pleasure in Greek thought, but here that association is extended in two ways. First, the provision of milk now comes to represent the provision of all manner of protection and safety. It is the guarantor of the Healer's promise to in every direction send averting charms [against] as many things as the broad Earth nourishes [and] much-groaning Amphitrite rears in the sea. Second, the 'provision of milk' that accomplishes this is itself a representation: it is not the liquid itself that will work the charm, but the ritualized inscription of the liquid's virtues upon a piece of tin. Letters (*grammata*) stand in for milk, which itself stands in for something much bigger.

This brings us to larger questions that deserve more attention than can be given in this chapter. If I am right that the Getty *historiola* was an experiment that works on the logic of the 'conceptual metaphor' rather than by the A : B :: a : b model that underlies other *historiolae*, and if I am right that this choice reflects the Greek attitude towards myth as a metaphoric discourse, then what windows does this open for us upon the broader Greek view of myths as 'useful' narratives within a ritual context—or useful narratives in any other way? Could the Greeks 'do things' with myths in anything like the same way that their Near Eastern neighbours did? And how might this Greek attitude towards the ritual potential of myth have affected the particular course that magic took in Greece?

Finally, to return to a question posed at the beginning of this chapter: why are variations of this *historiola* found so widely scattered throughout the Greek world and across such a broad span of time? First, it should be noted that all the places where it shows up are, like Selinus, open to frequent foreign exchange (Phalasarna on Crete; Himera on Sicily; Locri Epizephyrioi on the coast of Italy, and Oxyrhynchus in Egypt); the specific find-spot of the papyrus on which one example (*PGM* LXX.5–16) appears is unknown but is Egyptian as well. In other words, this *historiola* was carried to spots where what I have suggested is a hybrid product of *bricolage* might be more marketable than elsewhere—and even more importantly, places that might have been positively responsive to the Egyptian background of the story it told, and the technique of *historiolae* in general.

Second, it should be noted that the *historiola* as we see it in the Getty Hexameters does not always survive in what might be called its 'full Greek' form. Some combination of the goat, the milk, the garden, and the child are always present, even in our briefest examples, but Demeter and Persephone appear in only two other instances: the unpublished Latin version (which, according to reports by Jordan and Kotansky, 'translates' our lines 8–15)[99] and the Oxyrhynchus tablet (Bernabé A), which includes a close variation of our lines 8–11. Bernabé has proposed, in this volume, that our *historiola* evolved over time into the *Ephesia Grammata*; he suggests that the Getty text, where both the *historiola* in a lengthy narrative form and some of the *Ephesia Grammata* coexist, represents a stage after this has begun to happen. The other, shorter texts from Sicily that date to the fifth century (and are therefore either contemporary with or slightly earlier than the Getty Hexameters) retain less of the story and look more like *Ephesia Grammata* as we know them from later texts; the fourth-century texts from Locri Epizephyrioi and Phalasarna retain marginally more of the story; as stated, later texts (Oxyrhynchus and the Latin version) include mentions of Demeter and Persephone that are nearly identical with those in the Getty Hexameters. Thus, we should

---

[99] Jordan (1988) 256 and Kotansky (1994).

not imagine that the transformation from narration into *Ephesia Grammata* ran along a smooth chronological continuum, even within a single locale (the three tablets from Selinus alone contradict this). Rather, both the straightforward narrative, which could be understood in a traditional sense by anyone who heard it, and the *Grammata*, which must have sounded like the mysterious, technical language of ritual specialists to the average person, were contemporarily available for most of antiquity. The choice to use one or the other (or both, as in the Getty text) may have depended on a practitioner's knowledge, a client's willingness to pay to have the (longer) narrative inscribed, or a number of other factors. But in any case, the development and eventually widespread popularity of the *Ephesia Grammata* would probably have helped to carry abroad, and thus to preserve, a uniquely Greek *historiola*.

8

The Immortal Words of Paean*

Ian Rutherford

A conspicuous feature of the Getty Hexameters (and one that distinguishes it from related 'magical' texts, such as the 'Phalasarna hexameters'[1]) are the repeated references to a deity called 'the Healer', Paieon, hereafter simply 'Paean'. He is apparently mentioned four times in the text. On two occasions the name is extant, first, at lines 6–7:

Παιήων σὺ δὲ πάντοσ' ἀλέξιμα φάρμακα πέμπεις
καὶ τάδε φωνήσας ἔπε' ἀθάνατα θνητοῖσιν.

Paean, for in every direction you send averting charms,
even having spoken these immortal verses to mortal men...

These lines precede and seem to introduce the '*historiola*' about the child and the goat that follows, which must be the 'immortal verses' referred to (immortal because they are of divine origin). In this volume Sarah Johnston suggests that Paean might make a subsequent appearance as the god guided by Hecate in lines 13–15, in which case those lines would be outside Paean's speech.

---

* Thanks to the participants at the Getty Symposium.
[1] Jordan (1992). The later Greek Magical Papyri contain a few references to the deity Paieon/an/on, always apparently identified with Apollo, all of them embedded in hymns to the deity in hexameters or occasionally other metres: the iambic line at *PGM* I.297, which Preisendanz makes into a separate composition (Hymn 8), though it is probably the first line of a longer hexameter hymn (Preisendanz 23); see Betz *ad loc* and Bortolani (2012) (Hymn 1); Preisendanz Hymn 10 = *PGM* VI.26–38: I.296ff.: one iambic line; Preisendanz Hymn 10 = *PGM* VI.26–38: adapts Chryses' prayer in *Iliad* I; Preisendanz Hymn 11 = *PGM* II.81–101, 133–40, 163–6: long hexameter hymn to Apollo and Apollo Helios; Preisendanz Hymn 12 = *PGM* III.234–58: hexameter hymn to Apollo and Daphne. The word παιανίζω is used for invoking the deity at *PGM* III.192 (where it seems to introduce Preisendanz Hymn 5) and 304.

The second place where the name is extant (more or less) is lines 47–8 at the end of the text:

> Πα]ι[η]ων–ὁ γάρ αὐτὸς ἀλέξιμα φάρμακα πέμπεις–
> [οὐ]κ ἂν δε{ι}λήσαιτ' οὐδεὶς {ουδαι} πολυφάρ[μακ - - -]

> [Pa]i[e]on, for in every direction you [send] averting charms,
> Nor would anyone be harmed armed with much-cur[ing] ...

In both lines Paieon is associated with φάρμακα, which makes intuitive sense, and can be paralleled in Homer.

The name is restored two further times in lines 21–32, which it is worth quoting in full:

> [c.6–7]ωντ' ἀνόμων ο[ἴκ]ων ἄπο χε[c.13–14]
> [Παιήων·] σὺ δὲ πάντοσ' ἀλέξιμα φάρμα[κα πέμπεις ?
> [c.6–7]γου κατάκουε φ[ρ]άσιν· γλυκὺν ὕ[c.11–12]
> 25 [c.6 ἀ]νθρώποισιν ἐπιφθέγγεσθαι ἄν[ωγα]
> [c.5–6]ωι κἂν εὐπολέμωι καὶ ναυσίν, ὅτα[ν κῆρ]
> [c.7 ἀ]νθρώποις θανατηφόρος ἐγγύ[θεν ἔλθηι]
> [c.6–7]ι προβάτοις καὶ ἐπὶ τέχναισι βροτ[c.10–11]
> [c.6 φ]θέγγεσθαι ἐν εὐφρόνηι ἠδὲ κατ[c.10–11]
> 30 [c.6–7]ν ἔχων ὅσιον {σιον} στόματος θυ[c.10–11]
> [c.6 ἔ]σστι πόλει· τὰ γὰρ ἀρχῆς ἐστιν ἀριστ[c.10–11]
> [Παιήων· σὺ δ']ε πάντοσ' ἀκεσσφόρος ἐσσὶ καὶ ἐσθ[c.11–12]

> ....of/from lawless h[ou]ses....
> For you, [O Healer], yourself [do send ?] averting charms!
> Give ear to the utterance of...! sweet...
> 25 [command?] you to utter for mortals....
> whenever [doom] among the... good-at-war and the ships
> [comes] near bringing death to mortals.
> ... [and] near the flocks-and-herds and the handiworks of mo[rtals]
> ... utter in night and by [day]
> 30 ... keeping pure of mouth
> ... is for/to the city, for best are the things from the beginning(?).
> [Paean, for you] in every direction are cure-bringing and exce[llent].

The surviving part of line 23 is identical to the corresponding part of line 7, which strongly suggests that the *lacuna* at the start is filled out with Παιήων. In the following line, Paean is requested to listen to speech (φράσιν), and then in the line after that someone commands that someone utter (ἐπιφθέγγεσθαι) something to men. Lines 26–7 suggest that this utterance is made in the context of various forms of

The Immortal Words of Paean 159

disaster, which it is presumably intended to avert. In line 29 there is another instance of the word 'utter' (presumably [ἐπιφ]θέγγεσθαι again). This section of the poem seems to end at line 33 with the citation of the 'Ephesian Letters', leading into another *historiola* involving another goat and the Tetrax. Immediately preceding that, in line 32, is another line addressing a being as cure-bringing, and the lacuna at the start of this line seems also to invite the restoration 'Paean'. Thus a reference to Paieon introduces the ritual part of the text, as in line 7. In fact, the whole stretch of text from line 21 to line 32 is an extended introduction to the section that follows, setting out the circumstances for its delivery or performance.[2]

So much is clear, but it is not clear who does the commanding here and who the uttering, or what the utterance is. The analogy of lines 6–7 would suggest that the utterance comes from Paean, but in line 24 Paean is the listener. In line 5 the speaker of the prayer might be commanding (ἄν[ωγα]) Paean to speak (cf. *Iliad* V.899 where Zeus 'ordered Paean to heal' Ares [... Παιήον' ἀνώγειν ἰήσασθαι]), but it would be strange for a mortal to command a god in this way. More likely men are ordered to make the utterance, either by the speaking-subject of the Getty Hexameters or alternatively by Paean himself (ἄν[ωγας]?). As to the nature of the utterance, the easiest solution is to take it of the Ephesian letters plus *historiola* beginning at line 13, though the form of utterance with which Paean is most commonly associated is the paean-cry '*ie paian*', an appeal to the deity, often cast in the form of the refrain of a paean-song (see later on), and the standard Greek term for 'refrain' is none other than ἐπίφθεγμα.[3] However that may be, the overall force of this section of the text is to associate Paean with the ritual section that follows in lines 33ff., with the probable implication that he is the authority for it, as in line 7.

The four lines in which the theonym occurs can be set alongside each other like this:

> Line 6: Παιήων σὺ δὲ πάντοσ' ἀλέξιμα φάρμακα πέμπεις.
> Line 23: [Παιήων] σὺ δὲ πάντοσ' ἀλέξιμα φάρμα[κα πέμπεις?
> Line 32: [Παιήων σὺ δ]ὲ πάντοσ' ἀκεσφόρος ἐσσὶ καὶ ἐσθ[λός.
> Line 47: Πα]ι[η]ων–ὁ γάρ αὐτὸς ἀλέξιμα φάρμακα πέμπεις.

The first two are identical; the third and fourth introduce variety by altering first the second half of the line, and then the first.

---

[2] This is the structure assumed in Jordan and Kotansky (2011) 28–9.
[3] See Rutherford (2001) 71 with n.11.

The role of Paean in the Getty Hexameters thus seems to be that of a source of and authority for the ritual incantations. Ascription of a magical ritual to a deity has parallels in Near Eastern religion; thus, the *Utukku Lemnutu* series of Assyrian incantations attributes a special position to the deities Ea or Marduk, as we see, for example, in the following text:[4]

> I belong to Ea / I belong to Damkina, / and I am Marduk's messenger. My incantation is actually Ea's, /my spell is actually Marduk's, with Ea's master-plans being in my possession.

As Mark Geller comments:[5]

> The series relies most heavily on Marduk's powers over demons, in his divine role as Ea's son and emissary, while the human exorcist claims to be the emissary of Marduk, carrying out divine instructions.

In Greco–Egyptian magical texts, on the other hand, spells tend to be ascribed to human ritual experts, often from the semi-mythological past.[6]

In texts of the Classical period, Paieon or the shorter forms Paian or Paion (Attic-Ionic) is usually an epithet of Apollo and Asclepius, from the Hellenistic period also of other deities; in Latin, the usual form is Paean.[7] This usage is attested for Selinus in a fragmentary fifth-century text inscribed on a block described by the most recent editor as a 'fragment of a cornice (the *geison* of an altar?) found in the area comprising temples C and D':[8]

[— — Ἀπό]λλōνος Παιᾶνος
[— — Ἀθ]αναίας.

of Apo]llo *Paian*
of Ath]ene

---

[4] Geller (2007) 201. Similarly, in Hittite religion, for example, there seems to be a special relationship between the ritual practitioner known as 'the old woman' (^MUNUS^SU.GI) and the deity Kamrusepa, the Hittite or Hattic god of magic: Archi (1993).

[5] Geller (2007) xii.

[6] Such as Solomon (*PGM* 4.850), Pitys (*PGM* IV.1930, 2006, 2140), Pibechis (*PGM* IV.3007), or Jeu (*PGM* 5.96), Claudianus (*PGM* VII.862), Pythagoras and Demokritos (*PGM* VII.795), Astrapsoukhos (*PGM* VIII.1), Agathokles (*PGM* XII.107), Moses (*PGM* XIII.345). A possible case where a deity could be a source of ritual authority is *PGM* VI.42–3 (= Preisidanz Hymn 14, 4–5), where an appeal is made to goddess Daphne: 'haste to sing/ divine precepts to me...' (ἔπειγέ μοι ἀείσασθαι / θεσμοὺς θεσπεσίους...), but the text is uncertain.

[7] Rutherford (2001) 11–12; von Blumenthal (1942) 2341.

[8] Arena (1989) n. 36; *IG* XIV.269.

The Immortal Words of Paean

Sometimes it seems to be used as an alternative name for Apollo or Asclepius, as when Cicero describes the worship of Paean together with Asclepius at Syracuse, where Apollo is clearly meant.[9] At the same time, it has been argued that Paieon/Paian/Paion was a distinct deity, either in cult (in certain periods and areas) or in poetic imagination. Linear B texts from Knossos give us reason to think that in the Late Bronze Age 'Paiawon' (clearly an earlier form of the same name) was an independent deity, not as far as can be seen associated with Apollo (who may be attested in Linear B) or Asclepius (who is not).[10] Again, there are several references to Paean in early Greek poetry, apparently as an independent deity. He is mentioned three times in Homer: two instances of the same line at *Iliad* V.401 = 900:

> τῷ δ' ἐπὶ Παιήων ὀδυνήφατα φάρμακα πάσσων / ἠκέσατ'·
>
> For him Paean, spreading pain-killing drugs, / healed...

This is said first of Paean's healing Hades in the distant past when he was wounded by Heracles, and then of his healing Ares who has been wounded by Diomedes. A different role is attributed to him in the *Odyssey* (*Od.* IV.227-32), where, commenting on the drugs given to Helen during her sojourn in Egypt by Polydamna, wife of Thon, Homer adds that in Egypt every man is a skilled physician, 'for they are of the race of Paean' (ἦ γὰρ Παιήονός εἰσι γενέθλης).[11] There are two more instances: one in (Ps.?) Hesiod fr.307.2:

> εἰ μὴ Ἀπόλλων Φοῖβος ὑπὲκ θανάτοιο σαώσαι
> ἢ αὐτὸς Παιήων, ὃς ἁπάντων φάρμακα οἶδεν
>
> Unless Phoebus Apollo should save him from death,
> or Paean himself who knows the remedies for all things...

and one in an elegiac fragment of Solon, fr.11, where healers do the work of 'Paion':

> ...ἄλλοι Παιῶνος πολυφαρμάκου ἔργον ἔχοντες / ἰητροί.
>
> ...others are doctors knowing the function of Paion with many drugs.

---

[9] *In Verr.* 4.128; also IG IV², 424.10.
[10] Rutherford (2001) 11-12; Huxley (1975); Paiawon: Aura Jorro (1985-1993) II.69; Apollo in Linear B: Aura Jorro (1985-1993) II.113, s.v.]pe-ro₂-[.
[11] The name Paieon is speculatively given an Egyptian origin by Bernal (2006) 210, 456.

The epithet is the same as the one that occurs within a line of the name Paean in line 48 of the Getty Hexameters.[12] In all these passages Paean is often regarded as an independent deity, but in fact the reference could conceivably be to Apollo.[13] Equally, as far as cult is concerned, there is no evidence that Paieon/an/on ever had an independent existence after the Mycenaean period. The only instance known to me of the name appearing on its own where identification with Apollo or Asclepius seems unlikely is a Choes-vase from the late fifth century BC, where the fourth of four naked revelling boys is called 'Paian', the others being Kallos, Neanias, and Komos; here, 'Paian' may perhaps be the personification of the paean song or of music in general.[14] In the Getty Hexameters the name could either stand for Apollo or Asclepius, or it could be the independent healer deity. All things being equal, however, it seems likeliest that it would have been understood as referring to Apollo, as indeed seems to be the case in the inscription from Selinus cited above.

The deity or epithet Paean/Paieon/Paion is often associated with a special genre of poetry or song, the paean. In fact, a working definition of the paean would be a poem or song in which that divine name features prominently, usually as part of a repeated refrain addressed to the deity with some variation on the formula '*ie/io + paieon/paian/paion*'.[15] At their most basic, paeans are communal appeals to a deity invoked as 'Healer' to provide salvation, either generally or in a certain situation of crisis. Though associated most commonly with those healer gods par excellence Apollo and Asclepius, paeans can be directed to other deities as well, such as Poseidon in his capacity to preside over earthquakes. The uncertainty about whether Paean/Paieon/Paian/Paion is an independent deity or name for any of a number of other gods is a reflex of the close association between the theonym and name of the genre paean: any deity, but

---

[12] Applied to doctors in Homer, *Il.* XVI.28, to Circe at *Od.* X.276 and Hesiod, fr. 302.15.

[13] Burkert (1985) 145 takes them as independent, as did Usener (1929) 154–5. Von Blumenthal (1942) 2341 doubts whether an independent *Paieon/Paian/Paion* was ever worshipped in cult (but that was before the decipherment of Linear B). Fritz Graf pointed out to me at the Getty Symposium that even in Homer Paieon need not be distinct from Apollo.

[14] *LIMC* 7.1, 140, s. Paian 1 (A. Kossatz-Deissmann), *LIMC* 6.1, 95 s.v. Komos 3 (A. Kossatz-Deissmann). On the vase, see also Smith (2007).

[15] Ford (2006); on the refrain, Rutherford (2001) 69–70; Käppel (1992) 65–70.

especially Apollo and Asclepius, deserves the name in so far as he or she can be the addressee of paeans.[16]

In view of the link between name and genre, one obvious possibility is that the Getty Hexameters should be seen as a paean. For modern students of Greek literature the best known examples of the paean are grand choral paeans, such as Pindar's, designed for performance at festivals at such major sanctuaries of Apollo as Delos, and these do not resemble the Getty poem. But another common form of the genre, though not well represented among literary examples, was the apotropaic paean designed to avert a particular crisis, such as the Spartan paean to Poseidon, mentioned above, or Thaletas of Gortyn's paean, which was remembered as having neutralized a plague in Sparta.[17] A crisis is exactly what is implied in the Getty Hexameters, lines 26–7, cited earlier, which look as if they are describing the anticipated context or purpose of this text.

A related use of the paean was to effect purification through ritual, as we see from the testimony of Aristoxenus in his *Life of Telestes*:[18]

> The musician Aristoxenus says in his *Life of Telestes* that in the time of his visit to Italy, strange things were happening. One concerned the women: they were seized by such distraction that sometimes when seated at supper they would answer as if someone was calling and then dash out uncontrollably, and run outside the city. When the Lokrians and Rhegines consulted the oracle about relief from the condition, the god told them to sing twelve spring paeans each day for sixty days. That, he says, is why there were so many paean-writers in Italy.

Although this is not a form of therapy, Delphi is elsewhere known to have recommended, it cannot be regarded as unexpected in view of

---

[16] Burkert (1985) 74; Ford (2006); on the paean to Poseidon, Xen. *Hell.* IV.74.
[17] Earthquakes: Xen. *Hell.* IV.74; eclipses: Pindar, *Paean* 9; plagues: Ps.Plut. *De Musica* 1 (1146b) on Thaletas of Gortyn; madness and mental health: Aristoxenus fr. 117, Iamblichus, *Vit.Pyth.* 25. See Rutherford (2001) 36–8; Käppel (1992) 44–5.
[18] Aristoxenus, fr.117 = Apollon. *Mir.* 40; translation based on Campbell (1993), Telestes T5. Ἀριστόξενος ὁ μουσικὸς ἐν τῷ Τελέστου βίῳ φησίν, ὥπερ ἐν Ἰταλίᾳ συνεκύρησεν, ὑπὸ τὸν αὐτὸν καιρὸν γίγνεσθαι πάθη, ὧν ἓν εἶναι καὶ τὸ περὶ τὰς γυναῖκας γενόμενον ἄτοπον· ἐκστάσεις γὰρ γίγνεσθαι τοιαύτας, ὥστε ἐνίοτε καθημένας καὶ δειπνούσας ὡς καλοῦντός τινος ὑπακούειν, εἶτα ἐκπηδᾶν ἀκατασχέτους γινομένας καὶ τρέχειν ἐκτὸς τῆς πόλεως. μαντευομένοις δὲ τοῖς Λοκροῖς καὶ Ῥηγίνοις περὶ τῆς ἀπαλλαγῆς τοῦ πάθους εἰπεῖν τὸν θεόν, παιᾶνας ᾄδειν ἐαρινοὺς δώδεκα τῆς ἡμέρας ⟨ἐπὶ ἡμέρας⟩ ξ′. ὅθεν πολλοὺς γενέσθαι παιανογράφους ἐν τῇ Ἰταλίᾳ. For the text, see West (1990).

the close association between Delphi and the Apolline paean.[19] As for Telestes, his home city was none other than Selinus, and he is said to have been victorious in Athens in 402–401 BC, which means the period generally assigned to the Getty Hexameters corresponds closely to his lifetime.[20] Why Aristoxenus was interested in Telestes, an exponent of the despised New Music and in his trip to Italy is uncertain, but some contrast is likely to be implied between the traditional and wholesome quality of Apolline paeans and Telestes' own dithyrambic tastes. Up to the middle of the fifth century, though presumably less so by its end, South Italy, particularly the cities of Croton and Metapontum, was associated with Pythagoras and his disciples, who were also said to have used music and performed paeans (specified by Iamblichus as in the springtime) for the purpose of *katharsis* and healing. For all we know, the paean-writers of Locri and Rhegium had a Pythagorean background.[21]

Another text where we may find evidence for paean-incantations is lines 516–19 of the Homeric *Hymn to Apollo*, where the Cretan pirate-priests stamping out a march behind Apollo as he approached Delphi are said to have sung *ie paieon*, i.e. the paean, here a song of praise and jubilation:

> ... οἱ δὲ ῥήσσοντες ἕποντο
> Κρῆτες πρὸς Πυθὼ καὶ ἰηπαιήον᾽ ἄειδον,
> οἷοί τε Κρητῶν παιήονες οἷσί τε Μοῦσα
> ἐν στήθεσσιν ἔθηκε θεὰ μελίγηρυν ἀοιδήν.

And the Cretans, beating the ground, followed
to Pytho and were singing *iepaieon*
like the Cretan *paieones* in whose hearts
the goddess Muse places sweet-voiced song.

Controversy surrounds the word *paieones*. Some commentators, such as Cassolà, still want it to mean 'paeans', but it makes more sense if it can have the otherwise unattested sense of 'paean-singer', a view that

---

[19] Rutherford (2001) 24–9.
[20] Suda *T* 265 (iv 518 Adler) = Telestes T1 in Campbell (1993); see the discussion of Berlinzani (2008).
[21] Aristoxenus, fr.26W (music); Iamblichus, *Life of Pythagoras* 110 (paeans in spring). On Pythagoras in S. Italy, see Burkert (1972) 109–120. On possible Pythagorean background, see Berlinzani (2008), citing Aristoxenus, fr. 50W = Athenaeus XII.545a–546c on an embassy led by Polyarchus sent by Dionysius II of Syracuse to the Pythagorean philosopher Archytas at Tarentum.

goes back to German lexicographer Wilhelm Pape.[22] In a paper published in 1975 George Huxley endorsed that view, putting it in the context of evidence for Cretan healers and purifiers, such as Thaletas of Gortyn, and the Linear B evidence for a cult of Paiawon in Mycenaean Crete. On the basis of this, he posits that in early Crete '*paiawon*' was the name for a 'paean-singer' whose duties included healing by singing paeans or even the simple paean-cry. To quote him:[23]

> Thus Paieon, like Asclepius, had kinsfolk who were among the healers of mankind. One of their functions would have been the chant of incantation (ἐπωιδή) ἰηπαιάϝον when healing wounds and driving away plague.

In Huxley's view, the Cretan *paiawones* date back to a time before the deity *Paiawon* was ever associated with Apollo. It follows that the '*paiawons*' they sang would be the oldest forms of the paean genre, and the choral paeans that we are more familiar with ought to be seen as secondary imitations of the original ritual form.

Whatever one makes of Huxley's thesis about the Cretan *paiawones*, it is clear from Aristoxenus fr. 117 W and many other secondary sources that one form of the paean was a purificatory incantation, and that from the point of view of function, there is at least a general similarity between this and the Getty Hexameters. On the formal level, the case seems harder to make, because we do not usually associate 'lyric' paeans with hexameter poetry; on the other hand, the existence of the hexameter *Homeric Hymns* suggests that a hexameter paean is not a theoretical impossibility.[24] However, the key distinctive feature of the paean was the paean-refrain, a formulaic invocation of, and by implication a prayer to, the deity Paean/Paieon/Paian/Paion, usually occurring at the end of a triad or strophe (in the

---

[22] Pape (1884–91), 2.438 ('Päanen-sänger bei den Kretern'); cited in von Blumenthal. 1942, 2341. The same interpretation is found in Evelyn-White's Loeb (1950) 361. Von Blumenthal also thinks it might be a mistake for παραηδόνες (cf. Homer *Od.* XXII.348); for the meaning 'paeans', Cassolà (1975) 148–9.

[23] Huxley (1975) 121.

[24] Hexameter paeans are attested from the Roman period, e.g. the paeans to Asclepius and Telesphoros in *IG* II.2.4533; and cf. also the hexameter incantations in the Greek Magical Papyri (see n. 1); Rutherford (2001) 465–6. For a paean in lyric dactyls, Faraone (2011). Contrast the view of Costabile (1979), 531–2 who puts the paeans of Aristoxenus fr. 117 in the context of religious traditions at Rhegium relating to Apollo and Delphi.

case of non-triadic songs), and sometimes at the beginning.[25] In literary paeans, the place of this formula is sometimes taken by a reference to Paean/Paieon/Paian/Paion or the paean-genre, which can be thought of as a 'quasi-refrain'. Thus, at the end of the second triad of Pindar's *Sixth Paean*, young men are called on to 'send measures of paeans', and at the end of the third, Paian is requested to receive an offering (triad three).[26] Although not a single text of a paean-incantation survives, it seems highly likely that these would have featured regular paean-refrains as well, especially since elsewhere in Greek poetry the repeated use of a 'refrain' seems to have magical significance; thus in Theocritus *Idyll* 2, the love-sick Simaetha intensifies the force of her passion with two refrains, one addressed to the *iunx* and the other to the Moon. Another celebrated example of a refrain with magical force is the so-called 'binding-song' in Aeschylus' *Eumenides* (331–3, 344–6).[27]

We saw earlier that the Getty Hexameters are punctuated by lines addressing Paean and stating that he sends averting charms, or is a bringer of cures. These are not at the end of strophes or triads, which cannot occur in a hexameter poem, but they seem to divide the text into sections, marking the beginning of the two *historiolae*. One marks the end of the text, just as in choral paeans the end of the poem is a favoured place for paean-cries or refrains, either as the last refrain in a sequence, or as a stand-alone closural feature.[28] The lines of the Getty Hexameters that mention Paean are not all identical, nor do they occur at exactly regular intervals (*prima facie* the intervals are seventeen lines, nine lines, and fifteen lines), but similar variation in form and periodicity is found in Bion's hexametric *Lament for Adonis*.[29] Another difference between the references to Paean in the Getty poem and typical paean-refrains in lyric paeans is that in the latter the deity Paean/Paieon/Paian/Paion is invoked as a healer and crisis-fixer, while in the former he is represented as the source of incantations and magical formulas (lines 7ff.), which are not, as far as can be seen, directed towards him. That is, in an ordinary paean, Paean/Paieon/Paian/Paion is the addressee of incantations, whereas

---

[25] On refrains in Greek poetry, see the thesis of Burris (2004); also Morris (1979).
[26] Quasi-refrain: Rutherford (2001) 70–1.
[27] Faraone (1985). Another example of a refrain used for a magic purpose is the song of Alphesiboeus in Virgil *Ecl.* 8.68 etc.
[28] Rutherford (2001) 71.   [29] Estevez (1981).

in the Getty poem he is their origin. Even this difference may be more apparent than real, however, since in both cases, the deity is regarded as a source of deliverance (whether he provides it directly, or via incantations). And it is also worth remembering that in lyric paeans poets were not bound to use the conventional refrain based on '*ie paian*', and seem to have felt free to substitute other formulations ('quasi-refrains'), as long as some form of the theonym or the genre-term was included. Bear in mind also that the presentation of Paean as a source for the ritual authority of the singer, though it is attested only in the Getty Hexameters, could have been much more widespread. If an incantation-paean could be composed and performed on the instruction of the Delphic Oracle (like those described in Aristoxenus, fr.117 W), why would their singers not mention that Paean Apollo was the source of their ritual authority?

Thus, analysis of both formal features and implied function suggests that parts of the Getty Hexameters are resonant of paean-incantations. Other parts are not, however, namely the *historiolae*, sections of which are found without references to Paean in the hexameter texts from Locri (fourth century) and Phalasarna (Hellenistic); the simplest conclusion must be that the *historiolae* circulated in two forms, one with, and one without references to Paean, and they originally existed independently of them. A third, less significant, element in the composition are the Ephesian letters of line 33, in so far as these are distinct from the *historiolae*.[30] In this way, the Getty Hexameters could be seen as the result of a process of *bricolage* from different poetic or ritual genres.

Thus, depending on how much emphasis we give to each of the main elements, three ways of understanding the text present themselves. First, in so far as it contains resonances of the paean-incantation (which, as Aristoxenus fr.117 attests, was known in an area not far from Sicily in this period), and in so far as repeated references to Paean within the text would probably have been regarded as indications that it was a paean, it can be argued that an ordinary Selinuntian of 400 BC could be expected to have understood it as a paean-incantation, in fact the only example of this sub-genre to survive. The poet could even have been one of those to whom Aristoxenus might have applied the term 'paean-writer' (παιανογράφος), perhaps a descendant of Huxley's *paiawones*.

---

[30] On the Ephesian Letters, see Bernabé, this volume.

The second view would be that the Getty Hexameters is a hexametric ritual text of a reasonably common, though poorly understood type, to which have been added superficial references to Paean, without changing its essential quality;[31] thus, our ordinary Selinuntian is likely to have interpreted this as a ritual text, but not a paean. Someone who believed that paeans (at least at this early period) would not normally have been composed in hexameters might favour this view, but this is not certain.

The third and final view is that the Getty Hexameters should be regarded as an example of 'Kreuzung der Gattungen' between the genres of ritual *historiola* and incantation paean, resulting in something that would have been recognized as a hybrid. This would be in line with a tendency found elsewhere in this period for the formal features of the paean to be found in contexts where it might seem incongruous; the Delphic *Paean to Dionysus* by Philodamus of Scarpheia dating from 340–339 BC is the most conspicuous example, but similar experiments in genre can be found in Athenian tragedy already in the fifth century.[32] There may also be a parallel 'Kreuzung' going on between different stylistic and religious levels: on the one hand the poetics and ritual idiom associated with Apollo, and on the other hand the language of mystic cult. A rough parallel for this latter combination from many centuries later is a hexameter-incantation included in the Greek Magical Papyri (*PGM* VI.22–8), which seems to be a composite made up of the beginning and end of Chryses' famous prayer to Apollo in *Iliad* I.37–42, within which are sandwiched many un-Homeric epithets and *voces magicae*.[33]

---

[31] Chris Faraone's view, this volume, that the lines mentioning Paieon are rubrics connecting a short anthology of rituals also has the effect of minimizing the generic significance of references to the deity.

[32] Philodamus of Scarpheia: Rutherford (2001) 131–5; Stewart (1982); in tragedy, Rutherford (2001) 113–14.

[33] Hymn 10 in *PGM* II.2: κλυθί μευ, ἀργυρότοξε, ὃς Χρύσην ἀμφιβέβηκας / Κίλλαν τε ζαθέην Τενέδοιό τε ἶφι ἀνάσσεις. /χρυσοφαῆ, λαῖλαψ καὶ Πυθολέτα μεσεγκριφι, / Λατῶε, Σιαώθ, Σαβαώθ, μελιοῦχε, τύραννε, / πευχρη, νυκτε[ρόφ]οιτε, σεσεγγεν βαρφαραγ⟨γ⟩ης, / Ἀρβηθω πολύμορφε, φιλάρματε, Ἀρβαθιάω, / Σμινθεῦ, εἴ ποτέ τοι χαρίεντ' ἐπὶ βωμὸν ἔρεψα, / ἢ εἰ δή ποτέ τοι κατὰ πίονα μηρί' ἔκηα / ταύρων ἠδ' αἰγῶν, τόδε μοι κρήηνον ἐέλδωρ (Hear me, god of the silver bow, you who stand protector / Of Chryse and holy Cilla and are the mighty lord of Tenedos, / Gold-shining, hurricane and dragon-slayer, MESENKRIPHI I / Leto's son, SIAOTH, SABAOTH, MELIOUCHOS, ruler / PEUCHRE, night-wanderer, SESENGEN, BARPHARANGES, / ARBETHO, god of many forms, O you who're fond of chariots, ARBATHIAO, / Smintheus, if ever I have roofed a pleasing altar for you, / Or if I've ever burnt for you fat thighs / Of bulls or goats,

Besides probing the generic origins of the text, it is also useful to ask what was at stake in this 'paeanization' of an earlier magical and ritual text or texts. The answer is surely ritual authority: the references to Paean in the Getty Hexameters suggest that the poet was following the direction of instructions of the Delphic Oracle, which, as we know from Aristoxenus fr. 117, was capable of ordering the composition of paeans.[34] Since consulting the Delphic Oracle on matters of ritual and purification was standard practice at this period, it is to be expected that ritual texts deferring to the authority of Paean Apollo were common as well. The Getty Hexameters need not have been unique.

grant this my prayer! (Translation is indebted to Betz [1986] 111). The meaning of many of the *voces magicae* here is illuminated by the useful glossary in Brashear (1995), 3576–603; e.g. 'mesenkriphi' means in Egyptian 'child in his chapel', a regular invocation of the sun god (1995, 3592).

[34] Evidence for early relations between Delphi and Selinus is thin, but see the funerary stele for Arkhidamos son of Putheas, Arena (1989) n. 33.

9

Poetry and the Mysteries

Dirk Obbink

9.1 INTRODUCTION

Theseus in Euripides' *Hippolytus* 952–4 provides a scathing critique of the mysteries and their texts in his indictment of what he takes to be his son's religious practices:

> Ὀρφέα τ' ἄνακτ' ἔχων
> Βάκχευε πολλῶν γραμμάτων τιμῶν καπνούς.
>
> 'Play the *bakchos* with Orpheus as your master,
> In devotion to all his vaporous writings.'

As wrong as Theseus may be about his son's allegiances (he also accuses him of avoiding meat, for example—but Hippolytus is a hunter!), the passage sheds valuable light on a much-discussed aspect of the Orphic mysteries. As early as the fifth century BC there existed texts that were considered genuine compositions of Orpheus, a mythical religious leader. These provided the foundation for the mysteries, and knowledge of the texts could bestow semi-divine status on the initiate. Here both initiate or votary and god are called *bakchos*, so closely are the two assimilated. And here (to Theseus at any rate) devotion to Orpheus and knowledge of writings can be taken to define what it means to behave in the manner of an initiate.[1]

---

[1] Henrichs (2003). One wonders what makes Orphic texts so insubstantial to the outsider. Presumably the criticism is lack of comprehensibility and transparency of meaning, of the sort that necessitated, for the Derveni author as for many contemporary devotees, an allegorical understanding that could, for all we know, have been applied in a contemporary milieu to the Getty Hexameters. On allegory in this context see further Struck (2007); Obbink (2010).

The same could well be true of the Getty Hexameters, based on their content and what we know about the circumstances of their preservation. Thanks to the recent full publication of the Derveni papyrus,[2] we now know the kind of text Theseus had in mind in the quotation above, namely, a hexameter poem that purports to account in mythic terms for the origins of the gods and their relationship with mortals. Putting Theseus' remarks side by side with the Getty Hexameters shows, like the hexameter poetry quoted and explicated by the Derveni commentator, that mysteries provided a prominent context for the composition and performance of poetry in classical Greece, alongside the better recognized contexts of the symposium and public festivals (civic and religious), and, to a lesser extent, weddings and funerals.

The Getty Hexameters, as the essays in this volume attest, feature ritual cries or invocations of deities such as Paean, Demeter, and Hecate, magical formulae such as the *Ephesia Grammata*, instructions for both the performance of rites and the inscription of texts, *synthemata* and *symbola* (mystery catchwords and passwords), and myth encapsulated in semi-narrative (*historiola*) form as a paradigm for action. In what follows I survey the Greek tradition of employing poetry—often, though not exclusively, hexametrical—in the context of mystery cult, and argue that most of what we find in the Getty Hexameters is fully at home in such a context. This is, of course, not the same as proof that they do in fact derive from a mystery context, but other confirmatory evidence may emerge.

9.2 MYSTERY RITES AS A CONTEXT FOR CULT SONG

That mysteries (*teletai*) engendered a type of poetry with its own occasion, functionality, and stylistics has gone unrecognized, although it was well known to ancient critics who isolated in it a type of discourse distinctly aligned with poetry. Walter Burkert in his *Ancient Mystery Cults* (1987) does not include an index entry for poetry (or even hymns),[3] and neither does Charles Segal touch on mysteries in his

---

[2] Kouremenos et al. (2006).
[3] Reitzenstein (1927) had been more judicious in this respect.

chapters on early Greek literature in the *Cambridge History of Ancient Literature: Vol. 1 Greek Literature* (1985); nor do any of the authors in Oliver Taplin's *Literature in the Greek and Roman Worlds: A New Perspective* (2000) mention mysteries. Yet, as I argue, a significant number of early Greek poetic works belong to this seldom acknowledged but pervasively recognizable class of text. Some are well known, such as the Homeric *Hymn to Demeter*; others are lesser or even little known, such as the closely related Orphic *Hymn to Demeter*, while still others, such as the Getty Hexameters, are only lately becoming known to us.[4]

Our word 'mysteries' sums up a variety of ritual activities apparent in certain ancient cults, but derives from the activities of humans, the *mystai* or initiates who adhered to them. The terminology associated with the liturgy of the mysteries permits us to recognize this type of poetry as itself a sub-genre of hymnic discourse, replete with its own lexicon, formal properties, and set of generic expectations now different from and now parasitic upon those we recognize in other poetic genres of the period. My remarks mainly concern mysteries known in Greek culture from the late Archaic period down through the Church Fathers.[5] And although I will address Greece and West Greece in particular, it is important to remember that we have important evidence for mysteries in Roman culture from, for example, the *S. C. de Bacchanalibus* of 186 BC, from Virgil's portrait of a mystery eschatology in *Aeneid* VI, and from Horace's Bacchus ode, to name but a few.

It might be thought that there is no natural connection between poetry and mysteries. However, our earliest glimpse of mysteries comes accompanied by a poetic connection. Orpheus was a mythical singer and initiate par excellence, whose origins are perhaps lost in the Bronze Age. But the mysteries themselves as rites are generally considered to be post-Homeric. Neither the Greeks nor the Trojans in the *Iliad* celebrate mysteries, although they do celebrate games and other rites, and both banquets (Demodocus in *Odyssey* IX; Phemius in XVff.) and weddings (on the shield in *Iliad* XVIII) are represented as typical occasions for the composition and performance of poetry.

---

[4] Graf (1974) established that a large body of Orphic–Dionysiac poetry, now largely lost to us, had existed under the commission of the aristocratic elite in fifth-century Athens; cf. id. (2008); Obbink (1994). For the official cultic background: Clinton (1974). For the hymnic address to the Idaean Dactyls see IG XII,9 259 and Schaaf 2013.

[5] For the latter see especially Herrero de Jáuregui (2010).

Dionysiac rites are almost absent in the Homeric poems (the myth of Lycurgus in *Iliad* VI and the Cyclops' encounter with wine in the *Odyssey* being virtually the only exceptions). However, Odysseus' 'descent' to the underworld in *Odyssey* XI is considered to have all the characteristics of an initiatory mystery *Nekuia* by more than one scholar. The fact that Odysseus does not actually go anywhere, but 'sees' the underworld scenes in a pool of sacrificial blood, has been taken as comparable to dramatic visualizations of famous eschatological scenes enacted in mystery rites and witnessed by initiates.[6]

Outside of epic, it is not certain that any of the nine canonical Greek lyric poets before Pindar and Simonides composed for the mysteries. Dionysus and his rites are generally ignored in early Greek lyric (in Partheneia, for example), although not entirely: Alcman (fr. 56), describes a large *skyphos*, nocturnal celebrations, and the milking of a lioness (a Dionysiac epiphany-miracle), and may be addressed to a maenad. As such it could come from an aretalogy of Dionysus in an initiatory context.[7] However, it is with the Orphic eschatology of Pindar's *Second Olympian* and Ibycus' Orphic *Argonautica* (as reconstructed by M. L. West[8]) that the full mystery dimension of early Greek lyric can be glimpsed. In Pindar's case, we have not only the Orphic–Dionysiac mystery eschatology of the *Second Olympian Ode*, but also extensive remains of a dithyramb by the poet (fr. 70b) in which he narrated in mythic form the invention of the whirled instrument known as the *rhombus* by the nurses of Dionysus as an aetiology for Dionysiac mystery rites.[9]

At the same time, in the hymnic tradition, we know of a number of famous *hymnologoi* who worked at least as early as Homer and who composed hymns for mystery liturgies—Olen, Pamphos, etc. Whether or not any of these would have been performed chorally in the celebration of mysteries (as the examples from Pindar and

---

[6] One wonders whether the *historiola* narrated on Side A of the Getty Hexameters describes just such a scene to be witnessed by initiates.

[7] Cf. Anacreon *PMG* fr. 357, a cletic hymn in glyconics and pherecrateans, to Dionysus, who is asked to wisely advise Cleobulus to accept the singer's love. At 10–11 Dionysus is asked to be a σύμβουλος to the boy, obviously a pun on his name. But the epithet also recalls Dionysus Eubouleus, with the Orphic associations of that epithet. So too, Anacreon in *PMG* fr. 411a, despairing of help from love-troubles, goes on in fr. 411b to associate this (perhaps in a mythological exemplum) with the effects of madness inflicted on the Bassarai by Dionysus (another Dionysiac epiphany).

[8] West (2005).

[9] Obbink (2011b) 294 and the new Dionysiac Mysteries papyrus discussed there (291–2).

Plate 4. Orpheus, seated with lyre (now missing) and plectrum, life-size, in terracotta. Sicily, early 5th century BC (The J. Paul Getty Museum, Villa Collection, Malibu, California).

Simonides may have been), is open to doubt. It is at least worth asking whether the Getty Hexameters, with their instructions to invoke Paean, might have been sung chorally, as some paeans were.[10] That is what we might expect from poetry performed in a mystery context.

Here we are fortunate in having several preserved visual representations of mystery contexts for the performance of poetry and song. The first is the famous wall painting from Pompeii depicting the celebration of the Isis mysteries. A priest stands in the foreground at the

---

[10] See the chapter by Rutherford in this volume.

Plate 5. Orpheus, seated with lyre (now missing) and plectrum, and singing Sirens group, life-size, in terracotta. Sicily, early 5th century BC (The J. Paul Getty Museum, Villa Collection, Malibu, California).

centre, preparing to sacrifice. He is flanked on either side by choruses of initiates enraptured in the singing of a hymn. The second representation is the life-sized terracotta group in the Getty Museum of Orpheus (seated on a throne with a lyre) accompanied by a chorus of two bird-footed sirens. From a Sicilian tomb, the group is frozen forever in mystery song, perhaps performing for the deceased in the underworld.

More familiarly, Aristophanes in *Frogs* depicts a god from the private mysteries guided by a holy chorus of mystery initiates, the Frogs, who sing poetry. One wonders whether Aristophanes was skating on thin ice in portraying Dionysus as a buffoon and coming close to giving away vulgar details about the poetic texts of the mysteries that were restricted to the knowledge of initiates. But presumably Attic comedy was sufficiently carnivalesque to permit this, while the dramatic illusion of a world in which such details could be depicted in a vulgar way constituted the 'what if' or utopian quality of many of the escapist plays such as *Birds* and *Acharnians*. This is apparently so because instead of being indicted by the Athenians for impiety, Aristophanes was awarded prizes for his comedies.

No so lucky in his encounter with the mysteries was Alcibiades (for whom Euripides is supposed to have composed an epinician ode), let alone Diagoras of Melos, whose profanation of the mysteries earned him the verdict of death from the Athenians in absentia. This famous (and ill-understood) incident illustrates the often-stated contention of Burkert, Henrichs, and others that the fifth century Athenians, tolerant as they may have been of free speech under the democracy, were hypersensitive to anything approaching disrespect when it came to the Eleusinian mysteries. It is a significant fact (often ignored) that Diagoras was a lyric poet, with connections to Mantinea (he wrote an encomium of a prominent Mantinean). Whether or not the incident is due to strained relations between Athens and Mantinea in this period, the most likely context for the offence on Diagoras' part is in one of his poems: how else could the Athenians have known or had evidence of it? Aristoxenus (as reported by Philodemus in his *De pietate*) even tried to find aspects of the poetry he could attribute to Diagoras that might have been regarded by the Athenians as blasphemous. Thus a poem for or about the Eleusinian mysteries by Diagoras looks inevitable. Perhaps he composed one, perhaps not unlike the verses we find in the Getty Hexameters, on commission from another city for its protection or foundation of rites, and this was felt sufficiently similar to the text of the mystery songs sung at Eleusis to warrant his condemnation by the Athenians. This would be supported by the numerous formulaic parallels between the Getty Hexameters and similar texts including the Orphic gold leaves circulating in mystery contexts throughout the Greek world, as well as the numerous parallels between the Getty Hexameters and early Greek lyric and epic poetry.

The two texts most important for their connection with the mysteries are the Homeric *Hymn to Demeter* and its close relative, the Orphic *Hymn to Demeter*. The first is well known for its transmission of what would later become a canonical myth about the seasons—Persephone's alternation between the upper and lower worlds. But the hymn is curiously narrated: a *locus amoenus* is spoilt by a violent rape committed by an underworld divinity and a young girl is swallowed up; only another divinity with chthonic associations, Hecate, witnesses the event, but doesn't tell what happened. Demeter's mourning among mortals is unmotivated, as is her bizarre attempt to immortalize a human baby by magic; the connection with agriculture (which doesn't yet exist as Demeter hasn't yet brought grain) is tenuous, and the eating of the pomegranate seed has a wicked-stepmother fable-like quality akin to *historiolae*. Hecate is brought back in at the end to receive special honours and provide an aetiology for secret dread rites at Eleusis, which offers us tell-tale evidence of local composition.

The second is the lesser-known Orphic *Hymn to Demeter*, which survives on the reused verso of a Berlin papyrus, the recto of which is dated to the second century BC.[11] Substituting a number of Orphic–Dionysiac elements for those that appear in the Homeric hymn (for example, Baubo for Iambe), it is otherwise textually quite close, and Bruno Currie has recently argued on the basis of formulaic variants that the Orphic version should be seen as predating the Homeric one.[12] Here the differences are perhaps as telling as the similarities: one was composed (or perhaps evolved) for what later became civic mystery rites in which even women and slaves became initiates, the other (Orphic) hymn was the prerogative of elite aristocratic initiates. We might well see a similar transformation, both diachronic and synchronic, between the Getty Hexameters and the stylized form of paeanic discourse that emerged under the hands of Pindar and Bacchylides and became canonized as such by the Alexandrian critics and editors.

9.3. THE FORM AND CONTENT OF TELESTIC SONG

Armed with this evidence, let us sum up some of the expected features associated with mystery poetry, some of which it shares with hymns, prayers, and various rites sometimes deemed magical in nature:

(i) Invocation, deploying divine names and epithets, ritual cries
(ii) Myth, in semi-narrative (*historiola*) form, as a paradigm of action
(iii) *Synthemata*, catchwords, *Zauberwörter*, magical utterances
(iv) Aetiologies/rationalizations of rites and formulae
(v) Requests or spells for aid, or presence, or appearance (epiphany)
(vi) Instructions for performance of rites
(vii) Metre (non-complex), song.

---

[11] P. Berol. 13044 verso = OF 386–97 Bernabé.
[12] Currie (2012).

Some mystery texts emphasize one or more of these over another, while there has been much argument over the question of whether or not the mysteries had primarily only (iii), to the exclusion of any formal doctrine or dogma. One hastens to add inscription, that is objectification in writing, to this list, although this may be simply due to a coincidence of preservation—because of the requirement of secrecy, oral promulgation of such texts would have been tantamount to profanation, so the only way they can have come down to us is via inscribed, archaeologically surviving examples, together with tattling quotations in the secondary tradition, and the odd renegade survival of the collections of Homeric and Orphic hymns. All exhibit a concern for the salvation and safety of an individual or collective body as part of their overall ethos, but it is hard to frame this feature as a generic or formal requirement, since it is necessarily included as part of the initiatory context. Similarly, as a general feature, there is usually present an element of secrecy, restriction on knowing/hearing the song, or on concealment of the text, often among an in-group and from or against an out-group, either to activate the spell or to ensure its efficacy against interference from non-initiates and the unknowing.

The way in which the Homeric and Orphic hymns to Demeter fit this pattern is fairly obvious, each in its own way, as described above. Other texts that conform fairly closely include the verse-sequences woven into the texts of the Orphic–Dionysiac gold leaves,[13] and some of the poetic sequences in the more formal texts in the magical papyri, such as the famous 'Mithras liturgy' in *PGM* IV. The verses of the Orphic theogony expounded by the Derveni commentator would certainly fit, as would some of the choruses such as the Iakchos song in Aristophanes' *Frogs*.

Yet it remains to assess to what degree the new Getty Hexameters text fits this pattern. This text now has a claim to being crucial and primary, coming as it does almost as early as any of these texts (and only a century or so later than the Homeric and Orphic hymns to Demeter), and as such may be deemed one of the earliest texts to be exemplary for what constitutes the ancient poetic sub-genre of mystery or telestic poetry.

---

[13] Obbink (2011a).

Invocations, for example, in the Getty Hexameters are in evidence throughout (lines 6, 23, 32, 49, the last in third-person 'er-Stil' form), as well as the spontaneous ritual utterance (line 39). Divine names are carefully articulated throughout, with epithets strikingly chosen from the epic and formulaic tradition but with an appropriate connection to the act of inscription and dedication of the text, as prescribed in the opening lines of Side A. This inscription is presumably to be on a tomb or for the foundation of a temple, or at any rate within its precinct and enclosure walls. 'Paean' quite obviously fits the context of a request for healing and/or protection from harm. Hecate, too, with her underworld connections is appropriately invoked and honoured with praise and special status, as she is in the Homeric and Orphic hymns to Demeter, for notable actions ('coming through the night'), and her association with chthonic goddesses, especially Persephone (named in 9). Her garden (cf. 34) may suggest the idyllic opening meadow of the Homeric *Hymn to Demeter*, if it is not a euphemism for the realm of the dead itself, with which she is more closely associated. Likewise Heracles (not himself a god associated with mysteries, but cf. Ar. *Frogs*) is fittingly brought in, if we are right to identify him as the 'son of Zeus' (line 47), as the references to arrows and the Hydra (48) suggest: Heracles himself overcame death in visiting the underworld; arrows, in Apollo's case, bring plague (in the *Iliad*), but Heracles' arrows were tipped with the Hydra's poison—all enigmatically symbolic of the ills faced by those enacting the rite and the healing desired.

The most enigmatic divinity to be named in the text, however, is Amphitrite (line 5). She figures only in a minor way in the earliest Greek poetry, then goes virtually underground before resurfacing in Catullus and the Augustan Roman poets.[14] She may have been drawn into the text simply as part of a summary Homeric formula (= all creatures), and as such, she may be insignificant. However, she does seem to have been an initiatory figure in the cycle of Theseus myths.[15]

Myth, too, is present, albeit in a less palpable form than, for example, elements (i) and (iii). The reference to Heracles' killing of the Hydra (where the poisonous blood of the Hydra might be relevant) is a good example: fragmentary though the context is, it seems likely that this was

---

[14] Alessandro Barchiesi suggests to me that, on account of her rarity in poetry, Amphitrite might have been named here as, or have later become, a secret mystery divinity.

[15] See Faraone (forthcoming 2012) MS pp. 24ff.

a comparison in the context of Apollo being invoked as the 'far-shooter', as he is in *Iliad* I, as one whose arrows rain plague on the Greek forces on foreign soil. But the mythic elements in 8–17 and in particular the part of Paean (= Apollo?) in all of this seems almost beyond definition. Seminarrated in *historiola*-form, we seem to have more of a paradigm of action suggested for a divine epiphany to act as healer of the speaker's (or his/her city's?) troubles, than a narrative with a beginning–middle–end such as we might expect from any proper mythic story. The goat (10–11, 34) as attendant of Demeter suggests nothing so much as a sacrificial victim, with images of plenty and fecundity/milking surrounding it. Yet it may be no more than an image, resonant of the 'like a kid, I have fallen into the milk' utterance in the Orphic–Dionysiac gold leaves.[16] Lamps and night might suggest the underworld setting of a myth, such as that of Demeter (10) or Persephone (9), or even Heracles (who went there and back); or is it the darkness of mystery exclusion of the initiate before the blinding image of brightness and light of revelation? Hecate 'of the roadside' suggests not so much one particular myth about the goddess as a functionality that reminds us of her trivial 'crossroads' character spanning the interstice between the upper and lower worlds, that is the Hecate of the world of magical practice and discourse. This is not, of course, to ignore the possible connections with the local, archaic shrine of Hecate within the larger precinct of Demeter Malophoros at Selinus. Hecate had a similar close local connection in both cult and myth with Demeter at Eleusis, as we know from the Homeric and Orphic hymns to Demeter. In this case mention of Hecate in the Getty Hexameters might be comparable to the unusual invocation in song of Athena Soteira by the chorus of Aristophanes' *Frogs* at line 378: Athena has no other known connection with the mysteries at Athens, although in the Orphic tradition she is credited with saving the heart of Dionysus after his dismemberment by the Titans and their blasting by Zeus.[17] Both have strong local connections to their cultic environments, as well as being associated with other prominent local mystery divinities in their poetic texts.

Perhaps hardest to conceptualize, especially in the context of formal poetry, are the *synthemata*, catchwords, or *Zauberwörter*, magical utterances that fill lines 33–42.[18] In this context also belongs the reference to

---

[16] Faraone (2011a); Cabrera (2011).
[17] See Obbink (2011b) 294–5, and the new text discussed there (pp. 291–2).
[18] For the transmission of *synthemata* (apart from the *Ephesia Grammata* discussed extensively in the chapters of Bernabé and Edmonds in this volume) see Herrero de Jáuregui (2010) index s.v. *symbola/synthemata*, especially 149–52.

Damnameneus, the obscure Idaean Dactyl (if correctly restored). They would have resisted accurate transmission as poetry, as is evidenced by the breakdown in metre, especially towards the second half of side B. Yet they must have seemed powerful when activated by the ritual, and hence must be included. In this respect some form of aetiology or rationalization of ritual formula may be seen: ὅσσα[19] κατὰ σκιαρῶν in line 8 might well be a rationalization of or aetiology for the *aski kataski* formula in line 33, regularizing the powerful *Ephesia Grammata* (as they were known by the later tradition) into a hexameter mode that provided a greater chance of survival and ensured preservation of the text through both oral and written transmission, a kind of encoding of the secret formula into a performed poetic text.[20]

To the body of attested and recorded *symbola* or *synthemata* may now be added the new, lexical addendum 'alexima', used several times (lines 6, 23, 47) in the Getty Hexameters to describe formulaically the *pharmaka* that Paean brings (or is desired to bring).[21] 'Alexima' as neuter plural adjective (sing. 'aleximos, -mon') is (apparently) not a Greek word: it is not listed in LSJ or the Montanari lexicon, nor is it in any of Preisendanz's unprinted *Registeren* (indexes) to *PGM*. As such, it should probably not be accented at all, as though it were a *Zauberwort* or foreign word. If it were a real Greek word, as a neuter plural adjective modifying 'pharmaka', it should probably be accented with an acute accent (changing to grave) on the ultima (as twice in the original working text). However, it is close enough in sound to 'alexēma, -ēmatos', which is accented on the antepenult, to warrant giving it that accent, and perhaps it is a corruption of that word, in apposition with 'pharmaka', 'drugs, which are a defence'. ('Aleximon', neuter substantive = 'defence', also accented on the antepenult, appears as a v.l. for the synonymous 'alexion' once in Nicander.) Of course, 'alexēma pharmaka' won't scan: that is to say it cannot have been the original reading of the hexameter verse. One expects 'alexipharmaka' (the root of the old Homeric verb 'alexō' forms compounds easily)—

---

[19] There is no need to understand this word as a name: ὅσσα is a familiar alternative in epic language for ὅσα = ὡς, ὥσπερ (LSJ sv. ὅσος IV.7).

[20] This seems a more profitable line of explanation than that *aski kataski* is a later, abracadabra-like corruption of something that was originally linguistically intelligible when correctly transmitted, and allows us to see the composer of the hexameters working creatively on the poetic tradition.

[21] Cf. Photius s.v. *Ephesia Grammata* and *alexipharmaka*, cited by Edmonds in chapter 5 in this volume, n. 1.

but that won't scan either! Perhaps the best solution would be to think of 'alexi(ma)pharmaka' as a kind of *Zauberwort* like 'askikataski', similarly in this text semi-rationalized into a hexameter context.

There is certainly no shortage of requests, or spells for aid, or presence or appearance (epiphany), particularly in the section 23–31, where concern for the city (and mortals, their flocks, and herds) is also notably expressed. Whether or not a crisis or known historical threat (for example, the attested threats of Carthage or plague at Selinus) may be presumed or suspected, the request for aid does look like the primary purpose of the text. A community spirit is evinced, in which even the welfare of the city is at stake. ἀνόμων ῥ[ἴκ]ων in line 22 may even suggest civil or familial/class strife, together with their repercussions for government.[22]

Notably, the text begins with instructions for performance of rites: both the scripted form of the invocations—mythic 'narratives' and requests for aid—but it is also doubly determined, in that the physical text prescribing the rite is to be inscribed and dedicated, presumably to powers of the nether world in the form of a grave or foundation deposit. Comparable in many respects is the Derveni papyrus, which begins (as preserved) with a text that has textual affinities to a saying of Heraklitus' about cosmic justice, then discusses rites concerned with the Erinyes and Magoi, before continuing with an enigmatic theogony in traditional poetic language and attributed explicitly to Orpheus, its hexameters convincingly reconstructed by West.[23]

Both these instructions for activation of the spell as a physical object and the scripted form of the narrative with its invocations and requests, are expressed metrically, i.e., in song. Other, more formal cult regulations are occasionally found couched in verses.[24] Hexameters are the commonest form of formal expression in early Greek discourse. These have a number of close affinities with epic and lyric verse known from the transmitted canonical tradition. Several features still stand out. In line 4, for example, νιν, being largely Doric, is not

---

[22] If this is the correct restoration. I have also considered that ἀνόμων ὅ[ρκ]ων should perhaps be restored here, with similar overtones reminiscent of Pittacus' foreswearing himself in Alcaeus frr. 6 and 129.

[23] West (1983). On the language of the Derveni hexameters, see Sider (forthcoming 2012).

[24] Petrovic (2011); Petrovic et al. (2011b). For an example of more straightforward (and more extensive) prose cult injunctions, see Gawlinski (2011).

very common in hexameters.[25] This verse also gives a monosyllabic last word, and together with lines 5 and 7 shows three spondaic verses (with a spondaic fifth foot) in four successive lines. Similarly, it is not clear whether μελαναύγει in line 8 and φρικώδει in line 13 should be accented as spondees (making two more spondaic lines in close succession) or as dactyls (μελαναυγέϊ, φρικώδεϊ), as could be the case in Homeric verse. Line 5 violates Hilberg's law, but otherwise the hexameters, where they are transmitted as whole hexameters, are unexceptional. The preponderance of the masculine caesura is characteristic of Greek hexameters from the fifth century BC.

All things considered, it looks as though the Getty Hexameters, in spite of some ambiguities, perplexities, and contortions of transmission, exemplify pretty well the features we would expect to see from cult poetry of the mysteries of the fifth century BC. The connection with Demeter could be local to the Selinus cult and precinct, and Hecate may be relevant here as well. But they could just as well have been transferred from rites of Demeter elsewhere, from a composer who worked in an itinerant Panhellenic context. The appeal to Paean/Apollo, however, would have been ubiquitous, especially in times of crisis. The formulaic language, ritual utterances, and magical sequences are what we would expect from liturgies of rites that were supposed to be clothed in secrecy and security. We can be sure that we are about as close as one could get to the text of a poem, such as it is, for performance at a religious rite. One only wonders whether it worked.

[25] Noted by Sider (1997) 131 n. 7 with parallels and fuller discussion.

APPENDIX

The Inscribed Lead Tablet from Phalasarna, Crete (*Inscriptiones Creticae* 2.223–5 no. xix.7)

The text and translation below—with regularized spelling and a few other changes discussed in the notes to the translation—follow Jordan (1992), who suggests that 'the letter-forms, "epigraphical" as at Derveni and in the early Timotheus papyrus, suggest the 4th or perhaps early 3rd century'. The tablet was apparently fashioned to be wide enough to hold two dactylic hexameters side by side. The Arabic numbers below indicate the beginning of a new line on the tablet, while the letters in alphabetic order mark the start of each new hexametric verse. Thus the first line on the tablet holds two verses (A and B), as does the second (C and D). The scribe, however, seems to have lost his way at the end of verse F, where the coincidence of verse- and line-beginnings breaks down, to be briefly recaptured in lines 6 (= verses J and K) and 7 (= verses L and M), and then once again at the very end in line 11 (= verses S and T).

GREEK TEXT

A (1) ἀγγελίαν *ΑΝΑΓΑ*[⏑⏑–⏑⏑–τ]ῷνδε κελεύω
B [φε]ύγ[εμε]ν [ἡμ]ετέρων οἴκων [⏑⏑–]ων [ἀ̱]π[ὸ - -].
C (2) Ζῆνα τ' ἀλεξίκακον καὶ Ἡρακλέα πτολίπορθον,
D Ἰατρὸν καλέω καὶ Νίκην καὶ Ἀπόλλω[να].
E (3) αἰαῖ ἐγὼ δ' ἕλκει τε τράγος *ΠΥΞΥΤΥΑΙΤΑΓΑΛΙΣ*
F ἔπαφος, ἔπαφος, ἔπαφος, φεῦ[γ',] ἅμα φεῦγε, (4) λύκαινα·
G φεῦ γε, κύων ἅμα σ⟨ύ,⟩ καὶ *ΠΡΟΚΡΟΠΡΟΣΑΤΕ* vac. (5) σύνοικος.
H μαινόμενοι δάντων πρὸς δώματα αὐτοῦ ἕκαστος.
I ἀρκοῦ μεμ πομπα[ῖς..]*ΕΤΩΙΚΥΝΕ*
J (6) ασκι κατασκι {κατασκι} αασιαν ενδασιαν ἐν ἀμολγῶι
K [αἴ]ξ αἶγα βίαι ἐκ κήπου ἐλαύνε⟨ι⟩⟩ {τε}. τ[ῶι ὄ]νομα Τέτραγ[ος]·
L (7) ⟩σοὶ δ' ὄνομα Τρεξ. ⟨–⏑⏑–⟩ ἀνεμώλιος ἀκτή.
M ὄλβιο[ς̱]ῷι κ⟨α⟩τὰ δὲ σ[κ̱]εδαθῆι κατ' ἀμαξιτὸν 'ἰώ'
N κ[αὶ] φρεσὶν αὐτὸ[ς] (8) ἔχηι μακάρων {μακαρων} κατ' ἀμαξιτὸν α[ὑ̱]δάν
O "Τραξ Τέτραξ Τέτραγος
P Δαμναμε[ν̱]εῦ vac. (9) δάμασον δὲ κακῶς [ἀ]έκοντας ἀνάγκα[ι̱ς],
Q ὅς κέ με σίνηται καὶ οἳ κακὰ *ΚΟΛΛΟΒΑΔΟΙΣΙ*."
R ἱερακόπτε[ρον?] (10) πελειόπετον χιμ[αί]ρας ἀμίσαντον λεωκέρας λέωντος ὄνυξ,

186   *Appendix*

     λεοδράκοντος γλώσαν, γένειον.
S   (11) οὔ με καταχρίστ[ωι δ]ηλήσετοι οὔτε ἐπηνίκτ[ωι]
T   οὔτε πατῶι [οὔ]τ' ἐπατωγῆι, σ[ίν]τορ ἀπάντων.

TRANSLATION

A   ...message.... I command (you)
B   to flee from these houses of ours....
C   (I call upon) Zeus, the averter of ills and Heracles, the sacker of cities,
D   Iatros, I call upon, and Nike and Apollo.
E   Alas, I myself... the he-goat drags PUXUTUAITAGALIS
F   Epaphos, Epaphos, Epaphos, flee, flee at once, she-wolf!
G   And you, dog, flee at once and PROKROPROSATE[1] (vac.) associate.
H   Let them run maddened, each to his own house.
I   Ward off with escor[ts[2] ....]ETÔIKUNE[[3]
J   *aski kataski aasian endasian* at milking time
K   the she-goat from the garden with force drives the he(?)-goat. His name is Tetragos!
L   Your (sing.) name is Trex.... a windy promontory.
M   Blessed is the one, for whomever from overhead "Iô" is scattered along the carriage way
N   and whomever himself along the carriage way holds in his heart[4] the speech of the blessed.
O   Trax Tetrax Tetragos[5]
P   O Damnameneus! By necessity subdue those, who are evilly unwilling,
Q   whosoever is trying to hurt me and those who are evilly trying to *kollobadein*(?) me![6]

---

[1] Wünsch suggested that the end of the line can be restored as Πρόκλοπος ἅτε σύνοικος ('and the Deceiver, as their associate'), the name (otherwise unattested) deriving from προκλέπτειν ('to deceive'); see comments below on the final line where the word σίντωρ can mean 'spoiler' or 'thief'. Burglars would, of course, be a good target of a house amulet.

[2] As suggested by Brixhe and Panayotou (1995) *ad loc*. The word *pompê* ('escort') can be used for purification and scapegoat rituals that protect houses and cities; see Faraone (2004).

[3] It is tempting to see at the end of this line (*kune*) another reference to dogs (cf. line G).

[4] As suggested by D'Alessio (1993).

[5] For lines J–L and O–P we follow Bernabé's text as presented in this volume.

[6] Some third-person plural subjunctive verb lurks within these letters. There is a verb κολαβίζειν, 'to maim' (cf. the adjective κολοβός, 'maimed') and the LSJ supplement cites the verb κολλυβίζειν (Suda s.v. κολλάβους), which means 'to chop into small pieces', but neither κολαβίζωσι nor κολλυβίζωσι fits the metre.

Appendix 187

R   Hawk's feather, PELEIOPETON, white-horned(?) AMISANTON of a she-goat, claw of a lion, tongue of a lion-serpent, jaw (of a ?).[7]
S   Neither with ointment shall (he) harm me nor with application[8]
T   nor with drink nor with spell, the predator (or "thief")[9] of all things.[10]

---

[7] This line seems to be an unmetrical list of *materia magica*, as Jordan suggests. It also seems incomplete, as the 'jaw' (or 'mane') is not specifically linked with a wild animal, as is true for the previous two body parts, 'claw' and 'tongue'.

[8] For the translation of ἐπηνίκτ[ωι] as 'with application' see Maas (1944).

[9] Wünsch suggested that the word σ[ίν]τορ here is the equivalent of σίντωρ ('spoiler, thief') and σίντης ('predator, thief'), both derived from the verb σίνομαι ('to hurt, to harm').

[10] After ἁπάντων there is the remains of a single alpha, with little room for any other letters and there is a wide margin on the bottom. Jordan remarks: 'A number? This text the first of several?'

Bibliography

Albinus, L. (2000), *The House of Hades. Studies in Ancient Greek Eschatology* (Aarhus).
Allen, T. W. (1895), 'Descriptive Names of Animals in Greece', *CR* 9, 13.
Allen, T. W., Halliday, W. R., and Sikes, E. E. (1936), *The Homeric Hymns* (Oxford).
Archi, A. (1993), 'Kamrušepa and the Sheep of the Sun-God', *Orientalia* NS 62, 404–9.
Arena, R. (1989), *Iscrizioni greche arcaiche di Sicilia e Magna Grecia I. Iscrizioni di Megara Iblea e Seliunte I. Iscrizioni di Sicila* (Milan).
Arnold, C. A. (1989), *Ephesians: Power and Magic. The Concept of Power in Ephesians in Light of its Historical Setting* (Cambridge).
Aura Jorro, F. (1985-1993), *Diccionario Micenico* (2 vols.) 1–2 (Madrid).
Avram, A., et al. (2007), 'Defixiones d'Istros', *BCH* 131, 383–420.
Baumbach, M., Petrovic, A., and Petrovic, I. (eds) (2011a), *Archaic and Classical Greek Epigram* (Cambridge).
——(2011b), 'Archaic and Classical Greek Epigram: An Introduction' in Baumbach et al., 1–20.
Beekes, R. (2009), *Etymological Dictionary of Greek*, 2 vols. (Leiden).
Berlinzani, F. (2008), 'Teleste di Selinunte il ditirambografo', *Aristonothos* 2, 109–40 (available at: http://riviste.unimi.it/index.php/aristonothos/article/view/462).
Berman, D. W. (2005), 'The Hierarchy of Herdsmen, Goatherding, and Genre in Theocritean Bucolic', *Phoenix* 59, 228–45.
Bernabé, A. (2000), 'Tradiciones órficas en Diodoro', in M. Alganza Roldán, J. M. Camacho Rojo, P. P. Fuentes González, and M. Villena Ponsoda (eds), *EΠIEIKEIA. Studia Graeca in memoriam Jesús Lens Tuero* (Granada), 37–53.
——(2001), 'La experiencia iniciática en Plutarco', in A. Pérez Jiménez and F. Casadesús Bordoy (eds), *Estudios sobre Plutarco: Misticismo y religiones mistéricas en la obra de Plutarco (Actas del VII Simposio Español sobre Plutarco)* (Madrid–Málaga), 5–22.
——(2002), 'Orfeo. De personaje del mito a autor literario', *Ítaca* 18, 61–78.
——(2003), 'Ephesia Grammata: Génesis de una fórmula mágica', *MHNH* 3, 5–28.
——(2005), *Poetae Epici Graeci testimonia et fragmenta* II, *Orphicorum et Orphicis similium testimonia et fragmenta*, fasc. 2 (Monachii et Lipsiae).

Bernabé, A., and Jiménez San Cristóbal, A. (2001/2008), *Instructions for the Netherworld. The Orphic Gold Tablets*. Trans. Michael Chase. RGRW 162 (Madrid/[Eng. trans.] Leiden).

Bernal, M. (2006), *Black Athena. The Afroasiatic Roots of Classical Civilization. Vol. III: The Linguistic Evidence* (New Brunswick).

Betz, H. D. (1980), 'Fragments from a Catabasis Ritual in a Greek Magical Papyrus', *History of Religions* 19, 287–95.

—— (ed.) (1986/1992), *The Greek Magical Papyri in Translation, including the Demotic Spells*. 1st and 2nd editions (Chicago and London).

Bonner, C. (1910), 'Dionysiac Magic and the Greek Land of Cockaigne', *TAPA* 61, 175–85.

—— (1950), *Studies in Magical Amulets Chiefly Graeco-Egyptian*. University of Michigan Studies, Humanistic Series 4 (Ann Arbor).

Borghouts, J. F. (1978), *Ancient Egyptian Magical Texts*. Nisiba 9 (Leiden).

Bortolani, L. M. (2012), *Greek Magical Hymns: Egyptian Voices in Greek Dress? The Nature of Divinity in Graeco-Egyptian Magical Literature* (thesis, UCL).

Boyancé, P. (1972), *Le culte des muses chez les philosophes grecs*, 2nd ed. (Paris).

Brashear, W. M. (1995), 'The Greek Magical Papyri: an Introduction and Survey', *ANRW* II, 18, 5, 3380–684.

Bremmer, J. N. (2002), *The Rise and Fall of the Afterlife* (London and New York).

—— (2005), 'The Sacrifice of Pregnant Animals', in R. Hägg and B. Alroth (eds), *Greek Sacrificial Ritual: Olympian and Chthonian* (Stockholm), 155–65.

—— (2008), *Greek Religion and Culture, the Bible and the Ancient Near East* (Leiden).

—— (2010a), '*Manteis*, Magic, Mysteries and Mythography: Messy Margins of Polis Religion?', *Kernos* 23, 13–35.

—— (2010b), 'From Holy Books to Holy Bible: an Itinerary from Ancient Greece to Modern Islam via Second Temple Judaism and Early Christianity', in M. Popović (ed.), *Authoritative Scriptures in Ancient Judaism* (Leiden), 327–60.

Brixhe, C., and Panayotou, A. (1995), 'Le Plomb Magique de Phalasarna *IC* II–XIX 7', in C. Brixhe (ed.), *Hellènika Symmikta: Histoire, Linguistique, Epigraphie* 2 (= *Études d'archéologie classique* 8) (Nancy, Paris), 23–38.

Buck, C. D. (1955), *The Greek Dialects*, 2nd ed. (Chicago).

Burkert, W. (1972), *Lore and Science in Ancient Pythagoreanism*. Trans. E. L. Minar (Cambridge, MA).

—— (1983), 'Itinerant Diviners and Magicians: A Neglected Element in Cultural Contacts', in R. Hägg (ed.), *The Greek Renaissance of the Eighth Century B.C.: tradition and innovation*. Skr. Ath.[4] 30 (Stockholm), 115–20.

—— (1985), *Greek Religion. Archaic and Classical*. Trans. J. Raffan (Oxford).

—— (1987), *Ancient Mystery Cults* (Cambridge, MA).
Burris, S. P. (2004), *Refrains in ancient Greek poetry* (thesis, Cornell).
Cabrera, P. (2011), '"Ram, You Fell into the Milk" (OF 485.5–486.4). Possible Orphic Echoes in an Apulian Image', in Herrero de Jáuregui *et al.*, 187–203.
Cairns, D. L. (2010), *Bacchylides: Five Epinician Odes (3, 5, 9, 11, 13)* (Cambridge).
Calder, W. M. (1963), *The Inscription from Temple G at Selinus*. Greek Roman and Byzantine Monographs 4 (Durham, NC).
Calvo Martínez, J. L., and Sánchez Romero, M. D. (1987), *Textos de magia en papiros griegos* (Madrid).
Campbell, D. A. (1994), *Greek Lyric Poetry*, vol. 5, (Loeb Classical Library, London and Cambridge, MA).
Carnegie, H. (1908), *Catalogue of the Collection of the Antique Gems* (London).
Carroll-Spillecke, M. (1989), *Kepos: Der antike griechische Garten* (Munich).
—— (1992), 'Griechische Gärten', in *eadem* (ed.), *Der Garten von der Antike bis zum Mittelalter* (Mainz), 153–75.
Cassolà, F. (1975), *Inni Omerici* (Rome).
Clauss, J. J., and Johnston, S. I. (eds) (1996), *Medea. Essays on Medea in Myth, Literature, Art and Philosophy* (Princeton).
Clinton, K. (1974), *The Sacred Officials of the Eleusinian Mysteries*, TAPS 64.3 (Philadelphia).
—— (2005), 'Pigs in Greek rituals', in R. Hägg and B. Alroth (eds), *Greek Sacrificial Ritual: Olympian and Chthonian* (Stockholm), 167–79.
Collard, C. (1991), *Euripides: Hecuba* (Warminster).
Collins, D. B. (2008), *Magic in the Ancient Greek World* (Oxford and Malden, MA).
Cook, A. B. (1914), *Zeus: A Study in Ancient Religion* (Cambridge).
Costabile, F. (1979), 'Il culto di Apollo. Quale testimonianza della tradizione corale e religiosa di Reggio e Messana', *MEFRA* 91, 525–45.
—— (1999), '*Defixiones* da Locri Epizefiri; nuovi dati sui culti sulla storia e sulle istituzioni', *Minima epigraphica et papyrologica* 2, 23–76.
Currie, B. (2012), 'Perspectives on neoanalysis from the Archaic Hymns to Demeter', in Øivind Andersen and Dag T. T. Haug (eds), *Relative Chronology in Early Greek Epic Poetry* (Cambridge), 184–209.
D'Alessio, G. B. (1993), 'Note alla tavoletta plumbea di Phalasarna', *ZPE* 97, 290.
Daniel, R.W., and Maltomini, F. (1992), *Supplementum Magicum II* (Opladen).
Davies, O. (2004), 'French Charmers and Their Healing Charms', in J. Roper (ed.), *Charms and Charming in Europe* (New York), 91–112.

Dawson, W. R. (1932), 'Adversaria Aegyptiaca', *Aegyptus* 12.1, 9–16.
De Jong, A. (1997), *Traditions of the Magi: Zoroastrianism in Greek and Latin Literature* (Leiden).
Degen, A. A. (2007), 'Sheep and Goat Milk in Pastoral Societies', *Small Ruminant Research* 68, 7–19.
Deissmann, A. (1918), 'Ephesia Grammata', in W. Frankenberg (ed.), *Abhandlungen zur semitischen Religionsgeschichte und Sprachwissenschaft. Festschrift Baudissin zum 70. Geburtstage* (BZAW 33) (Giessen), 121–4.
Dieterich, A. (1891/1911), *De Hymnis Orphicis capitula quinque* (Marpurgi Cattorum) = *Kleine Schriften* (Leipzig) 69–110.
Dubois, L. (1989–2008), *Inscriptions grecques dialectales de Sicilie*. 2 vols. (Geneva).
Duhoux, Y. (1988), 'Les éléments grecs non doriens du Crétois et la situation dialectale grecque au IIe millénaire', *Cretan Studies* 1, 57–72.
Edmonds, R. G. (2004), *Myths of the Underworld Journey: Plato, Aristophanes, and the "Orphic" Gold Tablets* (New York).
Eitrem, S. (1922), 'Varia', *Nordisk Tidsk. Filol. Ser.* IV 10, 115.
Estevez, V. A. (1981), 'Ἀπώλετο καλὸς Ἄδωνις. A Description of Bion's Refrain', *Maia* 33, 35–42.
Evelyn-White, H. G. (1950), *The Homeric Hymns and Homerica* (Loeb Classical Library, London and Cambridge, MA).
Faraone, C. A. (1985), 'Aeschylus' *Hymnos Desmios* (*Eum.* 306) and Attic Judicial Curses', *JHS* 105, 150–4.
—— (1992a), 'Aristophanes *Amphiaraus* Frag. 29 (Kassel-Austin): Oracular Response or Erotic Incantation?', *CQ* 42, 320–7.
—— (1992b), *Talismans and Trojan Horses* (New York and Oxford).
—— (1995a), 'The Mystodokos and the Dark-eyed Maidens: Multicultural Influences on a Late-Hellenistic Incantation', in M. Meyer and P. Mirecki (eds), *Ancient Magic and Ritual Power* (Leiden), 297–333.
—— (1995b), 'The "Performative Future" in Three Hellenistic Incantations and Theocritus' Second *Idyll*', *CP* 90, 1–15.
—— (1996), 'Taking the Nestor's Cup Inscription Seriously: Conditional Curses and Erotic Magic in the Earliest Greek Hexameters', *CA* 15, 77–112.
—— (1999a), *Ancient Greek Love Magic* (Cambridge).
—— (1999b), 'Curses and Social Control in the Law Courts of Classical Athens', *Dike: Revista di storia del diritto greco ed ellenistico*, 113–15.
—— (2001a), 'The Undercutter, the Woodcutter, and Greek Demon Names Ending in *-tomos* (Hom. *Hymn to Demeter* 228–29)', *AJP* 122, 1–10.
—— (2001b), 'Handbook or Anthology? The Collection of Greek and Egyptian Incantations in Late Hellenistic Egypt', *Archiv für Religionsgeschichte* 2, 195–214.

—— (2001c), 'A Collection of Curses against Kilns (Homeric *Epigram* 13.7–23)', in A. Y. Collins and M. M. Mitchell (eds), *Antiquity and Humanity: Essays on Ancient Religion and Philosophy Presented to Hans Dieter Betz on his 70th Birthday* (Tubingen), 435–50.

—— (2003a), '*Thumos* as Masculine Ideal and Social Pathology in Ancient Greek Magical Spells', in S. Braund and G. Most (eds), *Ancient Anger: Perspectives from Homer to Galen*, Yale Classical Studies 32 (Cambridge), 151–60.

—— (2003b), 'New Light on Ancient Greek Exorcisms of the Wandering Womb', *ZPE* 144, 189–97.

—— (2004a), 'Hipponax Frag. 128W: Epic Parody or Expulsive Incantation?', *Classical Antiquity* 23, 209–45.

—— (2004b), 'The Collapse of Celestial and Chthonic Realms in a Late Antique "Apollonian Invocation" (*PGM* I 262–347)', in R. Abusch, A. Y. Reed, and P. Schäfer (eds), *Heavenly Realms and Earthly Realities in Late Antique Religions* (Cambridge), 213–32.

—— (2004c), 'Twisting and Turning in the Prayer of the Samothracian Initiates (Aristophanes *Peace* 276–79)', *Museum Helveticum* 61, 30–50.

—— (2006a), 'Magic, Medicine and Eros in the Prologue to Theocritus' Eleventh *Idyll*', in M. Fantuzzi and T. Papanghelis (eds), *Brill's Companion to Greek and Latin Pastoral*, Mnemosyne Supplement (Leiden), 75–90.

—— (2006b), 'Gli incantesimi esametrici ed i poemi epici nella Grecia antica', *QUCC* 84, 11–26

—— (2008), 'Mystery Cults and Incantations: Evidence for Orphic Charms in Euripides' *Cyclops* 646–48?', *RhM* 151, 127–42.

—— (2009), 'Stopping Evil, Pain, Anger and Blood: The Ancient Greek Tradition of Protective Iambic Incantations', *GRBS* 49, 227–55.

—— (2010), 'A Socratic Leaf-Charm for Headache (*Charmides* 155b–157c), Orphic Gold Leaves and the Ancient Greek Tradition of Leaf Amulets', in J. Dijkstra *et al*. (eds), *Myths, Martyrs, and Modernity. Studies in the History of Religions in Honour of Jan N. Bremmer* (Leiden), 145–66.

—— (2011), 'An Athenian Tradition of Dactylic Paeans to Apollo and Asclepius: Choral Degeneration or a Flexible System of Non-Strophic Dactyls?', *Mnemosyne* 64, 206–31.

—— (2011a), 'Rushing into Milk: New Perspectives on the Gold Tablets', in R. G. Edmonds III (ed.), *The "Orphic" Gold Tablets and Greek Religion* (Cambridge), 310–30.

—— (forthcoming 2013), 'Gender Differentiation and Role Models in the Worship of Dionysus: The Thracian and Thessalian Pattern', in A. Bernabé *et al*. (eds), *Redefining Dionysus* (Berlin).

Faraone, C. A., and Kotansky, R. (1988), 'An Inscribed Gold Phylactery in Stamford, Connecticut', *ZPE* 75, 257–66.

Fauth, W. (1985–86), 'Aphrodites Pantoffel und die Sandale der Hekate', *Gräzer Beiträge* 12–13, 193–211.
Flower, M. A. (2008), *The Seer in Ancient Greece* (Berkeley, Los Angeles, and London).
Ford, A. (2006), 'The Genre of Genres: Paeans and "Paian" in Early Greek poetry', *Poetica* 38, 277–95.
Frankfurter, D. (1995), 'Narrating Power: The Theory and Practice of the Magical *Historiola* in Ritual Spells', in M. Meyer and P. Mirecki (eds), *Ancient Magic and Ritual Power* (Leiden), 457–76.
—— (2004), 'The Binding of Antelopes: A Coptic Frieze and its Egyptian Religious Context', *JNES* 63, 97–109.
—— (2009), 'The Laments of Horus in Coptic: Myth, Folklore, and Syncretism in Late Antique Egypt', in U. Dill and C. Walde (eds), *Antike Mythen. Medien, Transformationen und Konstruktionen* (Berlin), 229–47.
Fridh-Hanson, B. M. (1987), 'Votive Terracottas from Italy. Types and Problems', in T. Linders and G. Nordquist (eds), *Gifts to the Gods* (Stockholm), 67–75.
Furley, W. D. (1993), 'Besprechung und Behandlung. Zur Form und Funktion von $E\Pi\Omega I\Delta AI$ in der griechischen Zaubermedizin', in G. W. Most et al. (eds), *Philanthropia kai Eusebeia. Festschrift für Albrecht Dihle zum 70. Geburtstag* (Göttingen), 80–104.
Gager, J. J. (ed.) (1992), *Curse Tablets and Binding Spells from the Ancient World* (Oxford).
Gawlinksi, L. (2011), *The Sacred Law of Andania: A New Text with Commentary*, Sozomena: Studies in the Recovery of Ancient Texts 11 (2011).
Geller, M. J. (2007), *Evil Demons: Canonical Utukku Lemnutu Incantations* (State Archives of Assyria. Cuneiform Texts 5, Helsinki)
Gordon, R. (1999), 'Imagining Greek and Roman magic', in B. Ankarloo and S. Clark (eds), *Witchcraft and Magic in Europe. Ancient Greece and Rome* (Philadelphia), 159–275.
Gow, A. S. F. (1950), *Theocritus*. 2 vols. (Cambridge).
Graf, F. (1974), *Eleusis und die orphische Dichtung Athens in vorhellenistischer Zeit* (Berlin and New York).
—— (1980), 'Milch, Honig und Wein', in G. Piccaluga (ed.), *Perennitas. Studi in onore di Angelo Brelich* (Rome), 209–21.
—— (1985), *Nordionische Kulte* (Rome).
—— (1997), *Magic in the Ancient World* (Cambridge, MA and London).
—— (2008), 'Orfeo, Eleusis y Atenas' in A. Bernabé and F. Cassadesús (eds), *Orfeo y la tradición órfica. Un reencuentro* (Madrid).
—— (2009), *Apollo* (London and New York).
Graf, F., and Johnston, S. I. (2007), *Ritual Texts for the Afterlife. Orpheus and the Bacchic Gold Tablets* (London).

Bibliography

Griffith, J. Gwyn (1960), *The Conflict of Horus and Seth from Egyptian and Classical Sources. A Study in Ancient Mythology* (Liverpool).
—— (ed., trans., and comm.) (1970), *Plutarch's De Iside et Osiride* (Cambridge).
—— (ed., trans., and comm.) (1975), *Apuleius of Madauros. The Isis-Book (Metamorphoses, Book XI).* EPRO 39 (Leiden).
Guarducci, M. (1990), 'Riflessioni sulle nuove laminette 'orfiche' della Tessaglia', *Epigraphica* 52, 9–19.
Hart, G. (2005), *The Routledge Dictionary of Egyptian Gods and Goddesses.* 2nd ed. (London).
Headlam, W. (1899), review of Nauck, *Tragicorum Fragmenta, CR* 13, 3–8.
Heim, R. (1892–3), *Incantamenta magica graeca latina. Jahrbücher für Class. Phil.* Suppl. 19.
Henrichs, A. (1991), 'Namenlosigkeit und Euphemismus: Zur Ambivalenz der chthonischen Mächte im attischen Drama', in H. Hofmann and A. Harder (eds), *Fragmenta dramatica* (Göttingen), 161–201.
—— (2003), 'Writing Religion: Inscribed Texts, Ritual Authority, and the Religious Discourse of the Polis', in H. Yunis (ed.), *Written Texts and the Rise of Literate Culture in Ancient Greece* (Oxford), 38–58.
Herjulsdotter, R. (2009), 'Swedish Snakebite Charms from a Gender Perspective', in J. Roper (ed.), *Charms, Charmers and Charming. International Research on Verbal Magic* (New York), 54–61.
Herzog-Hauser, G. (1932), 'Milch', in *RE* 15 (1932) 1569–80.
Hinz, V. (1998), *Der Kult von Demeter und Kore auf Sizilien und in der Magna Graecia* (Wiesbaden).
Herrero de Jáuregui, M. (2010), *Orphism and Christianity in Late Antiquity*, Sozomena Studies in the Recovery of Ancient Texts 7 (Berlin and New York).
—— et al. (eds) (2011), *Tracing Orpheus: Studies of Orphic Fragments in Honor of Alberto Bernabé* (Berlin).
Hornblower, S. (2008), *A Commentary on Thucydides III* (Oxford).
Hornung. E., and Bryan, B. M. (eds) (2002), *The Quest for Immortality. Treasures of Ancient Egypt* (Washington, DC).
Huvelin, M. (1901), *Les tablettes magiques et le droit roman* (Mâcon).
Huxley, G. (1975), 'Cretan Paiawones', *GRBS* 16, 119–24.
Jameson, M. H., Jordan, D. R., and Kotansky, R. D. (1993), *A Lex Sacra from Selinous. GRBS* Monographs 11 (Durham, NC).
Janko, R. (1982), *Homer, Hesiod and the Hymns: Diachronic development in epic diction* (Cambridge).
—— (1984), 'Forgetfulness in the Golden Tablets of Memory', *CQ* 34, 89–100.
—— (2000), *Philodemus, On Poems Book 1* (Oxford).
—— (2008), 'Summary and Historical Conclusions', in W. D. Taylour and R. Janko, *Ayios Stephanos: a Bronze Age and Medieval Settlement in South Laconia, BSA Supplementary Volume 44* (London), 550–610.
—— (2014), 'Hexametric Incantations against Witchcraft in the Getty Museum: an Integrated Restoration with *apparatus criticus*' (forthcoming).

Jeffrey, L. H. (1990), *The Local Scripts of Archaic Greece*. 2nd ed., revised by A.W. Johnston (Oxford). First published 1961.
Johnston, S. I. (1990), *Hekate Soteira. Hekate's Roles in the Chaldean Oracles and Related Literature* (Oxford).
——(1999), *Restless Dead: Encounters between the Living and the Dead in Ancient Greece* (Berkeley, Los Angeles, and London).
——(2011), 'Hecate, Leto's Daughter in Orph. Fr. 317', in Herrero de Jáuregui *et al.*, 123–6.
Jordan, D. R. (1985), 'A survey of Greek defixiones not included in the Special Corpora', *GRBS* 26, 151–97.
——(1988), 'A Love Charm with Verses', *ZPE* 72, 245–59.
——(1992), 'The inscribed lead tablet from Phalasarna', *ZPE* 94, 191–4.
——(1993), 'Curse Tablets at Selinous', in M. H. Jameson, D. R. Jordan and R. Kotansky (eds), *A Lex Sacra from Selinous* (Durham), 125–31.
——(2000a), 'Three Texts from Locri Epizephyrioi', *ZPE* 130, 95–103.
——(2000b), 'Ephesia Grammata at Himera', *ZPE* 130, 104–7.
——(2001), 'Notes on Two Michigan Papyri', *ZPE* 136, 183–93.
——(2002), 'New Evidence for the Early Written Transmission of Greek Hexameters', Newsletter No. 10 (Autumn) of the Centre for the Study of Ancient Documents, Oxford University, www.csad.ox.ac.uk/CSAD/Newsletters/Newsletters10.
Jordan, D. R., and Kotansky. R. D. (2011), 'Ritual Hexameters in the Getty Museum: preliminary edition', *ZPE* 178, 54–62.
Käppel, L. (1992), *Paian, Studien zur Geschichte einer Gattung* (Berlin).
Kellerman, G. (1986), 'The Telepinu Myth Reconsidered', in H. A. Hoffner and G. M. Beckman (eds), *Kanissuwar: a tribute to Hans G. Güterbock on his seventy-fifth birthday, May 27, 1983* (Chicago), 115–23.
Kingsley, P. (1995), *Ancient Philosophy, Mystery, and Magic* (Oxford).
Klöckner, A. (2010), 'Women's Affairs? On a Group of Attic Votive Reliefs with Unusual Decoration', in J. Dijkstra *et al.* (eds), *Myths, Martyrs, and Modernity. Studies in the History of Religions in Honour of Jan N. Bremmer* (Leiden), 179–91.
Koenen, L. (1962), 'Der brennende Horosknabe: Zu einem Zauberspruch des Philinna-Papyrus', *Chronique d'Egypt* 37, 167–74.
Kotansky, R. D. (1991), 'Incantations and Prayers for Salvation on Inscribed Greek Amulets', in C. A. Faraone and D. Obbink (eds), *Magika Hiera. Ancient Greek Magic and Religion* (Oxford), 107–37.
——(1995), 'Greek Exorcistic Amulets', in M. Meyer and P. Mirecki (eds), *Ancient Magic and Ritual Power* (Leiden), 243–77.
Kotansky, R. D., and Curbera, J. B. (2004), 'Unpublished Lead Tablets in the Getty Museum', *MedAnt* 7, 681–91.
Kotansky, R. D., and Jordan, D. R. (2011), 'Ritual Hexameters in the Getty Museum: Preliminary Edition', *ZPE* 178, 54–62.

Kouremenos, T., Parassoglou, G. M., and Tsantsanoglou, K. (2006), *The Derveni Papyrus* (Florence).
Kraay, C. M., and Hirmer, M. (1966), *Greek Coins* (New York).
Kuhnert, E. (1905), 'Ἐφέσια γράμματα', *RE* V.2, 2771–3.
Lakoff, G., and Johnson, M. (1980), *Metaphors We Live By* (Chicago).
Lanata, G. (1967), *Medicina magica e religione popolare in Grecia fino all'età di Ippocrate* (Rome).
Lejeune, M. (1972), *Phonétique historique du mycénien et du grec ancien* (Paris).
Levi, D. (1922), 'Silloge in corsivo delle iscrizioni metriche cretesi', *SIFC* N. S. 2, 321–400.
Luck, G. (1985), *Arcana mundi* (Baltimore and London).
Maas, P. (1942), 'The Philinna Papyrus', *JHS* 62, 33–38.
—— (1944), 'Ἐπένικτος', *Hesperia* 13, 36–37.
McCown, C. (1923), 'The Ephesia Grammata in Popular Belief', *TAPhA* 54, 128–140.
Maehler, H. (2004), *Bacchylides: A Selection* (Cambridge).
Manni Piraino, M. T. (1976), 'Le iscrizioni', in N. Allegro et al. (eds), *Himera*, II, *Campagne di scavo 1966–1973* (Rome), 665–701.
Martín Hernández, R. (2010), *Orfeo y los magos: la literatura órfica, la magia y los misterios* (Madrid).
Meiggs, R., and Lewis, D. (1969), *A Selection of Greek Historical Inscriptions to the end of the fifth century B.C.* (Oxford).
Méndez Dosuna, J. (2009), '¿Un nuevo testimonio de αἶζα 'cabra' en una lámina órfica?', in A. Martínez Fernández (ed.), *Estudios de Epigrafía Griega* (La Laguna), 369–75.
Merkelbach, R., and Stauber, J. (1996), 'Die Orakeln des Apollon von Klaros', *EA* 27, 1–53.
Meyer, M., and Smith, R. (eds) (1994), *Ancient Christian Magic: Coptic Texts of Ritual Power* (San Francisco).
Montet, P. (1928), *Byblos et l'Egypte*. Bibliothèque Archaeologique et Historique 11 (Paris).
Moritz, H. E. (1979), 'Refrain in Aeschylus. Literary Adaptation of Traditional form', *CPh* 74, 187–213.
Obbink, D. (1994), 'A Quotation of the Derveni Papyrus in Philodemus' *On Piety*', *Cronache Ercolanesi* 24, 111–35.
—— (2010), 'Early Greek Allegory', in R. Copeland and P. T. Struck (eds), *The Cambridge Companion to Allegory* (Cambridge), 1–18.
—— (2011a), 'Poetry and Performance in the Orphic Gold Leaves' in R. G. Edmonds III (ed.), *The "Orphic" Gold Tablets and Greek Religion: Further Along the Path* (Cambridge), 291–309.
—— (2011b), 'Dionysos in and out of the Papyri' in R. Schlesier (ed.), *A Different God? Dionysos and Ancient Polytheism* (Berlin and Boston), 281–95.
Ogden, D. (1999), 'Binding Spells: Curse Tablets and Voodoo Dolls in the Greek and Roman worlds', in B. Ankarloo and S. Clark (eds), *Witchcraft and Magic in Europe. Ancient Greece and Rome* (Philadelphia), 1–90.

Osborne, R. (1992), 'Greek Gardens', in J. D. Hunt (ed.), *Garden History: Issues, Approaches, Methods* (Washington), 373-91.
Pack, R. A. (1967), *The Greek and Latin Literary Texts from Greco-Roman Egypt*. 2nd ed. (Ann Arbor, MI).
Pape, W. (1884-94), *Griechisch-Deutsches Handwörterbuch* (3 vols), 3rd Auflage ed. M. Sengebusch (Braunschweig, F. Vieweg).
Parker, R. (1996), *Athenian Religion: a history* (Oxford).
——(2011), *On Greek Religion* (Ithaca and London).
Petrovic, A. (2011), 'True Lies of Athenian Public Epigrams', in Baumbach *et al.* 202-16.
Pfeiffer, R. (1968), *History of Classical Scholarship from the beginnings to the end of the Hellenistic Age* (Oxford).
Pfister, F. (1924), 'Epode', *RE* Suppl. 4, 323-44.
Picard, C. (1922), *Éphèse et Claros* (Paris).
Pinch, G. (1994), *Magic in Ancient Egypt* (Austin, TX).
——(2002), *Egyptian Mythology. A Guide to the Gods, Goddesses and Traditions of Ancient Egypt* (Oxford).
Pirenne-Delforge, V. (2010), 'Nourricières d'immortalité: Déméter, Héra et autres déesses en pays grec', *Paedagogica Historica* 46.6, 685-97.
Pócs, E. (2009), 'Miracles and Impossibilities in Magic Folk Poetry', in J. Roper (ed.), *Charms, Charmers and Charming. International Research on Verbal Magic* (New York), 27-53.
Podemann Sørensen, J. (1984), 'The Argument in Ancient Egyptian Magical Formulae', *Acta Orientalia* 45, 8.
Preisendanz, K. (1961), '*Ἐφέσια γράμματα*', *RAC* V (Stuttgart), col. 515-20.
Pugliese Carratelli, G. (2003), *Les Lamelles d'or orphiques* (Paris).
Race, W. H. (2000), 'Explanatory δέ-Clauses in the *Iliad*' *CJ* 95, 205-27.
Reitzenstein, R. (1927³), *Die Hellenistische Mysterienreligionen* (Leipzig).
Renehan, R. (1992), 'The Staunching of Odysseus' Blood: The Healing Power of Magic', *AJP* 113, 1-4.
Richardson, N. J. (1974), *The Homeric Hymn to Demeter* (Oxford).
Richter, W. (1972), 'Ziege', in *RE* II.19, 398-433.
Ritner, R. K. (1993), *The Mechanics of Ancient Egyptian Magical Practice*. Studies in Ancient Oriental Civilization 54 (Chicago).
——(1997), 'The Cult of the Dead,' in D. Silverman (ed.), *Ancient Egypt* (Oxford), 132-47 and 244.
——(1998), 'The Wives of Horus and the Philinna Papyrus (*PGM* XX)', in W. Clarysse, A. Schoors, and H. Willems (eds), *Egyptian Religion. The Last Thousand Years. Studies Dedicated to the Memory of Jan Quaegebeur*. Volume II (Leuven), 1027-41.
Rocca, G. (2009), *Nuove iscrizioni da Selinunte*. *Hellenica* 31 (Alessandria).
Roper, J. (ed.) (2004), *Charms and Charming in Europe* (New York).
——(ed.) (2009), *Charms, Charmers and Charming. International Research on Verbal Magic* (New York).

Roscher, W. H. (1901), 'Weiteres über die Bedeutung des E zu Delphi und die übrigen γράμματα Δελφικά', *Philologus* 60, 81–101.
Ruipérez, M. S. (1952), 'Desinencias medias primarias indo-europeas', *Emerita* 18, 8–31.
Rutherford, I. (2001), *Pindar's Paeans: A Reading of the Fragments with a Survey of the Genre* (Oxford).
Sarian, H. (1992), 'Hekate', in *LIMC* VI.1, 985–1018.
Scarpi, P. (1976), *Letture sulla religione classica: L'inno omerico a Demeter* (Florence).
Schaaf, I. (2013), 'Trick and Trade? The Eretrian "Hymn to the Idaean Dactyls" (IG XII,9 259)', in: Harder M. A., Regtuit R. F., Wakker G. C. (eds), *Hellenistic Poetry in Context*, Hellenistica Groningana 20 (Leuven) 305–24.
Schironi, F. (2004), *I frammenti di Aristarco di Samotracia negli etimologici bizantini*. Hypomnemata 152 (Göttingen).
Schmidt, K. F. W. (1937), 'Papyri in the University of Michigan Collection', *Göttingische gelehrte Anzeigen* 199, 149–50.
Schultz, W. (1909a), *Rätsel aus dem hellenischen Kulturkreise*, I, (Leipzig) 84–9.
—— (1909b), 'Ἐφέσια und Δελφικὰ γράμματα', *Philologus* 68, 210–28.
Sider, D. (1997), 'Heraclitus in the Derveni Papyrus', in A. Laks and G. W. Most (eds), *Studies on the Derveni Papyrus* (Oxford), 129–48.
—— (2012), 'The Poetry of the Derveni Papyrus', in *The Derveni Papyrus at the Center for Hellenic Studies, Classics@* [online publication, print version forthcoming].
Siebourg, M. (1915), 'Zu den Ephesia Grammata', *Archiv für Religionswissenschaft* 18, 594.
Smith, A. C. (2007), 'Komos Growing Up among Satyrs and Humans,' in A. Cohen and J. B. Rutter (eds), *Constructions of Childhood in Greek and Roman Antiquity* (Princeton), 153–71.
Smith, M. (1984), 'The Eighth Book of Moses and How it Grew (*P. Leid.* J 395)', in *Atti del XVII congresso internazionale di papirologia* (Naples), 683–93.
Sommerstein, A. H. (1989), *Aeschylus Eumenides* (Cambridge).
Stewart, A. (1982), 'Dionysos at Delphi. The Pediments of the Sixth Temple of Apollo and Religious Reform in the Age of Alexander', in B. Barr-Sharrar and E. N. Borza (eds), *Macedonia and Greece in Late Classical and Early Hellenistic Times* (Washington, DC), 205–27.
Stickel, A. (1860), *De ephesiis litteris linguae Semitarum vindicandis commentatio* (Jena).
Strandberg, Å. (2009), *The Gazelle in Ancient Egyptian Art. Image and Meaning*. Uppsala Studies in Egyptology 6 (Uppsala).
Struck, P. T. (2004), *The Birth of the Symbol: Ancient Readers at the Limits of their Texts* (Cambridge).
Teodorsson, S.-T. (1989), *A commentary on Plutarch's Table Talks* (Göteborg).
Threatte, L. (1980), *The Grammar of Attic Inscriptions*. I. *Phonology* (Berlin and New York).

Todisco, L. (2002), *Teatro e spettacolo in Magna Grecia e in Sicilia* (Milan).
Tortorelli Ghidini, M. (2006), *Figli della Terra e del Cielo stellato* (Naples).
Tsantsanoglou, K., and Parassoglou, G. M. (1987), 'Two Gold Lamellae from Thessaly', *Hellenika* 38, 3–16.
Turchi, N. (1923), *Le religioni misteriosofiche del mondo antico* (Rome).
Tzifopoulos, Y. (2010), *'Paradise' Earned: The Bacchic–Orphic Gold Lamellae of Crete* (Washington, DC).
Usener, H. (1902), 'Milch und Hönig,' *RhM* N.F. 57, 177–92.
——(1929), *Götternamen. Versuch einer Lehre von der religiösen Begriffsbildung* (Bonn).
Ustinova, Y. (2009), 'Apollo Iatros: A Greek God of Pontic Origin', in K. Stähler and G. Gudrian (eds), *Griechen und ihre Nachbarn am Nordrand des Schwarzen Meers* (Münster), 245–99.
Versnel, H. S., 'Die Poetik der Zauberspruche', in T. Schabert and R. Brague (eds), *Die Macht des Wortes* (Munich), 233–97.
Visconti, A. (1999), *Aristosseno di Taranto. Biografia e formazione spirituale* (Naples).
Von Blumenthal, A. (1942), 'Paian', in *RE* 18, 2340–62.
Wachter, R. (1998), *Non-Attic Greek Vase Inscriptions* (Oxford).
Watkins, C. (2009), 'The Milk of the Dawn Cows Revisited', in K. Yoshida and B. Vine (eds), *East and West: Papers in Indo-European Studies* (Bremen), 225–39.
Wessely, K. (1886), *Ephesia Grammata aus Papyrusrollen, Inschriften, Gemmen, Jahresber. Franz Joseph-Gymnasc.* (Vienna).
West, M. L. (1970), 'The eighth Homeric Hymn and Proclus', *CQ* N.S. 20.2, 300–4.
——(1975), 'Zum neuen Goldblättchen aus Hipponion', *ZPE* 18, 229–36.
——(1982), *Greek Metre* (Oxford).
——(1983), *The Orphic Poems* (Oxford).
——(1990), 'Ringing Welkins', *CQ* N.S. 40.1, 286–7.
——(2003), *Greek Epic Fragments from the Seventh to the Fifth Centuries* BC (Cambridge, MA and London).
——(2005), 'Odyssey and *Argonautica*', *CQ* n.s. 55, 39–64.
——(2007), *Indo-European Poetry and Myth* (Oxford).
Willi, A. (2008), *Sikelismos* (Basel).
Wilson, P. (2007), 'Sicilian Choruses', in idem (ed.), *The Greek Theatre and Festivals* (Oxford), 351–77.
Wortmann, D. (1968a), 'Neue magische Texte', *BonnJhb* 68, 56–111.
——(1968b), 'Die Sandale der Hekate-Persephone-Selene', *ZPE* 2, 155–60.
Wünsch, R. (1900), 'Neue Fluchtafeln', *RhM* 55, 73–85.
Ziebarth, E. (1899), 'Neue attische Fluchtafeln', *Nachrichten von der Gesellschaft der Wissenschaften zu Göttingen, Phil.-hist. Klasse*, 129–32.
Zuntz, G. (1971), *Persephone. Three Essays on Religion and Thought in Magna Graecia* (Oxford).

Subject Index

abracadabra 3, 9, 76, 182
accusative 42, 49, 53, 95
Achilles 58
Acragas 55; *see also* Agrigentum
Adrastea 92
Aeolic 51
Aeolus 143
Aeschylus 5, 22, 25-26, 29, 47-51, 53, 63, 108, 117, 143, 148-49, 166
Aetna 50
Agamemnon 20, 22
Agrigentum 23, 25; *see also* Acragas
Alcibiades 177
Alcman 51, 174
alpha 48-49, 51-52, 90
alphabet 1, 32, 33, 84, 87, 95
Alpheios 26
altar 26, 152, 160, 168
Amalthea 35, 41, 143
Amphitrite 11, 41, 58, 99, 122, 136, 154, 180
amulet/amuletic 2, 57-65, 68-70, 101, 107-13, 116-19, 128, 129, 136, 146
amulet case 69
Amun 135
analogy/ analogical/ analogous 36, 50, 122, 124-29, 132, 135, 139, 145-48, 150, 159
ancestor 24, 69
Androcydes the Pythagorean 51, 53, 73, 75-77, 88, 94, 99, 102
anger 58, 136
anthology 7, 23, 107-13, 118-19, 168
Aphrodite 25, 60, 63, 115
Apollo/Apolline 4, 7-8, 23-24, 36, 38, 41, 43, 53, 61-63, 90, 98-99, 102-3, 106, 108-9, 112-18, 123-24, 127, 143, 145, 149-50, 157, 160-65, 167-69, 180-81
Arcadian 54
archaic 26, 38, 61, 88, 110-11, 173, 181
archetype 5, 28, 31, 38-56 122
Archilochus 48, 51
Archytas 164
Ares 51, 159, 161

aretalogy 174
Aristarchus 47-48
Aristophanes 9, 22, 32, 38, 66-67, 176, 179, 181
Aristoxenos 163-69, 177
Army/armies 2, 35, 68, 69
arrow 4, 36-37, 43, 91, 180-81
arsis 49
Artemis, Ephesian 74
Asclepius 4, 8, 36-37, 43, 54, 108, 143, 160-63, 165
aspirate 32, 39, 42, 44-45, 50
assimilation/assimilated: 4, 45, 134-35, 137, 139, 171
Assyria 160
Asteas 39
Astydamas 51
Athena 181
Athens/Athenian 9, 29, 33, 35-38, 50, 55, 63, 79, 99, 105, 118, 164, 168, 173, 176-77, 181
Attica /Attic 33, 44, 46-52, 54-55, 67, 74, 160, 176
Attis 141
Augustan 110, 180
Autolykos 62

baby 64, 125, 144, 177
Babylonia/Babylonian 75
Bacchus /Bacchic: 22, 92, 141-42, 173
Bacchylides 8, 25-26, 49, 56, 146, 178
barbarian voice 59
barren 132
battlefield 69
bear 26, 95, 101, 105-6, 111, 118, 143
Betz, Hans Dieter 45, 71, 76, 78-79, 100, 103, 157, 169
bird 9, 28, 32, 38, 50, 66, 87, 108, 176
blood/bleeding 47, 63, 174, 180
boast/boasting 2, 6, 57-65, 67, 69-70, 105, 110, 113-15, 118
book-rolls 33
Branchus 27, 150
breast 134-35, 141, 149, 154
bronze 61, 105-6

Bronze Age 161, 173
brother 37
bull 92, 140–42, 168
Byblos 133, 138–9

Caecilia Secundina 68
Caesura 35, 46, 65, 184
camel 27
Carthaginians 5, 24–25, 37
cattle 78, 135, 149
Celeus 65, 133
citizens 55
city/cities 1, 4, 12, 31, 34–35, 37, 38, 43, 55, 61, 74, 99, 108, 112, 133, 146, 158, 163–64, 177, 181, 183
charm 6, 11–13, 22, 36, 55, 57–58, 63–64, 66–67, 69–70, 79, 98, 100–1, 105–6, 110–18, 121, 126, 131, 149, 151, 154, 157–58, 166
child 12, 27, 35, 41, 46, 63, 65, 78, 80, 84, 105, 121–22, 130–36, 138, 141, 143–44, 148–51, 154–55, 157, 169; *see also* youth
chorus/choral 6, 8, 46, 50, 62–63, 65, 67, 105, 113, 163, 165–66, 174–76, 179, 181
Christ 125–26, 146, 148, 152
Christian/Christians 74, 109, 126, 135
Chromius 50
chthonic 29, 32, 34, 97, 106, 177, 180
Classical period 2, 65, 67, 70–71, 84, 110, 112, 118–19, 160, 172
Clement of Alexandria 52, 72, 74–75, 79, 85–86, 89, 102–3
coast/coastal 32, 133, 155
coda 22, 66–67, 111
cognate 31
coin 27
Cologne 31, 45, 47, 48–50, 78, 98, 100, 103, 105
colonization/colony 9, 24
comedy 65, 176
command 12–13, 36, 41, 43, 59, 60–62, 65, 68, 108–9, 112–14, 116–18, 121, 129, 131, 135, 158–59
community 2, 8, 91, 183
composer/composition 1–9, 23, 25–26, 28, 38–39, 46–47, 49, 55–56, 57, 63, 68–70, 77, 88, 107, 110–11, 115, 117, 157, 167–69, 171–74, 177–78, 182, 184
composite 5, 7, 107, 109–10, 113–15, 118–19, 168

conditional 58, 118
consonant 39, 45, 51, 87
Coptic 127–28, 135, 151–52
copyist 6, 48, 86
cosmogony 53
couplet 66, 111
court 63
Crete/Cretan 1–2, 4, 27, 31–32, 45, 50, 54–55, 64–65, 70, 91, 103–4, 123, 143, 155, 164–65
cretic 104
crisis 32, 62, 99, 113, 162–63, 166, 183–84
Croesus 55–56, 73–74, 102, 107
cross 27
crossroads 41, 181
Croton 164
cult 3, 4, 7–9, 28–29, 32, 36, 38, 74, 79, 97, 103, 106, 137, 139, 141, 150, 161–62, 165, 168, 172–73, 181, 183–84
cure 4, 12, 43, 62, 70, 116–18, 125, 133, 144–45, 149, 152, 154, 158–59, 166
curse 37
curse tablet 24
Cyprogeneia 66
Cyprus 32

Dactyls 7, 35, 43, 56, 72, 74, 79, 88, 93, 95, 98, 101–6, 165, 184
dactylic metre 47
Damnameneus 35, 43, 59, 71, 75–76, 79, 80–81, 95, 97–98, 101–3, 182
Danger/dangerous 1, 61–62, 64–65, 69
Daphne 157, 160
Daphnis 27, 150
dark/darkness 12, 26–27, 46, 52–53, 75–76, 78, 80, 98, 102, 111, 121, 131, 181
dative 48, 50–51
daughter 25, 28, 94, 132
day/day-break 12, 35, 43, 61, 63, 104, 158, 163
death 12, 43, 60–61, 68–69, 119, 137, 142, 158, 161, 177, 180
declension 49, 53
deer/doe 125, 132, 138, 143, 145, 148
defense/defensive 100, 103
defixio 23, 31, 35, 98, 100, 103, 105, 118–19, 125, 129, 138, 148
deictic 59, 62, 98, 114–15, 117
Delphi/Delphic 163–65, 167–69

Subject Index

Demeter 3, 5–6, 7, 9, 12, 21–22, 25–29, 32, 41, 48, 55, 59, 63–67, 69, 70, 78, 81, 91, 94, 105–6, 113, 121–22, 130–32, 138–39, 147–51, 154–55, 172–73, 177–81, 184
demon/daimon 64–65, 72, 77, 91–92, 98, 100–1, 104, 112–13, 160
demonic/daimonic attack 7, 98, 101, 134
Demophoon 149–50
Demosthenes 37
Demotic 134
Derveni Papyrus 5, 45, 49, 91, 104, 171–72, 179, 183
desert 136–37, 149, 152
dialect 1, 36, 39, 43–46, 49–50, 52–56, 68, 109
die-cutter 32
Diagoras of Melos 177
digamma 5, 45
Diodorus 103–4, 150
Diomedes 161
Dionysus/Dionysiac 2, 5, 9, 140–42, 168, 173–74, 176–79, 181
disaster 61, 90, 159
disease 5, 36, 55, 70, 109, 113, 144
dithyramb/dithyrambic 164, 174
dittographies 39, 45, 89
doctor 55, 161–62
dog 112, 143, 179
doom 12, 41, 60, 62, 68, 118, 122, 158
door 43, 51
Doric/Dorian 1, 24–25, 52–56, 183
drug 41, 43, 62, 64, 161, 182
dusk 26

Ea 160
efficacy/efficacious 6, 34, 57–58, 60, 63, 65–67, 69, 99, 102, 110–11, 147, 153, 179
Egypt/Egyptian 7–8, 22, 24, 31–32, 67, 78, 99, 123, 126–27, 129, 132–39, 141, 144, 152–55, 160–61, 169
Einodia 60, 105; *see also* Hekate Einodia
elegy/elegiac 46–48, 51, 161
Eleusis/Eleusinian 3–4, 105, 132, 138, 149, 150, 177–78, 181
Empedocles 2, 6, 23, 26, 46–47, 51, 55
engraving/engraved/engraver 23, 34, 54, 74, 113
enjambed/enjambment 46, 54, 59
Ephesia Grammata (Ephesian letters), 3, 5–6, 7, 35, 37, 43, 51–53, 55–56, 62, 64, 71–77, 79, 84–85, 89–91, 94, 97–106, 107–9, 112–14, 116–18, 124, 155–56, 159–67, 172, 181–82
Ephesus/Ephesian 73–74
epic 37–38, 45–46, 48–55, 58–59, 70, 87–88, 147, 174, 177, 180, 182–83
epichoric 56
epigram 23, 50, 53, 113
epigraphy/epigraphic 38, 56, 69, 89, 97
Epimenides 2, 38, 55
epithet 8, 23, 32, 36, 48–49, 59, 61, 95, 160, 162, 168, 174, 178, 180
Epizephyrioi/Epizephyrian 31, 36, 81, 88, 99, 132, 155
epsilon 32
Erinyes 183; *see also* Furies
Euboean 38, 44
Euripides 5–6, 25–26, 28–29, 47, 50–51, 55, 65, 67, 69, 105, 143, 147, 171, 177
evil/evilly 13, 37, 38, 43, 61, 74, 99, 101, 112, 123, 125, 131, 136, 137, 144
evil eye 125
eye 65, 105, 111, 125, 134, 136–37, 144–45, 151–52, 154

falcon 134–35, 138
family 69, 137–38, 146
fever/feverish 36, 43, 125, 132–34, 144, 154
fire 65, 105, 111, 134
firebrand 65
flocks 2, 12, 27, 35, 43, 61, 99, 122, 150, 158, 183
flood 2
forever 42, 53, 129, 176
formula 3, 6–7, 37, 46, 48–49, 51, 54, 67–68, 71–95, 97–100, 102–3, 105–6, 109, 112–14, 116, 162, 166–67, 172, 177–78, 180, 182
formulaic 112, 165, 182, 184
France 61, 152
Frankfurter, David 121, 124, 127–28, 135, 137, 147, 152
Furies 60, 63, 69, 108, 114, 117, 119; *see also* Erinyes

Gadara 111, 114
Ganymede 150
garden/gardens 3, 12, 24–25, 35, 41, 43, 59, 78, 80–83, 91–92, 94, 104, 121–22, 130–32, 148, 151, 155, 180
gatekeeper 68

Subject Index

gazelle 136–39, 152–54
Gela 33
gem/gemstone 52, 76, 83, 87, 89, 101, 113
genitive 48–49, 87, 95, 112
Getty Museum 5, 15, 17–18, 31, 121, 175–76
Getty Villa 4, 21, 97, 113
goat 3, 8, 12, 24, 26–27, 35, 40–41, 43, 78, 80, 81–83, 87, 91, 92, 94, 103–4, 112–13, 121–22, 130–33, 138–40, 142–45, 148, 150, 153–55, 157, 159, 169, 181
goatherd 27, 150
gold 2, 5, 31, 34, 38, 39, 67–69, 79, 88, 91, 103–5, 109–10, 115–19, 140–42, 150, 168, 177, 181
gold-shining 168
golden-sandaled 106
Graf, Fritz 23–24, 26, 31, 39, 121, 129, 140–43, 162, 173
grandson 36, 43
graphemes 39
grave 41, 69, 141–42, 182–83
grove 91

Hades 35, 68, 161
handbook 7, 9, 64, 66, 107, 109–10, 115
handicrafts 2, 61
handiworks 12, 61, 158
Hathor 133–39, 147–48, 150–51, 153–54
head 4, 36, 43, 101, 104, 113, 116, 134, 136–37
headache 111, 113, 116–17, 125
healer 4, 55, 60, 99, 121, 128–31, 154, 157–58, 161–62, 165–66, 181
healing 4, 7–9, 24, 37–38, 41, 43, 58, 59, 62–3, 106, 111, 113, 128, 133, 137, 161, 164–65, 180
health 108, 136, 163
Hecate 3, 12, 27–28, 32, 34–35, 37, 41, 50, 59–60, 97, 100, 105, 121–22, 130–32, 157, 172, 177–78, 180–81, 184
Hecate Einodia ('Hekate of the Roadside', 'Hekate of the Crossroads'), 60, 105
Hellenistic period 2, 7, 67, 94, 112, 118, 160
Hera 149–50
Heraclea 32

Heracles 4, 36–37, 43, 54, 99, 105, 112–13, 124, 146–47, 150, 161, 180–81
Heracles the Sacker of Cities 99
Heraclitus 51
Hermes 26, 136
heroes 63, 122, 148, 152–53
Herodotus 22, 48, 102
Hesiod 7, 23, 25–26, 28–29, 48, 161-2
Hesychius 48, 51–52, 75–76, 85–87, 89, 98
hexameter 1–9, 15–19, 21, 24–25, 31–33, 35–39, 43, 51–53, 55–58, 60–61, 63–64, 67–71, 77, 80, 84, 89–90, 97–98, 100–1, 104–7, 109–12, 114–15, 118–19, 121–24, 128–32, 129, 142, 145, 146–47, 153, 155, 157, 159, 160, 162–75, 177–84
hiatus 35, 46, 48, 90
hieroglyphics 74, 137
Hiero of Syracuse 26, 36
hieros logos 3, 22, 129
Himera 2, 21, 31–3, 38, 52, 70, 82, 99, 108, 122, 132, 155
Hippocrates/Hippocratic 51, 144
Hippolytus 171
Hippomolgoi 142–3
Hipponax 50
Hipponium 34, 68
Hittite 160
holy 3, 12, 23, 26, 35, 40–43, 48, 53, 65, 76, 78, 81, 91, 98, 121, 131, 149, 168, 176
Homer 23–24, 26, 29, 45–46, 51, 53, 55, 161–62, 165, 174
Homeric 6, 9, 22–26, 44–48, 50–51, 54–55, 63, 66, 113, 138, 158, 164–65, 168, 173–74, 177–82, 184
homophone 95
honey 24, 140, 142, 144
horse 26, 111
Horus 125, 128, 132–38, 148, 151, 153
house 1, 2, 4, 11, 23, 27, 34, 41, 58, 61, 65, 68, 70, 107–8, 110, 112, 118–19, 123, 129, 134
human skill 35
Hydra 4, 13, 36, 43, 180
hymn 3, 6, 9, 13, 25–26, 37–38, 49, 54, 58, 61, 63, 65, 66, 70, 108, 113, 117, 138, 157, 160, 164–65, 168, 172–74, 176–81
hyparchetype 45, 52
hypnosis 35

Subject Index

iamb/iambic 54, 105, 157
Iambe 178
Iamblichus 163–64
Iatros 7, 24, 112–13
Ida/Idaean 7, 35, 43, 55, 72, 74, 79, 88, 93, 95, 98, 101, 103–6, 150, 182
idiom 44, 168
illness 69, 112
immolation 56
immortal 8, 12, 23–24, 41, 58, 60, 62, 98, 102, 106, 116–17, 121, 129, 130, 142, 157, 159, 161, 177
incantation 2–8, 11, 23, 41, 57, 61–70, 73–74, 77, 84–85, 88, 91, 93–95, 101, 105–16 118–19, 160, 164–68
Indo-European 53–54
initiate 68, 111, 115, 140–42, 171, 173–74, 176, 178–79, 181
initiated 22, 79, 93
initiation, initiatory 21–22, 55, 103, 106, 174, 179–80
inscription 28, 31–33, 37, 65, 68, 103, 113–15, 119, 141, 145, 147, 154, 162, 172, 179–80
inscribed text 1, 2, 6, 11, 34, 50, 57, 65, 119, 123, 125, 129, 156, 160, 179, 183
interment 34
invention 9, 25, 60, 72, 76, 79, 174
invocation 7–8, 35, 59, 89–90, 109, 113, 165, 169, 172, 179–81, 181
Ion 28, 47, 49, 50–51, 142, 144
Ionia/Ionian 24, 37, 62
Ionic 32–3, 38, 45–49, 51–52, 55, 160
Isis/ Isiac 111, 125, 127–28, 133–39, 141, 145, 147–51, 153, 175
Italy/Italian 2, 68, 91, 94, 103, 155, 163–64
iunx 60, 63, 108–9, 115, 166

Jahweh 110
Jason 63, 144
Jordan, David 2, 21, 26, 28, 31–35, 38, 42, 44–45, 54–55, 64, 76, 78–82, 84–5, 87, 89, 99–100, 103–4, 106–7, 110, 119, 124, 155, 157, 159

kids (young goats) 27, 91–92, 104, 140–42, 181
Kore 21–22, 106
Kotansky, Roy 21, 26, 28, 31–35, 38, 42, 44–45, 55, 68–69, 71, 80–81, 84, 88, 92, 106–7, 110, 155, 159

Laconian (dialect), 68
lamella 104
lamp 12, 121, 130–31, 181
land 12, 24, 46, 76, 78, 80, 99, 121, 131, 132, 142
laryngeal 45
Late Antiquity 6
Latin 61, 85, 124, 131–32, 155, 160
lead sheet/tablet/amulet 64, 70–71, 78–82, 84, 99, 103, 107–10, 112, 118, 132
lexicographer 90, 101, 165
life 5, 53, 103, 127, 134, 137, 143, 163–64
Linear B, 161–62, 165
lion 111–3, 174
lips 35
literary/literature 6, 8, 21–25, 28–29, 45, 57–58, 62, 66, 69, 71, 97, 107–8, 163, 166, 173
litigant 63
litotes 69
liturgy/liturgical 3, 7, 79, 111, 173–74, 179, 184
Locri/Locrian 2, 31, 36, 45, 50, 53, 64, 70, 81, 86, 88, 99, 108, 132, 155, 164, 167
love 63, 66, 72, 108, 124, 150–51, 166, 174
Lycambes 48
Lycurgus 48, 174
lyric 8–9, 46, 47, 50–51, 165–67, 174, 177, 183

Maas, Paul 64, 79, 110–11, 113, 122–23
Macedonia 5
maenads 24, 174
Magi 22
magic 1–2, 7, 9, 43, 51, 53, 63, 74, 79, 88, 94, 97–100, 102, 106, 113, 122, 155, 160, 166, 177
magical 1, 3–7, 9, 23, 31–32, 34, 53, 58, 61, 64–67, 70–71, 74, 76, 85–86, 88–89, 90, 93–95, 97–98, 100–2, 105–6, 109, 113, 115, 118, 122–25, 131, 133–35, 145, 148, 150–51, 153, 158, 160, 164–66, 168–69, 172, 178–79, 181, 184
magician 102, 105–6
magistrates 37
Magna Graecia 31–32
malaria 36, 43
Malophoros 181
Marathon 37

Subject Index

Marduk 160
mare 93, 143
Mary 125, 149, 151–52
meadow 91, 150–51, 180
Medea 49, 63
medical 23, 134, 144–45, 153
medieval period 6
Mediterranean 32, 123, 142, 150, 153
Melissos 147
mercenaries 37
metagrammatism 32
Metapontum 164
metaphor/ metaphorical 37, 141, 144–46, 154
meter/metrical 44, 63, 77, 79, 84, 91, 110, 113–14, 117
Michael 125, 145, 148
Milesian 33, 73
milk/milking 3, 8, 12, 24, 26–27, 35, 41, 43, 46–47, 52–53, 78, 80–82, 91–92, 94, 103–4, 121, 131–48, 150, 153–55, 174, 181
Minoans 32
Mithras 179
moon 105–6, 166
morning 26, 135; *see also* day-break
morpheme 49
mortal/mortals 12, 23–24, 35–36, 41, 43, 58, 60–61, 68, 92, 98–99, 106, 116–17, 121–22, 130, 140, 157–59, 172, 177, 183
Moses 109–110, 160
mountain 8, 12, 24–27, 41, 78–80, 103, 111, 121, 131, 133, 136–37, 148, 150–52
Mount Ida 104, 150
Mount Sinai 110
mouth 12, 43, 51, 152, 158
Musaeus 38
Muses 58, 70, 164
music 72, 101, 162–64
Mycenaean 23, 54, 162, 165
mysteries 3–4, 7–9, 22, 55, 105–6, 140–42, 150, 171–77, 179–81, 184
mystery 1, 3–7, 9, 29, 79, 93, 97, 106, 172–81
myth 3, 7–8, 104, 111, 122, 124–29, 132–39, 141, 143–48, 150–55, 160, 171–74, 177–78, 180–81, 183

narrative 3–5, 7–9, 58, 60, 63, 70, 77, 98, 106, 124, 151–52, 154–56, 172, 178, 181, 183

navy 61
Near East /Near Eastern 92, 111, 123, 126, 133, 155, 160
neck 36, 43, 69
Nephthys 134, 148
Nestor's Cup 114–15, 117–18
Nicander 182
night 3, 12, 35, 41, 43, 61, 104, 121, 158, 168, 180–81
Nike 112–13
noblewoman 68
nomads 27
nominative 49, 60, 87, 89, 91, 95
nonsense 3, 5, 88
noun 22, 25–26, 43, 46, 48, 59, 73, 84, 116, 122, 129, 131
nurse/nursemaid 36, 63, 66, 91, 149, 174
nymph 27, 143, 149

Ôamoutha 61
oath 47–48
ode 5, 26, 142, 147, 173–74, 177
Odysseus 62–3, 65, 174
ogre 6
Olympian/Olympic 5, 26, 107, 146, 174
omega 32
omen 50
optative 65
oracle 9, 25, 32, 35, 38, 43, 53, 61–62, 113, 116, 131, 163, 167, 169
oracular 2, 61, 109, 113–14, 118
oral 2–3, 5–6, 39, 47, 53, 57, 64–65, 67–69, 74, 110–11, 113, 118–19, 123, 129, 179, 182
oral performer/performance 6, 65, 110
oral tradition 47, 53, 64, 67, 111
order 27, 33, 35, 37, 43, 46, 75, 77, 102, 109, 159, 169
Orestes 63
Orpheus 7, 65, 67, 69, 76, 90, 92–3, 98, 102–6, 171, 173, 175–76, 183
Orphic 2, 5–7, 22, 25, 31, 34, 38–39, 46–49, 67–8, 76, 90–93, 102–6, 115–17, 119, 130, 142, 171, 173–74, 177–81
Ossa 35, 41

Paean 4, 6–8, 11–2, 35–38, 41, 43, 54, 58–62, 69–70, 98–99, 102–3, 106, 108–9, 114–17, 121, 124, 157–63, 165–69, 172, 175, 180–2, 184

Subject Index

paean/ paeanic 4–5, 8–9, 37–38, 61–62, 70, 106, 108–9, 117, 159, 162–69, 175, 178
Paestum 39
Paian 159–62, 165–67
Paiawon 161, 165, 167
Paieon 157–62, 164–66, 168
paieon 162, 164
Paiêôn 23–24
Paion 160–62, 165–66
paion 162
pantheon 123, 133
panther 143
Panyassis 49, 55
papyrus/papyri 5, 7, 31, 44–45, 47, 49, 66–67, 76, 88, 91, 94, 98, 100, 102, 104–5, 109–11, 113–14, 117, 123, 128, 133–34, 136–38, 148, 150–51, 155, 157, 165, 168, 172, 174, 178–79, 183
paradigm 124–28, 132, 137, 145, 148, 152, 172, 178, 181
paradise 142, 144
Paris 7, 143
Parke, H.W., 22, 36, 61
parody 66
Pasikrateia 32
passport 69
path 27, 35, 41, 91
pentameter 49–50
Persephone 3, 12, 24–28, 32, 35, 41, 55, 59, 78, 80, 91–92, 94, 103–4, 121–22, 130–32, 148, 150–51, 154–55, 177, 180–81
Persephoneia 25
Perseus 113
Phalasarna 1, 4, 7, 13, 31, 42, 50, 52–54, 59, 64, 79, 88, 99–100, 105, 107, 112–14, 118–19, 131, 155, 157, 167
Pherenicus 26
Philinna 110–11, 113–14, 117, 123
Philosopher/philosophical 101–2, 104, 164
Phoebus 61, 161
Phoenicia/Phoenicians 24, 133, 139, 153
phoneme 39
phonetic/ phonic 3, 85–87, 89, 93–95
Photius 72, 74, 97, 101, 182
pig 26
Pindar 5, 8, 25–26, 28–29, 36, 50–51, 54, 63, 66, 146–47, 163, 166, 174, 178
plague 2, 61, 163, 165, 180–81, 183
play 3, 48–49, 65–66, 86, 93, 95, 114, 130, 132, 135, 146, 171, 176

Pliny 61, 144
plosive 54
poet 2, 48–50, 55, 58, 60, 63, 67, 69, 101, 167, 169, 174, 177, 180
poetry/poem/poetic 1–3, 5–6, 8–9, 26, 44–45, 53–56, 71, 87–88, 90, 95, 111, 146, 161–62, 165–68, 172–73, 175–84
poison/poisonous 5, 36–7, 55, 99, 113, 144, 180
Polyphemus 138
Porphyry 103, 105, 131
Poseidon 162–63
potion 64
prayer 37–38, 54–55, 59, 63, 104, 109–10, 112–13, 147, 152, 157, 159, 165, 168–69, 178
Priam
priest 55, 164, 175
pronoun 46, 59, 116
Propylaea 28
protection 3–4, 61, 65, 79, 92, 99, 102, 106, 113, 118, 132, 136, 144, 146, 154, 177, 180
protective 2, 7, 36, 43, 62–3, 65, 69, 98–101, 109, 112–13, 116–19, 124, 137
prose 3, 6, 110, 112, 183
psilosis 44
pyre 55, 73–74, 102, 107
Pythagoras/Pythagorean 22, 51, 73, 75–76, 102–3, 160, 164

ram 92, 104, 140–42
Re 136
recitation 4–5, 100, 147
refrain 4, 7–8, 35, 37–38, 62, 69, 108–9, 116–17, 159, 162, 165–67
religion/religious 1, 3, 8–9, 24, 38, 122, 133, 160, 165, 168, 171–72, 184
repetition 7, 23, 60, 86, 89, 116–17
Rhegium/Rhegines 33, 163–65
rho 33
rhombus 109, 174
ring 60, 113, 135, 145
rite 6, 9, 21–22, 55, 102–3, 105–6, 172–74, 177–78, 180, 183–84
ritual 1, 3, 5–6, 8, 24, 34, 38, 60–61, 103–4, 106, 109, 113, 126–27, 129, 130, 133, 135–36, 138, 141, 144, 146–47, 154–56, 159–60, 163, 165, 167–68, 169, 172–73, 178, 180, 182, 184

Subject Index

rubric 7, 109–18, 168
Roman 3, 9, 32, 61, 68–69, 71, 109, 112–13, 137, 142–43, 165, 173, 180

sacred 3, 11, 26, 41, 58, 60, 62, 70, 76, 91, 98, 123, 129
safety 4, 8, 108, 144, 154, 179
salvation 3, 162, 179
Samos/Samian 33, 46
Samothracian 22
sanctuary 5, 7, 25, 138, 151
sandals 105
Sappho 46, 50–51
Sarah 127, 132
satyr 6, 65–67, 69
scansion 54
scapegoat 92, 113
scorpion 145, 149
scribal 23, 107
scribe 38–9, 44–45, 55, 108
Scodel, Ruth 45, 54
sea 11, 32, 41, 46, 58, 76, 99, 104, 122–23, 136, 154
Seaford, Richard 9
season 75, 102, 177
seer 32, 55
Selene 102
Selinus/Selinuntine 1–2, 5, 7, 21, 23–26, 28, 31–33, 35, 37–39, 46, 50, 70, 80, 82, 88, 97, 99, 108, 118–19, 122, 132–33, 138–39, 148, 154–56, 160, 162, 164, 169, 181, 183–84
serpents 38, 112
Seth 136
sheep 26–27, 135, 138–39, 150
ships 2, 12, 35, 41, 60, 99, 122, 158
shrine 9, 34, 181
Sicily/Sicilian 1, 2, 5, 7, 24, 26–29, 31–32, 38, 50, 55–56, 99, 104, 138, 146, 150–51, 155, 167, 175–76
sickness 64, 117
simplex 28, 58
singer 58, 60, 164–65, 167, 173–74
skull 65, 105
Solon 23, 54, 161
song 2–5, 8–9, 12, 29, 41, 57, 62, 70, 84, 98, 101, 104, 108, 114, 117, 119, 159, 162, 164, 166, 175–79, 181, 183
Sophocles 26, 28–29, 49–50, 61
sorcerer 64, 69, 72, 91, 95, 101
speech 6, 12, 24, 41, 55, 57, 59–60, 68, 119, 125, 128–30, 146, 157–58, 177

spell 7, 35–36, 39, 41, 43, 47, 49, 52–56, 60, 63–64, 69, 73–74, 79, 93, 98–100, 102–6, 108–12, 114–15, 118, 122–24, 127–28, 132–35, 145, 148–49, 151, 153, 160, 179, 183
Sphinx 26
spring 27, 111, 163–64
stallion 26
Stesichorus 50
stream 12, 26, 47, 76, 78, 81, 121, 144
sun 75–76, 98, 102, 169
swamp 36, 43
symbola 105, 172, 181–82
synthemata 172, 178, 181–82
Syracuse/Syracusan 7, 23, 26, 29, 36, 109, 161, 164
Syria/Syrian 32, 111, 114, 117

taboo 25
Tarentum 33, 164
technology 60
Telestes 163–64
telestic 178–9
temple 25, 28–29, 32, 138, 160, 180
terracotta 175–76
Tetragos 12, 80–83
Tetrakos 81
Thaletas of Gortyn 163, 165
theater 5, 29
Theocritus 7, 9, 54, 56, 108, 166
Theognis 51, 54
theogony/ theogonic 5, 22, 92–93, 179, 183
Theseus 171–72, 180
Thessaly 111, 114, 116, 141
thigh 62, 168
Thôsouderkou 61
thunder-stone 104
Thurii 33, 39, 91–92, 104
Timoleon 27
tin 11, 23, 41, 58, 65, 70, 118, 123, 129, 146, 154
tomb, 34, 68, 176, 180
torches 3, 27, 35, 41, 106
trade route 32, 55
tragedy 9, 46, 48, 55, 147, 168
transcript/transcription 44
transliteration 32
transmission 2–3, 5–6, 38–39, 46, 49, 55–56, 74, 85, 110, 123, 133, 177, 181–84

Subject Index

trimeter 47, 105
Trojan 26, 173
Tryphon the grammarian 52

'undercutter' 63, 64
underworld 3, 25, 35, 68, 100, 102, 104, 141, 151, 174, 176–77, 180–81
unguent 64, 134, 145
utter/utterance 12, 22, 35–36, 39, 41, 43, 50, 59–62, 68, 117–18, 147, 121, 125, 129, 147, 152, 158–9, 178, 180–81, 184

verb, 22–3, 26, 28, 50, 54, 58, 61, 65–66, 113, 182
victor 146–47, 164
victory 26, 37, 147
Victory 99; *see also* Nike
vocalism 45, 47–49, 51–52
vocative 59, 89, 95
vowel 87, 49

water 12, 36, 43, 111, 140
Watkins, Calvert 26
weather 2
West Greece 1–2, 9, 45, 65, 173
West, Martin 22–23, 27, 46, 48, 51, 54, 68, 103, 115, 163
wine 24, 142, 174
witchcraft 5, 35–37, 54–55, 63–64, 66
wolf 112, 143, 150
'woodcutter', 63–64, 66
worship 21–22, 36, 105, 139, 161–62
written text 1, 9, 31–34, 36, 57, 64, 69, 74, 110, 115

Xenophon (of Athens), 28, 50–51
Xenophon of Ephesus 74

Youth 24; *see also* child

Zeus 7, 13, 25, 36, 43, 99, 104, 112–13, 124, 143, 150, 159, 180–81

Index of Ancient Works and Texts

Acusilaus
  2F19 149
Ael. Dion ε 79 55, 73
Aelian, *N.A.* XII.9 (=Aristophanes fr. 29 K-A) 66–67
  VH XII.42 143
  XIII.1 143
Aeschines Socraticus fr. 11 142
Aeschylus, *Ag.* 426 26
  1021 22
  Cho. 350 53
    369 51
    653 148
  Eumenides 63, 108, (117)
    331–3, 344–6 166
  Lycurgus 48
  Psychagôgoi, F 273a.13 Radt 25
  Psychostasia: 47, 48
    F 280 Radt 47, 48
    F 420 Radt 48
    fr. adesp. 333a 48
  Supp. 985 26
    1022 26
  F 168 Radt 149
  fr. 280 Radt 48
  fr. 420 Radt 48
Aesop no. 210 Perry 150
Alcaeus
  Fr. 6 183
  Fr. 129 183
'Ammonius' on *Il.* XXI.195 = *P. Oxy.* 221 col. ix 1–2 49
Anacreon
  PGM (= PMG?) fr. 357, 10–11 174
  fr. 411a 174
  fr. 411b 174
Anaxilas
  fr. 18.6–7 K-A 72
  The Harp-Maker (II 268 K) (= Ath. *Deip.* XII.14.12–18) 101
Andocides, *De myst.* 29 50
Anecd. Ox. iv. 331, 21 Cramer 39
Anthologia Graeca IX.341 23
  Appendix 200,7 53

Anthologia Palatina App. 678 23
Apollodorus
  I.4.5 149
  I.5 143
  II.7.4 143
  III.4.3 149
  III.10.4 149
Apollonius Rhodius
  I.1129 (scholiast) 103
Apollonius Sophistes
  Lex. 28, 24–5 Bekker 47
    35, 18 Bekker 53 n. 105
Archilochus fr. 322 West 48 no.81
Orphic *Argonautica* (of Ibycus?) 174
  513 25
  1192–6 150
  schol. Theoc. 10.18e 48
Aristophanes, *Ach.* 176
  Av. 9, 32, 38, 176
    488 87
    959–991 32, 38 (citing 32)
  Eq. 9, 32, 38
    1000–1097 32, 38 (citing 32)
  Frogs 9, 176, 179
    373 151
    378 181
    449 151
    838 v.l. 51
    1344 (scholion) 149
  Amphiaraus, fr. 29 K-A 66–67
Aristotle, *Eudemian Ethics* 1238a28 90
Aristoxenus, fr. 117W 163, 165, 167, 169
  fr. 26W 164
  fr. 50W 164
Astydamas, Fr. 6, 2 51
Athenaeus:
  9.398c (Alex. Mynd.) 87
  9.398f 87
  XII.545a-546c (=Aristoxenus fr. 50W) 164
  XII.14.12–18.548C (=Anaxilas *The Harp-Maker* II 268K) 101
  XIV.633a-b (=PMG lyrica adespota fr. 36b1 Page) 50

Index of Ancient Works and Texts

Bacchylides 3.1-2 25
   3.3 50
   5.180 26, 49
Callimachus, *Ep.* 22 Pf. 27
   fr. 466 Pf. 130
   Hy. 1.45-8 143
   Hymn to Apollo 38
   Hy. Ap. 40-6 38
   Hy.Ap. 55-7 38
   Hy. Ap. 99-104 38, 38
Carcinus TrGF 70 F 5.1 25
Catullus 90.5 22
Chaldean Oracles:
   fr. 163 des Places 25
   fr. dub. 219 131
   fr. dub. 220 131
   fr. dub. 221 131
   fr. dub. 222 131
   fr. dub. 223 131
Choerilus of Samos fr. 22, 30 Bernabé 46
Cicero
   In Verr. 4.128 161
Clem. Alex. *Strom.*
   I.6 103
   I.73.1 35, 72, 79
   V.8.45 74
   V.(8.)45.2 51, 53 (citing 51), 73, 75, 88
   V.45.2-3 102
Conon
   FGrH 26 F 33 27
   Narr. 33 150
Curtius Rufus
   III.3.9 22
   V.1.22 22
Cypria fr. 7, 12 46
   fr. 9, 12 46
Damascius
   De princ. 123 bis (III 161.8 Westerink = OF 77) 92
Demosthenes, *De corona* 218 37
Dio Chrys.
   XXXVI.39 22
   XXXVI.42 22
Diodorus Siculus
   III.52.1 143
   III.64.3-4 149
   IV.43.1 93
   IV.48.6 93
   V.4.2-3 150
   V.49.6 93
   V.64.4 (=Ephorus FGrH 70 F104) 93
   V.70.2 143
   V.70.2-3 104
   XVI.66.3-5 27
Dionysius Scytobrachion
   fr. 18 Rusten (= D.S. IV.43.1) 93
   fr. 30 Rusten (= D.S. IV.48.6) 93
Dioscorides, *De Materia Medica*
   II.142 90
   IV.41.1 90
   V.99 144
Empedocles, Fr. 115, 10-11 VS 55
   Fr. 146, 1 VS 55
   On nature I, 298 47
Epicharmus 42.3 = 85.2 K.-A. 87
Ephorus FGrH 70 F104 (=D.S. V.64.4) 93
Etymologicum Magnum
   I.49 90
   402.22 73
   402.28 74
Euboulos F 64 K/A 25
Euphorio, *Suppl. Hell.* 430 ii 24 Lloyd-Jones/Parsons 24
Euripides, *Andr.* 1148 50
   Bacchae
     142 142
     704-11 142
   Cyclops 6, 105
     630-31 65
     645-48 105
     646-48 65-(66)
   El. 476 47
     477 26
   F 63 Kannicht 25
     223.143 Kannicht 25
     308 49
     308.4 28
   Hecuba 28, 50, 55
     152 25, 47
   Hel. 376 26, 47 (376b)
     1306-7 25
   Hipp. 225 25
     653 25
     952-54 171
     1202 50
     1216 50
   Ion 1005 51
     1048 28
     1048-50 49
     1204 28, 50
   Melanippe 143
   Or. 37 25
   Phaethon F 781.268 Kannicht 28

Euripides, *Andr.* 1148 (*cont.*)
  Phoen. 792 26, 47
    808 26, 47
  Rh. 963 25
  Suppliant Women 147
  Telephus 143
  Tro. 516 26, 47
Eusebius *Praep. Ev.*
  V.6.2–7.2 131
  V.8.3–4 (= Ch. Or. fr. dub. 219) 131
  V.8.5 (= Ch. Or. fr. dub. 222) 131
  V.8.6 (= Ch. Or. fr. dub. 221 and 223) 131
  V.8.7 (= Ch. Or. fr. dub. 220) 131
  VI.2.1 53
Eustathius
  2.201–2 = *in Od.* 1864.19 *ad* Hom. *Od.* XIX.247 73–74, 101
  1205.27 87
  p. 1681 ad *Od.* XI.253 143
Greek Anthology, IX.341 23
Herodotus
  I.122 143
  I.132.3 22
  I.216 143
  II.48.3 22
  II.51.4 22
  II.81.2 22
  IV.192 138
  VII.69 138
  VII.191 22
Hesiod, *Cat.*
    fr. 23a 6 49
    150.15 143
    151 143
  Fr. 54 M/W 149
  Fr. 282 M/W 88
  Fr. 302.15 M/W 162
  F 307 M/W 23, 161 (307.2)
  Th. 19 49
    371 49
    381 28
    582 46
    767 25
    914 25
  Works and Days 7
    465 48
    590 27
Hesychius,
  Lex. α 8335 Latte (= Aeschylus frr. 280 and 420 Radt) 47, 48
  Lex. ε 7401 Latte s.v. Ἐφέσια γράμματα 51, 75–76, 98
  Lex. τ 287 47
  Et. Gud. 90
Homer, *Iliad* 173, 180
  I 157, 181
  I.37–42 168
  I.157 24
  IV.167–8 22
  V.216 53
  V.401 23, 161
  V.899 159
  V.900 23, 161
  VI 174
  VIII.70 48 (scholiast)
  X.334 143 (scholiast)
  XI.741 23
  XIII.5 143
  XIV.274 25
  XVI.28 162
  XVIII 173
  XXI.195 49 (commentary of 'Ammonius')
Homer, *Odyssey*
  IV.227–32 161
  VII.268 24
  IX 138, 173
  X.276 162
  XI 174
  XI.253 143 (scholiast)
  XII.97 23
  XV 173
  XVIII.345 22
  XIX.247 73–74 (scholiast), 101 (scholiast)
  XIX.455–58 62–63
  593 23
  XXII. 137 51
  XXII.348 165
  Hymn to Apollo 21 46
  Hymn to Aphrodite
    4–5 46
    280 46
  Hymn 30.3 46
Horace
  Odes II.19.10 142
  Bacchus Ode 173
Homeric Hymns
  Hymn to Aphrodite
    4–5 46
    280 46
  Hymn to Apollo

Index of Ancient Works and Texts

4 54
21 46
516–19 164
Hymn to Demeter 6, 9, 54, 65, 113, 138, 173, 177, 179, 180, 181
7 150
24–8 130
52–9 130
56 25
101 149
227 13
227–30 63–(64)
228 54
228–229 66
235–7 149
360 25
368 51
438–40 130
439 48
Hymn to Hermes
450 26
Hymn 8 to Ares (Proclus)
4 51
Hymn 30
3 46 (???)
Hyginus *Fabulae*
87 143
139 143
167 149
179 149
182 143
187 143
252 143
Ion of Chios, fr. 5.5 47
Lex. 7401 51
Longinus, *De sublimitate* 16.2 37
Longus I.7 27
8 27
10 27
Lucian
Dial. Deor. 10 150
Pseud. 16 92
Vera Historia 1.24 143
Vera Historia 2.3 142
Vera Historia 2.13 142
Vera Historia 2.26 142
Menander
fr. 274 K-A 72
Paidia fr. 313 Kock 101
Meropis, F 4.3 (23)-24, 51
Nonnus, *Dionysiaca*
XXXIII.326 88
XLV.306 142

Oppian
I.559 (scholiast) 23
Orphic Argonautica (by Ibycus)? 174
12f. (= OF 99) 93
513 25
1192–6 150
Orphic Hymns 49, 179
Orphic Hymn to Demeter 173, 177, 178, 179, 180, 181
Hy. 1. 1 49
Orphic Fragments
43 22
45 22
77 92
99 93
110 92–93
317 130
386–397 178
387 150
485 92, 104, 140
486 140
487 91, 140
488 92, 140
489B 104
519–523 93
650 22
664 141
830a.1–5 78, 100
830b 78–79, 100
830c 79–80, 99
830e 81
830f 82
Orphic Theogony (5), 92, 93, 179, 183
Ovid
Met.
I.111 142
III.256–315 149
V.391–2 150
Fasti
IV.420–42 150
IV.445 132–(133)
IV.511 27
IV.517–18 149
V.115 143
Panyassis
fr. 28 Matthews 49
Parmenides
B 1.21 D.-K. 93
Pausanias Periegetes
II.26.3–5 143
V.27.5 22
VI.20.18 105
IX.31.9 150

Pausanias Periegetes (*cont.*)
  X.16.5 143
Pausanias (Lexicographer)
  17 Erbse 47
Pherecydes
  3F35 149
  3F131 149
Philostratus
  Imagines I.14 142
  VA VI.10 142
Philoxenos
  fr. 7, 21 Theodoridis 47
Phoronis fr. 2,3 Bernabé 35, 88
Photius *Lexicon*
  α 14 Theodoridis 90
  ε 2403 Theodoridis 55
  II 226 Theodoridis 73
  II 227 Theodoridis (s.v. Ephesia grammata) 72, 97, 182
  s.v. Alexipharmaka (= Menander Paidia fr. 313 Kock) 101, 182
Pindar:
  F.70b 174
    95.3 Maehler 26
    129 Maehler 25, 151
    165 Maehler 28, 50
  I. 4.49–53 147
  N. 3.8 26
    3.78 142
    5.48 37
    9.3 50
  O. 1 146
    2 5, 174
    3 146
    3.14 25
    3.18 25
    6.96 25
    9.27 25
  P. 3 36
    4.213–19 63
    5.24 25
    9.53 25
    12.2 25
  Paean 2.49 130
    9 163
Plato, *Alc*. 132b 23
  Leg. XII.957d 23
  Pol.279–80 23
Plutarch
  De Is. 15–16 139
  De Is. 20 136
  Mor. 85 B (Quo modo quis…15) 56, 71, 79, 101–102
  Quaest. Conv. VII.5.4 = *Mor.* 706D 72, 91
  Quaest. Conv. 706E 101
  Nic. 29 29
  Tim. 8.1.3–4 27
[Plutarch]
  De Musica 1 (*Mor*. 1146B) 163
PMG
  lyrica adespota fr. 36*b*1 Page 50
Porphyry
  Life of Pythagoras
    17 103–104
  Peri Agalmatôn
    8.58–65 105–106
  fragments
    fr. 347 131
Proclus
  Hy. 8. 4 51
  in Plat. Remp. II 207.27 Kroll (= OF 110) 92–93
Prodicus of Phocaea, *Descent of Pirithous (Minyas)* 46
Sappho, fr. 55, 3 50
Satyrus
  Vit. Eur. = F 6 Fr. 39 XIX Schorn 29
Seneca
  Oedipus 494 142
Sextus Empiricus
  Adv. math. I. 169–74 39
Solon, fr. 11 West[2] 23, 161
Sophocles
  Ajax
    571 25
  Antigone
    1001–2 28, 50
  Electra
    110 25
    292 25
  Oedipus Coloneus
    1548 25
  Oedipus Rex
    90 61
    965 28
  Rhizotomoi 55
    F 353.2 28
    Fr. 535 Radt. 49–(50)
  Fr. 89 143
Sophron, F 3 K/A 23
Strabo
  VIII.7.5 (p. 387) 143
  10.3.22 103
  XIV.1.45 151
  XV.3.14 22

Index of Ancient Works and Texts

Testamentum Salomonis
  7.4 52, 77
Theocritus, *2nd Idyll* 7, 9, 108, 166
  2.12 130 (scholiast)
  10.18e 48 (scholiast)
  18.44 25
Theognis 364 46
Varro F 252 Cardauns 27
Xen., *Anabasis* IV.5.4 28
  Cyr. VIII.1.23 22
  Hell. IV.74 163
Xen. Eph. I.5.6 74
CEG
  10 [iii], 4 50
  103, 151
  102, 250
  112 39
  342 49
IC
  II (19) 7 79
IG
  I^2, 355 37
  I^2, 355a 37
  II.2.4533 165
  IV^2, 424.10 161
  IX^2, 65 141
  XIV.256 23
  XIV.269 160
ML (Meiggs-Lewis)
  no. 30 37
  no. 38 32
  no. 54 (=IG I^2 355, 355a) 37
P. Amherst
  ii, Col. II(A) 110, 123
P. Berol.
  7504 110, 123
  13044 verso (= OF 386–397) 178
P. Derv.
  col. vi 104
  VI 2ff. 91
  23, 11 49
P. Mag.
  II 163 88
  III 80 88
  III 100 88
  III 443 88
  III 511 88
  IV 2772 88
  IV 2779 88
  VII.450 76, 85, 90
  VII.450ff. 94
  LXX.12 (= OF 830b) 78–79

P. Oxy.
  221 col. Ix 1–2 49
  Ined. 123
PDM
  xiv.594–620 127
  xiv.1078–89 134
  xiv.1219–27 152
PGM
  I.1–42 135
  I.42–195 131, 135
  1.296f. 157
  II.2 168
  II.81–101 157
  II.133–140 157
  II.163–166 157
  III.192 157
  III.234–258 157
  III.304 157
  IV 7, 179
  IV.52–85 131
  IV.94–153 128, 151
  IV.850 160
  IV.1930 160
  IV.2006 160
  IV.2140 160
  IV.3007 160
  IV.3125–71 135
  V.96 160
  VI.1–47 123, 127
  VI.22–28 168
  VI.26–38 160
  VII 105
  VII.451–458 102
  VII.795 160
  VII.862 160
  VIII.1 160
  XII.107 160
  XII.201–269 135
  XIII 109
  XIII.345 160
  XX 110–12
  XX.i.26–7 66, 67
  XX.ii.25 66, 67
  XX.4–12 152
  LXX 100, 103, 105
  LXX.5–16 155
  LXX.11–15 131
SEG
  34.971 28
  38.1837 78, 100
  42.818 79–80
  43.615 79

Index of Foreign Words

αασια 89, 90, 95
agathos 67
ἄγειν 32
ἅγιος 48
aition 63, 88, 129, 147, 149
αἴξ 87, 92, 94–95
αἰών / Αἰών 53, 93
ἀκαμαντορόης 48–49
ἀκεσφόρος 51
ἀλεξίκακος 36
ἀλέξιμα 23
alexima pharmaka 7, 61, 69, 97–98, 106
alexipharmaka 97, 99, 101, 182
ἀμολγός 26, 46, 47, 52, 56, 89
ἀνεμώλιος 53, 56
ἄνωγειν 61
aski 43, 71, 76–84, 97–98, 100, 182–83
ἄτη 95
αὐδήν 53
αὐτοκέλευστος 28, 50
γάρ 59
γράμμα 23
γράφει 23
Δαμναμενεύς 88, 89, 95
δέ 59
defixio 23, 31, 35, 98, 100, 103, 105, 118–19, 125, 129, 138
digamma 5, 46
dirae Teiae 37
Εἰνοδία 28, 49
Ἑκάτη 28, 49
ἐκκλάζειν 28, 50
ἐπαείδειν 22
epaoidê 22
epôidê 75
epithegma 108
esthlos 67
εὐπόλεμος 50 n.92
εὐφρόνη 51
ἐφιέναι 75
θεόφραστος 28, 50
hieron epos 129
hieros logos 4, 22, 129

historiola 4, 8, 24, 52, 54, 106, 123–39, 144–57, 159, 166–8, 172, 174, 178, 181
hymnologos 174
hymnos desmios 63, 108
iota mutum 52
iunx 60, 63, 108–9, 115, 166
katadesmos 100
κατακούειν 50
κελεύειν 61–62
κῆπος 25
κολάπτειν 23
λαμπάς 26
legomena 21, 106
lex sacra 31, 32, 32, 38, 110
μελαναυγής 25, 47
νιν 45, 183
Νύξ 93
ὄνομα / ὄϙνυμα 52
ὄπηδός 48
ὄσσα / ὄσα 182
παῖς 27
Περσεφόνη / Φερσεφόνη 25, 46
pestis 61
pharmaka 7, 58–62, 69, 97–99, 106, 116, 182–83
polis 61
polypharmakos 64
πολυφάρμακος 36
sandhi 45
scriptio continua 36
σκιερός / σκιαρός 25, 45, 85–86
ταδε 59
τελειν 22
temenos 28
τετραβάμων 26, 47
tetrax 71, 75–77, 80–81, 97–98, 101–2, 15
ὕδρης 54
ὑλοτόμος 64
ὑποταμνόν 64
φάρμακα 158
φρήν 50
φρικώδης 50